M · A · R · X
and the
FRENCH REVOLUTION

M · A · R · X
and the
FRENCH REVOLUTION

François Furet

Translated by Deborah Kan Furet

With Selections from Karl Marx
Edited and Introduced by Lucien Calvié

The University of Chicago Press • Chicago and London

FRANÇOIS FURET is former president of the Ecole des
Hautes Etudes en Sciences Sociales in Paris and
professor in the Department of History and the
Committee on Social Thought at the University of
Chicago. Among his previous books, *In the Workshop
of History* was published in English translation by the
University of Chicago Press (1984).

Originally published as
Marx et la Révolution française, © Flammarion 1986.

The University of Chicago Press, Chicago 60637
The University of Chicago Press, Ltd., London
© 1988 by The University of Chicago
All rights reserved. Published 1988
Printed in the United States of America

97 96 95 94 93 92 91 90 89 88 5 4 3 2 1

LIBRARY OF CONGRESS CATALOGING-IN-PUBLICATION DATA

Furet, François, 1927–
    Marx and the French Revolution.
    Translation of: Marx et la Révolution française.
    Includes index.
    1. France—History—Revolution, 1789–1799—
Influence. 2. Marx, Karl, 1818–1883—Views on the
French Revolution. I. Calvié, Lucien. II. Marx,
Karl, 1818–1883. Selections. English. 1988.
III. Title.
DC148.F8613 1988   944.04   88-20439
ISBN 0-226-27338-5

In memory of
KOSTAS PAPAIOANNOU,
with whom I first conceived this project·

Contents

Translator's Note

In the following work, I have translated all of part 1 and, in part 2, Lucien Calvié's introductions and notes. Translations of the selections have, wherever possible, been drawn from English-language editions of Marx's writings. The British spelling of those versions has been preserved. Most of the editorial notes to the previously published translations have been omitted or replaced by those of Mr. Calvié. Where Marx's own notes are included, these are identified.

The source note to each selection refers both to the German edition consulted by Mr. Calvié—for the most part, Karl Marx and Friedrich Engels, *Werke* (East Berlin: Dietz, 1956), abbreviated "MEW"—and to the English version. Where no English-language edition is cited, the translation is my own.

I would like very much to express my gratitude to Keith Baker and members of the University of Chicago Press for their invaluable aid as both readers and friends. Needless to say, any remaining imperfections are my own.

Deborah Kan Furet

Preface

Marx never did write a book on the French Revolution, although from the beginning to the end of his life and works he devoted numerous comments and allusions to this colossal event. Thus it seemed necessary, since such a project had never been undertaken, to gather and publish Marx's passages on the French Revolution along with an analysis of his ideas on the subject. As such, this book consists of two separate parts, the first being a synthetic essay on Marx and the Revolution, the second a critical edition of selected writings of Marx presented in chronological order. Since one comments upon the other, the two parts of this book are not mutually independent: they may, however, be read separately.

Since I am not a specialist on Marx, much less a Germanist, I have asked a colleague and friend, Lucien Calvié, who is an expert in these areas, to assemble and introduce the Marx selections. He has done so less with an eye to providing an exhaustive collection—for some of Marx's passages on the French Revolution are very brief or repetitive—than to situating within the overall context of Marx's thought his reflections on this event. Mr. Calvié's introductions, in turn, place these passages within their historical and philosophical contexts. I would like to thank him for his collaboration, which was at once rigorous and pleasant; because of his efforts, the dossier on Marx's interpretation of the French Revolution is now complete and accessible.

The first half of this book, for which I was responsible, is an attempt to present an interpretation of that interpretation; to make an inventory, through this array of writings, of the questions posed about the Revolution and the concepts used to treat them; and, finally, to trace the evolution of these questions and concepts in Marx's intellectual life. Within this brief framework I felt it unnecessary to include a bibliography of Marx's works; I have taken the liberty of referring only to the books and articles essential to my endeavor.

FRANÇOIS FURET

P·A·R·T O·N·E
INTRODUCTION

1

The Young Marx and the French Revolution

All Marxist interpretations of the French Revolution postdate Marx. While this paradox demonstrates that, like all great doctrines, Marxism has escaped its founder, it also brings to mind that although Marx considered writing a book on the French Revolution[1]—and, indeed, commented all his life, in various contexts, on the events of late eighteenth-century France—he never did write the book. This gap, between the book never written and the remarks that took its place throughout his work, will be my point of departure: it may allow us to free Marx's thought from its offspring and to reestablish its direction and the problems with which it dealt.

First, as to genealogy: to understand the young Marx's intellectual labor on the French Revolution, we may start with two central ideas put forth in early 1844 in an article devoted to Hegel's *Philosophy of Right* that was published in the *Franco-German Yearbooks*.[2] The first idea is an obsession with German backwardness. Marx shared all German intellectuals' passion to erase one day the kind of practical nonexistence of his country's history that had been underlined by its contrast to the universal visibility of the French Revolution. He was preoccupied with the notion of inventing a new revolution—this time a German one—which would, in its historical function, go beyond and complete the French emancipation. Hence the prior intellectual necessity to elaborate a critical philosophy of the French Revolution.[3]

1. See Maximilien Rubel's note on Marx's project of writing a history of the Convention and the reading he did in connection with this project, in Karl Marx, *Oeuvres,* Pléiade ed. (Paris: Gallimard, 1982), 3:1615.

2. Karl Marx, *Early Writings,* ed. Quintin Hoare (New York: Vintage Books, 1975), 245–59.

3. For a complete discussion of the problem of German backwardness and the role it played in intellectuals' fascination with the French Revolution, see Lucien Calvié, "Révolution française, misère allemand et révolution allemande chez le jeune Marx et quelques-uns de ses contemporains" (untranslated paper delivered

But he labored at this task by means of what one might call a critical doubling, installing himself within the Feuerbachian critique of Hegel. This was less a matter of rethinking the history of the French Revolution itself than of rethinking the interpretation of that history put forth by the Master of Jena, beginning with the *Philosophy of Right*. The result was a new concept of the state produced by a radical critique of the Hegelian state. This new concept is the second key idea of the 1844 article on the *Philosophy of Right,* and it is also to be found in a more elaborate form in the "Critique of Hegel's Doctrine of the State," a text drafted by Marx in the summer of 1843, but not published until 1927 (see discussion below and selection 3).

Let us first examine the idea of German backwardness, which seems ill matched, given the assumption that Reason unveils itself in historicity, to the idea that German philosophy was privileged with an understanding of the real. Marx, like Hegel—even more than Hegel—blasted Savigny and the historical school of law for confirming tradition and the status quo (see selection 1). Moreover, the Germany before his eyes was no longer the enlightened Prussia of 1818–20 but the reactionary Prussia of 1830–40. Fearing a revolution without having made one, Germany was an object of history that had never been able to become, like France, its subject: "We have been restored firstly because other nations dared to make revolutions and secondly because other nations suffered counterrevolutions: on the one hand, because our masters were afraid and on the other, because they were not afraid. With our shepherds to the fore, we have only once kept company with freedom, on the *day of its interment*."[4] If there was a lesson in German history, it was precisely that of its backwardness, which the philosopher had to make clear to all. The ancien régime, which met its tragedy in France, "plays its *comic* role as a German phantom"—the first appearance in Marx of the idea that history plays its great scenes several times, first tragically (as in France), then comically (as in Germany); the tragic manifests the arrival of a new era, the comic survival of the old one in its final phase, so that "mankind may part *happily* from its past."[5]

But then, why not condemn all of this wretched German history? For two reasons. The first is related to Germany's peculiarity in having experienced its future (what Marx calls "posthistory") in

at the colloquium "Marx et la Révolution française" sponsored by the Institut de recherches marxistes, Paris, April 1985).

    4. Marx, *Early Writings,* 245.
    5. Ibid., 247–48.

thought, in the form of philosophy. Germany is the theoretical conscience of other peoples; even its revolutionary past is philosophical, since it consists of Luther and the Reformation. As to the present, Germany is mired down in the ancien régime, paralyzed by its vices, but capable, thanks to its philosophy, of analyzing the flaw in the modern state as practically invented by the French. Even as it intellectually liquidates German archaism, the *Philosophy of Right* extends its critique to include the state of the French Revolution. But Marx, and this is the second reason, needed to go beyond Hegel by breaking the German curse of having to substitute intellectual history for real history—he needed to proceed, in other words, to the negation of philosophy through its realization: here we find the debate with Bruno Bauer in the making. Marx saw in the very defects of German backwardness the conditions for a revolution more radical than the French Revolution, one which would, in consequence, be on a par with German philosophy. The French Revolution was only "partial," "merely political," since it emancipated only a portion of civil society—the property-owning bourgeoisie—and did not create a "universally human" emancipation: here Marx recommended in his own manner the critical analysis of the *Philosophy of Right*. In contrast, owing to the very fact of its backwardness, the German ancien régime combined principles and classes, putting none in a dominant position and all in a sort of reciprocal neutralization. There, no one class could play the role of a general representative of society in order to realize a partial emancipation, in the French style. The paradox of this cowardly and "philistine" social world is that only a general emancipation is possible, an emancipation to be realized by a class laden with "*radical chains,*" with nothing below it, no residual humanity to exclude, and thus bearer, this time, of the emancipation of man. The idea of the proletariat springs up in Marx as the opportunity to bring German praxis to the level of German philosophy.

Marx returned to this idea in an article occasioned by the Silesian workers' revolt of June 1844 and published several months later during his stay in Paris (see selection 6). Arguing against an earlier article in *Vorwärts*[6] that was, in his eyes, guilty of underestimating the capacity of the Silesian weavers, he praised, along with the "brilliant" writings of Weitling, the theoretical mind of the German proletariat,

---

6. *Vorwärts!* was a German-language newspaper published in Paris, twice weekly, from January to December of 1844. Marx took part in its publication from the summer on. On an order from Prussia, the Guizot government expelled Marx and the journal's principal collaborators in January 1845.

in which he perceived the promise of the French-style political revolution's being transcended by a German-style social revolution. The first was the revolution of the citizen, the second would be that of man. In the first case, the French bourgeois were separated from the political community of the ancien régime. In the second, German workers would be separated from the human community, from the species-being of man, from his very nature. Hence this extraordinary parallel:

> It must be granted that the German proletariat is the *theoretician* of the European proletariat just as the English proletariat is its *economist* and the French is its *politician*. It must be granted that the vocation of Germany for *social* revolution is as *classical* as its incapacity for *political* revolution. For just as the impotence of the German bourgeoisie is the *political* impotence of Germany, so too the capacity of the German proletariat—even apart from German theory—is the *social* capacity of Germany. The disparity between the philosophical and political development of Germany is nothing *abnormal*. It is a necessary disparity. Only in socialism can a philosophical nation discover the praxis consonant with its nature and only in the *proletariat* can it discover the active agent of its emancipation.[7]

This passage is interesting for several reasons. First, because Marx here "resolved" the existential problem of German intellectuals by making the Silesian weavers' revolt an occasion for a vast generalization regarding the historical capability of the German proletariat. Second, because he displayed a sort of rhetorical prestidigitation that he was among the first to introduce into modern philosophical speculation, and that had more to do with preemptory sophistry than with reasoned demonstration. To Marx, the starting point was the philosophical superiority of the Germans, their specialization in the universal, the benefit of which he extended, by *petitio principii,* to the "people" as a whole, which thus became through him, "philosophical." For this philosophical people also to have a history outside of pure ideas, it is necessary and sufficient that it have a universal objective: the emancipation of man, and not just of the bourgeois, effectuated by the only class with no other interests than those of all humanity—the proletariat. Suddenly the Silesian revolt reveals the particular vocation of German workers for this task inseparably

7. Marx, *Early Writings,* 415–16.

philosophical and historical; here is a "theoretical" proletariat, already Marxist—without knowing it—through its praxis. Here also is a Germany where even the bourgeoisie is exonerated for being nonexistent, since by definition it can only have set itself bourgeois objectives and not philosophical ones.

And so, beginning with the distinction between the two emancipations, the political and the social, and through this succession of extravagant ascriptions, Marx promoted Germany to the avant-garde of European history, finally filling the gap that separates its philosophical history from its real history. The plus-side of Germany's radical political backwardness was that she had the best philosophers and the most "theoretical" workers, a combination which was to find its natural finality in the socialist revolution, an equally radical emancipation but of a radically different type—no longer political, but human.

The German revolution would thus be the sublation of the French Revolution. Savigny saved Germany by taking shivering refuge in a reactionary exaltation of the past. Marx returns the advantage to Germany on the very terrain on which she had been humiliated by the French. But to accomplish this, it was not enough for him to have ridiculed the historical school of law; he had to criticize Hegel's analysis of the French Revolution in the *Philosophy of Right*.

If the German revolution must be a negation of the French-style democratic political state, it is not for the benefit of a new concept of the state-community, the incarnation of the spirit of the people by a world-historical figure serving the spirit of the age; on the contrary, it is to lead society to the end of the state and to the reabsorption of politics in social activity freed from relationships of domination. The Marx of 1843–44 was full of Feurbachian enthusiasm; his object was to criticize the Hegelian conception of the state, to do with the Hegelian state what Feuerbach had done with religious alienation.

Between Marx and the French Revolution we must here take a detour through the work of the great mediator. The writings of the young Marx were devoted to a "critique" of the master in whose books he learned how to read universal history. Intellectual history, though rich in conflictual filiations, has rarely produced a philosopher so saturated, so obsessed, with the books of a predecessor. The young Marx knew Hegel line by line, and it was through Hegel that he first encountered the French Revolution before studying it in French historiography; it was, after all, Hegel who had put the idea of the state at the center of the history of the Revolution and its failure. In his eyes, the political instability inherent in the French events was characteristic of the revolutionaries' inability to disengage themselves from civil society in order to conceive of the state. Napoleon's greatness was to have accomplished just this, though only momentarily; the Hegel of the *Philosophy of Right,* in 1818, was more convinced than ever that the failure of the French Revolution was linked to its lack of comprehension of the "thought-concept" of the state. Thus, in his own critique of the Hegelian concept of the state, Marx inevitably returned to the question of the French Revolution.[8]

What did the *Philosophy of Right* actually say? Hegel presented his conception of the state through a critique of the classic theses of political philosophy. He immediately rejected Savigny, and Burke along with him: to found the state on custom, on the sedimentation of practices accumulated over centuries, was to consider it a random social product. Hegel, who looked upon the English system with little indulgence (in this respect he presaged Nietzsche's contempt for that "not very philosophical people"), lent this critique a tone all the more strident because he was simultaneously aiming for German reactionary thought: after Burke, Savigny. As he saw it, England had never emerged from the sphere of civil society to elevate itself to the level of a state. As to religion, that other classic foundation of the concept of the state, its private character and exaltation of the hereafter were not at all conducive to the public function it was supposed to fulfill. Its logic, on the contrary, was to separate the public and private worlds, thereby leading to political indifference. The subject of the king was the public face of the believer.

But in fact Hegel preserved his principal criticism for political economy, the utilitarian conception according to which the state is the guarantor of the property and safety of the citizens: a dominant idea at the end of the eighteenth century after the *Aufklärung*'s efforts to undermine religion allowed only *homo oeconomicus* to survive, defined by the universality of needs—which could hardly constitute a source of social unity. The concept of utility ended inevitably in the division of individuals—since what is useful to one is not so to another—and to the instability of power. At the time of the Constituant Assembly the king was defined by his utility to the social body, but he did not long survive the inconsistency of the principle upon which his position rested.

Having disposed of these interpretations of the state, Hegel still

---

8. See especially, apropos of this subject, Lucio Colletti's introduction in Marx, *Early Writings,* 1–56, esp. 28–46.

confronted one privileged interlocutor: Jean-Jacques Rousseau. The Genevan philosopher had attempted to found the state on Reason and to give it a spiritual principle, the will. He had thus broken with earlier explanations, rejecting what they had attributed to utility and externality. This gigantic stride made Rousseau in Hegel's view the first modern theorist of the state. Rousseau had made the mistake of retaining from his predecessors the idea of contract. For if the general will resulted from a contract, it was derivative from individual wills and the state remained contingent on civil society: a curious simplification of Rousseau (Hegel found it in Fichte) if one marks the care the author of the *Social Contract* took to distinguish the general will from the will of all. Nevertheless, only one fundamental difference separated Rousseau from Hegel, and it was less the conception of the general will than the idea that a "denaturation" was necessary to make a man a citizen—the *Second Discourse* and *Emile,* rather than the *Social Contract,* were alien to Hegel. In his view, man is a citizen of the state by birth, that is to say, in essence, since it is in the state that self-consciousness finds its substantive liberty. The hypothesis of a state of nature prior to the state itself was as abhorrent to Hegel, even as a theoretical postulate, as it would have been to Aristotle. The state is the modern *polis*. It can no more be conceived on the basis of an individual anterior to it than could the city of antiquity. Hegel wanted to effect the reconciliation of the public and the private spheres after their long divorce born of Christianity.

The French Revolution precisely illustrated for him Jean-Jacques's error, which was to have "reduce[d] the union of individuals in the state to a contract and therefore to something based on their arbitrary wills." From this, Rousseau could derive only abstractions: "For this reason, when these abstract conclusions came into power, they afforded for the first time in human history the prodigious spectacle of the overthrow of the constitution of a great actual state and its complete reconstruction *ab initio* on the basis of pure thought alone, after the destruction of all existing and given material. The will of its refounders was to give it what they alleged was a purely rational basis, but it was only abstractions that were being used; the Idea was lacking; and the experiment ended in the maximum of frightfulness and terror."[9] The work of Rousseau thus anticipated the "unprecedented" grandeur and the fatal defeat of an enterprise that had as its goal the

9. G. W̊. F. Hegel, *Hegel's Philosophy of Right,* trans. T. M. Knox (London: Clarendon Press, 1952; New York: Oxford University Press, 1967), 157.

10

INTRODUCTION

construction of the state on the basis of thought and thought alone, for the first time giving a rigorously philosophical character to a historical event—a French audacity that put 1789 way ahead of the English institutional tinkering of 1688, so celebrated by Burke. But in casting the general will as an alienation of the natural will, as a denaturation, a new beginning, Rousseau and the Revolution made it appear a purely external form that limited individual liberties instead of revealing the substantive character of liberty in the state. In the course of the Revolution, the Rousseauean abstraction was to lead to a result directly contrary to its aim, to the despotism of liberty, to the Terror. The French Revolution, in its ambition to create a new state founded solely on Reason, sought to incarnate the universal in the particular; that is why in the end it no longer recognized individual self-consciousness: in 1793, heads fell like cabbages.[10]

There was another consequence of this drama: the political instability characteristic of the postrevolutionary period. Like all his contemporaries, Hegel considered the inability to found a lasting state a failure of the revolutionary enterprise. This problem, renewed in everyone's minds by the fall of Napoleon, was posed by Hegel in existentially melancholy terms: "I am exactly fifty years old, I have passed thirty of them in this eternally agitated time of fearing and hoping, and I hoped that for once this fearing and hoping would be done with. Now I am forced to see that it goes on without halt."[11] For Hegel, as for Guizot during this same era, political stabilization was the postrevolutionary problem par excellence, the problem the era had to resolve.

Thus, as the *Philosophy of Right* illustrates, Hegel constructed his theory of the state on the basis of a critique of the French Revolution. The state had to succeed at what the Revolution had tried and failed to do: to realize Reason in modern history. He was concerned not with the state's historical origin but with the definition of its "concept," retaining the right part of the *Social Contract,* that Rousseauan intuition according to which the state is a self-determining will. It was inconsistent with this intuition to see the state as originating from a reality anterior to itself, because it possesses a fundamental philosophical anteriority to the individuals it unites. The state makes possible a

10. G. W. F. Hegel, *The Phenomenology of Mind,* trans. J. B. Baillie (New York: Harper and Row, Torchbook, 1967), 605.
11. Letter cited in Joachim Ritter, *Hegel and the French Revolution,* trans. Richard Dien Winfield (Cambridge, MA: MIT Press, 1984), 43.

rationally organized society. Hegel says, further, that the state is "absolutely rational inasmuch as it is the actuality of the substantial will" and that a "substantial unity is an absolute unmoved end in itself, in which freedom comes into its supreme right."[12] A "hieroglyph of reason," that is to say, something that must be deciphered by philosophy because its end—at once its limit and its goal—is to illuminate history, the state is what gives history its meaning as the history of man's liberty: the "contingent flower" of the Greeks, the private universality of Christianity, the abstract universality of the French Revolution, the substantive liberty of the modern state.

In this way, as has recently been noted,[13] the distinction Hegel made between civil society and the state took on a different sense than it had among liberal authors like Benjamin Constant. The Hegelian state is a totality that encompasses and transcends civil society. It has nothing to do with the liberal state, that product of civil society that must simply guarantee the "rights" of the former. The irony of this semantic confusion is that it was by way of the Marxist critique that it insinuated itself a posteriori into Hegelian philosophy. Indeed, in the manuscript written in the summer of 1843, long unpublished, which Marx devoted to a criticism of the *Philosophy of Right,* he recovered the distinction between the state and civil society from Hegel, but his criticism of Hegel's concept of the state made him fall back precisely on the liberals' version of that distinction. In order to apply the Feuerbachian treatment to the thought of the Master, and to find the bourgeois reality behind an illusion of the state-totality, Marx went by way of English political economy and French Thermidorian liberalism, Adam Smith and Benjamin Constant. It is through Marx that the precedence of the social over the political acquired its speculative dimension.

Marx retained Hegelian chronology. In his view, the concept that made possible the idea of the separation between state and civil society dates from the end of the city of antiquity, in which public and private were intermingled, and from the moment when the private individual was born with Christianity. In the Middle Ages, a public or political character was attached to every sphere of private life: the hierarchy of power between individuals was organized according to their respective membership in groups engaged in material

12. Hegel, *Philosophy of Right,* 155–56.
13. Luc Ferry and Alain Renaut, *Philosophie politique,* 3 vols. (Paris: Presses Universitaires de France, 1984), 3:96.

activity—serfs, feudal proprietors, corporations. In his own manner and in his own place in society, each man constituted the political state, and in this sense the Middle Ages was a democracy. But since no one was at liberty to alter his position, it was a "democracy of unfreedom."[14] For Hegel, this was the historical high point in the fusion of civil and political society prior to their modern dissociation.

"The abstraction of the *state as such* was not born until the modern world because the abstraction of private life was not created until modern times."[15] Indeed, modernity is inseparable from the free individual, who is master not only of his labor but also of his position in society. The abstraction of private life—that is, its radical separation from the political system—has brought about the abstraction of the state—that is, its radical separation from men's material activity. But Hegel, as we have seen, retained the idea that the state constitutes the principal figure of history and of the realization of the Idea. While civil society is the site of individual conflicts and, therefore, the potential seat of political revolutions, the state, which is the site of the interest of all, incarnates a superior rationality as the central institution of continuity and of the community. The contradiction between the state and civil society masks a unity of opposites in the Idea; and the state is the site of their reconciliation. Hence Hegel's rejection of all popular sovereignty, his admiration for Napoleon (conceptualized as chargé d'affaires of the universal spirit), and the idea of a rational monarchical state, represented by the Prussian state. In Hegel, to use the vocabulary of the young Marx, the political towers over the social, since it gives the social its meaning.

In Marx, as a result of the Feuerbachian reversal, the opposite is true. Civil society has priority over the state, and this very priority constitutes the essence of modernity. For the reality, in a modern civilization characterized by the dissociation of state and society, is the individual left to his own needs and interests—the man of the marketplace. This is the fact from which the famous Hegelian distinction originates as revealed by history and English political economy. It is under this form that Marx conceptualized modern individualism and reworked in his turn the central problem of modern political philosophy: What is a society (or a human community, in the young Marx's terms) if one can only conceive of its constituent units in terms of elements defined by particularity? For Marx as for Benjamin Constant,

14. Marx, *Early Writings*, 90.
15. Ibid.

whom Marx read pen in hand,[16] or for Tocqueville,[17] whom he studied more superficially, the private individual is the prototypical invention of modern civilization, a monad locked up in his own interests, calculations, and pleasures, cut off from his fellow men and a stranger even to the idea of a community. This individual is no longer the providential bearer of a final harmony born of the private universe of ownership (Locke) or competition (Smith). Rousseau, whose work Marx also read closely,[18] elaborated on the extraordinary difficulty of the natural individual's passage to the community of man: the social contract required nothing less than the denaturation of the individual. But whereas Rousseau was responding to Locke, Marx had Adam Smith in mind: *homo oeconomicus* must reconstruct his lost political dimension. But, how?

For the young Marx, the great modern rift between the social and the political operates to the benefit of the social. Whereas for Hegel it left the concept of the state intact as an expression of the reconciliation of opposites, for Marx it signified above all the birth of a new society, founded on the development of wealth and the dislocation of human relations by money. From this individualistic society, founded on particular interests, the modern state—a subordinate figure—arises as it was seen to emerge from the French Revolution, in the form of a representative democratic state succeeding the monarchical state. Its representative character reflects the separation of society from the state, and its democratic (universal) character reflects the abstraction of egalitarian citizenship in relation to the actual situations of

16. During his studies in Bonn, Marx noted extracts from Constant's *De la religion considérée dans sa source, sa forme et ses développements,* a work he contrasted flatteringly to the theses of the historical school of law in his article in the *Rheinische Zeitung* of 9 August 1842. Rubel, in his edition of Marx's works, points to other borrowings (see, for example, his note on Marx's article on the law concerning the stealing of wood, in Marx, *Oeuvres,* 3:1457), but it is clear that Marx was also familiar with Constant's work in general and especially with *De la liberté chez les Anciens et chez les Modernes.*

17. Marx took from Tocqueville's *Democracy in America* the idea that religious emancipation from the modern political state is not incompatible with the survival of religion in the form of the private belief of individuals. See, for example, *On the Jewish Question* (selection 4) and Rubel's note in Marx, *Oeuvres,* 3:1570. I am inclined to believe, on the basis of the manner in which he employed this text, that Marx read only the first part of *Democracy,* which was published in 1835, and not the second, 1840.

18. See especially in *On the Jewish Question* (selection 4), Marx's analysis of Rousseau as the lucid theoretician of the abstraction of democracy.

individual members of the social body. From real history, that of economic inequality and bourgeois domination, the representative democractic state fashions the illusion of community. Individuals cut off
from modern civil society alienate themselves in the imaginary community of the state, just as men, according to Feuerbach, project
in God the chimerical image of themselves. Reversing Hegel, Marx
extended the Feuerbachian critique to profane forms of alienation:
"Thus the criticism of heaven turns into the criticism of earth, the
criticism of religion into the *criticism of law* and the *criticism of theology*
into the *criticism of politics*" (see selection 5).

In so doing, Marx, in contrast to Hegel, preserved the preeminent historical dignity of the idea of revolution. Indeed, since the
forms of the state—for example, the passage from the monarchical to
the representative state—are subordinate to actual conditions of social
life, revolutions, which function precisely on the level of civil society,
are the midwives of history. The French Revolution, in overturning
the ancien régime, created modern politics, a characteristic of market
society. But since politics is an illusion produced by the alienation of
"democratic" citizens in the new state, the French Revolution must in
turn give way to a "real" revolution, one that will destroy the political
by absorbing it into the social. The revolution will result not simply
in one more transformation of the state, but in its abolition. It will
return man to what Marx calls his "species-being"—his humanity, in
other words—by destroying the intermediate expression of his alienation in the political illusion of citizenship. And so Marx rediscovers,
in the sublation (*Aufhebung*) of the French example, the future of the
German revolution.

A historical illustration of these analyses can be found in the August 1844 article in *Vorwärts!* that I have already cited. There Marx
refutes the argument of his friend Ruge—with whom he was breaking at the time—who explained the fatalism that marked the reaction
of Frederick William IV and German society to the savage revolt of
the Silesian weavers as a consequence of the primitive character of
Germany's relation to politics: seeing nothing more than a local catas-
trophe comparable to a natural disaster, they did not pursue solutions
on a national scale. Marx criticizes this interpretation, using first the
English, then the French example. The English bourgeoisie, supremely political, had faced worker's pauperism since Elizabeth; but if
they were incapable of finding any solutions other than expedients
identical to those devised by the King of Prussia—administrative or
charitable measures—it is precisely because there is no political cure
for social problems save a transformation of society. Napoleon, the

other hero of modern politics, decided one fine day to eradicate begging in France, with the same result. Even the Convention, which Marx sees as embodying *"the maximum of political energy, political power* and *political understanding"* (see selection 6), embraced the project of suppressing pauperism by order, with the sole result that it was besieged the following year by starving women.

An illusory project, but intellectually consistent if one accepts the young Marx's interpretation of the French Revolution: that the Revolution represents the apogee of the political spirit, as of the characteristic illusion of politics—the belief that it is possible to transform civil society by politics, whereas politics is, in fact, the mystification of society. It seemed possible to reform inequality and poverty because politics was by definition capable of everything, even though the "antisocial nature" of civil society was the very condition of existence of the political. Through this unmasking, Marx constructed a systematic critique of the French Revolution, which did not stop him from continuing to admire radicalism, especially that of 1793, not only because it displayed moral heroism but also because it offered an ideal laboratory for the reflection of the philosopher:

> "The *classical* period of political understanding is the French
> Revolution. Far from identifying the principle of the state as
> the source of social ills, the heroes of the French Revolution
> held social life to be the source of political problems. Thus
> Robespierre regarded great wealth and great poverty as an ob-
> stacle to *pure democracy*. He therefore wished to establish a
> universal system of *Spartan* frugality. The principle of politics is
> the *will*. The more one-sided, i.e., the more perfect, *political*
> understanding is, the more completely it puts its faith in the
> *omnipotence* of the will. The blinder it is towards the *natural* and
> spiritual *limitations* of the will, the more incapable it becomes of
> discovering the real source of the evils of society. (See selection 6)

Jacobinism, and to an even greater extent, Robespierrism, because they represent the illusion of the priority of the political over the social in its most complete form, reveal the truth of the French Revolution. Marx, starting from different premises, here reemployed the Hegelian idea that the revolutionaries' abstract voluntarism could lead only to the guillotine.

The most accomplished and subtle exposition of this dialectic between state and society characteristic of French revolutionary emancipation can be found in a piece Marx wrote just after *A Contribution to*

the Critique of Hegel's Philosophy of Right and published in Paris in the
Franco-German Yearbooks in early 1844—*On the Jewish Question* (see
selection 4). Recently arrived in Paris, Marx immediately immersed
himself in the study of political economy, French socialists, and the
history of France.[19] Critical reference to the French Revolution is all
the more frequent in his writings of this time because he was considering writing a history of the Convention (see note 1 above); and the
problem of the relation of the French political revolution to the social
revolution of tomorrow is at the heart of *On the Jewish Question*. This
little book was occasioned, as always, by Marx's reaction to another
text: this time, he set out to refute the thesis of Bruno Bauer—one of
the leaders of the Hegelian left—who held that the claim of German
Jews to legal emancipation was doubly contestable. As long as the
Prussian state remained a Christian state (Protestant, in this case),
Bauer demanded, how could it renounce its religious prejudice for the
sake of the Jews? Moreover, if the Jew remained a Jew, that is to say,
religiously Jewish, how could he be fit for modern citizenship? The
Jews were demanding citizenship from a state oblivious to the principle of citizenship, in the name of a confessional particularity at odds
with their very demand.

  Marx found in this argument an idealized conception of political
emancipation that led Bauer to take what the French Revolution said
and thought of itself at face value and to consider citizenship as the
final form of man's liberation. In Marx's view, political emancipation
is thus simply the product of the dissociation of state and religion,
making one the trustee of a laicized public sphere and the other a private affair, determined on the basis of individual choice. This dissociation does not entail the end of religious alienation or of the
religiosity of the citizen, as is shown by the American example in
which the neutrality of the state in respect to confessional membership coexists with unanimous belief in God. The modern religious
man lives his own life, alongside that of the citizen, as he lives the life
of a bourgeois, a landowner, or a wage earner. Political emancipation
does not signify the reunification of man, his reconciliation with his
species-being, his nature, but, on the contrary, his division into public man and private man, into the sphere of the state and that of civil
society.

  When political emancipation comes about through violence, of

19. On this period of Marx's life, see J. Grandjonc, *Marx et les communistes
allemands à Paris* (Paris:1974), and Auguste Cornu, *K. Marx et F. Engels,* 4 vols.
(Paris: 1962), vols. 2 and 3.

course, it may tend to reclaim the entire private sphere within the public sphere and to reduce the entire activity of individuals to their capacity as citizens. For the revolution that institutes citizenship, proclaiming the annihilation of religion is thenceforth on the same order as decreeing a ceiling on prices, the confiscation of goods, "the abolition of life (by the guillotine)." Again transposing Hegel's analysis into his own language, Marx saw the Terror as an attempt by "political life . . . to suppress its presupposition, civil society."[20]

But because this endeavor negates that which has allowed it to exist, it is incapable of lasting, and society will soon impose the priority of its existence. The French Revolution is simply the paroxysm of violence by which modern politics, pitting itself against the ancien régime, attempts to negate what it has produced. But this illusion of "*permanent* revolution" ends in the return of private man, religion, property, and all the other things that alienate man from his own creations, sacred and profane.

Marx was thus the triple heir to Adam Smith, Hegel, and Benjamin Constant; he sees at work in the "political" (i.e., the French) revolution the slow ripening of the conditions of production, the development of interests and needs, and the affirmation of individualism. Modern citizenship is a product of what the eighteenth century called "civilization." Thus, far from obliterating individuals' interests and egoism, modern citizenship is their abstract expression—something that has succeeded religion and now fulfills its functions on a collective level, since, like religion, it arises from the communal and universalistic aspirations of man. The democractic state temporally realizes Christianity's human foundation, but at the price of a new deception: it leads to the belief that political emancipation is the emancipation of the whole man, while it is but a new form of his alienation.

Thus Marx shared the same point of departure as English and French liberal thinkers: individualism as the essence of modernity, and modern man defined as the center of a network of private interests which make him a self-sufficient being, isolated from his fellow men. Beginning from this point the liberals reconstituted the political state in one or another of two ways: either by a *petitio principii,* according to which the totality of conflicting individual interests creates a general harmony, i.e., a society; or by default, in limiting the public sphere and restraining as far as possible the intervention of the state in individuals' activities.

20. K. Marx, *Early Writings,* 222.

These two paths are, nevertheless, not incompatible and proceed from the same spirit, since the first extinguishes the political by reducing it to the social, while the second restricts the political to the management of a residual public sphere. What separates Marx decisively from this liberal political philosophy is his introduction of the Rousseauean critique within it. But in his view, Rousseau's theory extends only to the abstract democratic state (see selection 4). Marx, having been nourished on Hegel, proceeded in his turn, to criticize the state from the perspective of an anthropological vision of history: politics is the new form of alienation in the modern era, while it is at the same time the imaginary expression of bourgeois society, and inseparable from it. This society—perpetually eroded by money and made up of aggregations enclosed in their particularity, is by definition incapable of conceiving of itself as a society, and so it invents an imaginary space where it can found the state as the locus of its fictitious and necessary unity—the space of citizenship and democratic equality. The meaning of the French Revolution lies in its invention of the political form of modern society.

Characterized, in contrast, by the identification of the state with religion, and by the existence of a king representing God, the ancien régime was founded on the nonexistence of man as a sovereign being. It recognized only subjects. There man had projected his humanity into the imaginary realm of religion. The modern state secularized the religious spirit by transposing the Christian idea of equality to the political level: here Marx retrieved an idea classic to French political philosophy and to the historiography of the Revolution in particular, only, as always, to submit it to a philosophical "critique." Indeed, as we have seen, the state does not realize Christianity but its human content, its "human foundation." Nor does it tear private man away from religion, the oldest of his alienations. In consequence, political emancipation is an improvement over the ancien régime and can thus be acquired, contrary to Bruno Bauer's thesis, by those who remain Catholics, Protestants, or Jews—in other words, religious—as private individuals. But at the same time, on the collective level, emancipation can only substitute political alienation for religious alienation. The bourgeois is the truth of the citizen, as the subject was the truth of the believer.

This explains why in the *Declaration of the Rights of Man and of the Citizen,* the charter of the French Revolution par excellence, the man, the member of civil society, constantly takes precedence over the citizen, the unit of the new democratic state. The rights of man, as distinct from those of the citizen, do not so much address man in general as they do the egoistic man of bourgeois society, the "man separated from other men and from the community" (see selection 4). In the "Declarations" of 1791, 1793, and 1795, for example, liberty and equality are defined as a framework destined to guarantee each individual his private satisfactions. "Political life," comments Marx, "declares itself to be a mere *means* whose goal is the life of civil society" (see selection 4). Nevertheless, revolutionary practice offers numerous examples that contradict the theory of the rights of man; violation of the privacy of correspondence, requisitioning of property, and breaches of individual liberties were the stock-in-trade of the French Revolution. For Marx, however, this provisional usurpation of the civil by the political constitutes one of the characteristic traits of the revolutionary emancipation. Indeed, the Revolution is the event that severed the bond rendering the political inseparable from the civil in feudal society; it is the straining and rending by which the citizen first affirms what Marx called the "idealism of the state" (see selection 4). The Revolution systematically abolished the corporative structure of the ancien régime—that expression of the separation of individual from the community, and of the political character of civil society. And it recovered, to its advantage, the political spirit freed from the fragmenting effects of feudalism, which, once emancipated, was capable of constituting the general sphere of the collectivity. At its apogee, which for Marx was 1793 and the Jacobin dictatorship, the Revolution manifested the absolute domination of the new idea of the community over the particular interests of civil society. But the same notion that constitutes politics as an autonomous domain also frees society itself from restraints on the free play of individual egoism. Political emancipation emancipates civil society from politics and opens the way for the unfettered materialism of interests. In this unequal match, where social man is the actual basis for the imaginary man of politics, society naturally ends up recovering what the political revolution has provisionally usurped. Hence the cycle running from the Year II to Thermidor. Setting out to be the Feuerbach of politics, the young Marx instead wound up sketching the outlines of a critical theory of the French Revolution.

The last elements of this theory can be discerned in *The Holy Family* (selection 7), which, although it appeared a few months after *On the Jewish Question,* belongs to the same intellectual cycle. Marx, Feuerbachian as ever, set his sights on the idealism of the "critical criticism" of Bruno Bauer and of the Hegelian Left. We have seen elsewhere that he was intensely interested during his stay in Paris—precisely in the period between *On the Jewish Question* and *The Holy*

Family—in the history of the French Revolution, although no one has as yet found a convincing explanation why he never wrote the history of the Convention he had in mind. He had at hand, like everyone else at the time, Buchez and Roux,[21] a fundamental source for all left-wing historiography of the era, and perhaps also (according to Rubel—see note 1 above) Cabet's *Histoire populaire de la Révolution française de 1789 à 1830*. In lieu of a history of the Convention per se, a portion of his new polemic with Bauer was devoted to this very period of the French Revolution.

Marx first put forth the idea, appearing here for the first time in his work but current in French historical literature of the time, that the Revolution generated ideas that went beyond its own achievements—that the Revolution was the source of the idea of communism, "of a *new world order*" (see selection 7), an idea that proceeded from the *Cercle social* in 1789 to Babeuf in 1795, and thence by way of the left wing of the Parisian popular movement, Leclerc and Roux. He did not dwell on this conception but used it to extend to "practical" and "political" revolutionary France the German privilege of possessing speculative thought going beyond the real situation and its representation. His essential commentary focused anew on the state–civil society dichotomy, the heart of his interpretation, and he sought to specify its significance in relation to the Robespierrist period as if to deposit there the material for his would-be history of the Convention.

Bauer saw in the state, especially in the virtuous state of Robespierre and Saint-Just, the means to hold together the diverse egoistic atoms of society. But as this alleged virtue could only be imposed by the Terror, contradictions brought the dictatorship to its demise. Marx rebels against this oversimplification: it is not the state that binds individuals together, he argued, but interest, the need of individuals one for another to satisfy their needs, civil and not political life. If the state is necessary, it is because the individuals within it con-

---

21. The *Histoire parlementaire de la Révolution française,* a vast publishing enterprise begun in 1834 by the Christian socialist Buchez and his friend Roux-Lavergne—an ex-Saint-Simonian like himself—was a compilation of documents from the revolutionary period consisting primarily of the minutes of the parliamentary debates. Each volume (there would be forty of them, 1834–38) until the thirty-fourth (the fall of Robespierre) was preceded by a preface by Buchez, who commented on their contents. This group of sources was systematically used by all historians of the French Revolution in the mid-nineteenth century, even by those such as Quinet who were the most hostile to the type of interpretation Buchez presented.

sider themselves to be self-sufficient beings, separate from their fellow men, and because they create a space in which they conceive of themselves as a community. The state does not maintain civil society; it is the other way round. Bauer mistook the heaven of the imagination for earth of reality.

As we have already seen in *On the Jewish Question,* a similar error explains Robespierre's failure: he hypostasized the political state in order to make it the central reality of history and society while it was but a literary figure. But in *The Holy Family* Marx added to this characterization of the Jacobin dictatorship an explanation of a cultural sort, the seed of which he probably found in the works of Benjamin Constant (see note 16 above). Reworking in his own language an idea dear to the author of *De la Liberté chez les Anciens et chez les Modernes,* Marx showed that Robespierre's and Saint-Just's illusion was fed by the example of antiquity. The revolutionary Terror was the product of an anachronism: "Robespierre, Saint-Just and their party fell because they confused the ancient, *realistic-democratic commonweal,* based on *real slavery,* with the *modern spiritualistic-democractic representative state,* which is based on *emancipated slavery, bourgeois society*" (see selection 7). By this somewhat elliptical formula Marx meant that in the ancient republics social activity and productive labor were the business of slaves; free men were exclusively concerned with politics and entirely defined thereby. Civil society and the state thus existed as two self-enclosed domains constituted by contradictory but non-mystifying principles, liberty and nonliberty: classical democracy was "realistic." In contrast, modern civil society rests on salaried labor, which conceals the domination of the property-owning bourgeoisie under the apparent liberty of personal contract. Thus, under the symmetrically illusory appearance of equal political rights, there arises a state that is "representative" (i.e., separate from those who are supposed to endow it with sovereignty) because there is no direct suffrage, and "spiritualistic" because it fails to recognize its nature and foundation: democracy is based upon the salaried worker, and political equality upon social inequality. Robespierre thought to found a classical-style democracy on the rights of man characteristic of modern society, as is evinced by his references to Greece and Rome in his speeches of 1793–94. His fatal error thus came from the gulf that separated the abstract equality implied by modern democracy from the actual inequality characterizing bourgeois society. In the modern world, as Constant observed, citizenship was no longer coextensive with liberty; but by means of the Terror the Jacobins wanted at any price to reduce this historically produced gap. Revolutionary violence thus became part not only of the nature of the Revolution, which was the provisional domination of the social by the political, but also of the repudiation by the drama's actors of what they were in the process of accomplishing. In taking eighteenth-century France for ancient Rome, they were confusing societies: anachronism is another name for Jacobin ideology.

By definition, a power founded on such anachronism could not last, because in the end society has the last word. It was, indeed, after the fall of Robespierre, and because of it, that the truth of the Revolution revealed itself: politics yielded to society. "Freed," under the government of the Directory, from "the trammels of feudalism and officially recognized (by the Revolution itself) in spite of the *Terror's* wish to sacrifice it to an ancient form of political life," bourgeois society "broke out in powerful streams of life" (see selection 7). The Enlightenment began, with Thermidor, to realize itself "prosaically." The bourgeoisie reigned over society and state all the more completely since it had been liberated by the "hammer of the Revolution" from all the structures of feudal society; and, as though by accident, the rights of man, the famous rights of man, finally became real because they were guaranteed by a political state in conformity with the society that founded them both.

But this rediscovered harmony, so perfect, was shattered on 18 Brumaire. Bonaparte put an end to the period during which bourgeois society found itself represented and led by the bourgeoisie: "It was not the revolutionary movement as a whole that became the prey of Napoleon of 18 Brumaire. . . . it was the *liberal bourgeoisie*" (see selection 7). Marx meant that the state recovered a certain measure of autonomy from civil society. Certainly, Napoleon was aware of the nature of the postrevolutionary state and all that it owed to bourgeois interests; and he put a great deal of stock in it—this was the *nouveau propriétaire* side of the Empire. But at the same time he did not hesitate to sacrifice, if necessary, the material and moral interests of the bourgeoisie and its representatives, whether industrialists or ideologues. The state he imposed on the bourgeoisie had ends other than their interests, had its own ends, or, better, was itself its own end, civil society being only its "treasurer." In this way Napoleon recovered the meaning of the Terror, which is the hypostasized autonomy of politics from society. But in reinventing the Terror, he gave it a different content, substituting conquest for virtue: "He *perfected* the *Terror* by *substituting permanent war* for *permanent revolution*" (see selection 7). The imperial dictatorship was an administrative version of the Terror, at the price of a change of objectives.

THE YOUNG MARX AND THE FRENCH REVOLUTION

Thus, in contrast to Bruno Bauer, the young Marx joined the historiographical tradition that analyzed Robespierrism and Bonapartism in terms of their direct relationship.[22] In his view, both regimes were characterized by the state's independence from civil society. In the first case, the regime of the permanent revolution of virtue, this independence expressed the springing up of modern politics in opposition to the ancien régime, but masked by the classical reference. In the second, continuing as a characteristic feature of the revolutionary cycle, it announced the end of permanent revolution, but at the price of its conversion into permanent war; virtue was replaced by the cult of the state as such.

In this way, the history of the revolutionary state remained distinct from the history of civil society and itself constituted the essential content specific to this period. The French Revolution, for the young Marx, was the *genesis of the modern state*.[23] Though the mutation of civil society was and remained the fundamental characteristic of European history, the study of the French Revolution revealed the other facet of this mutation, both dependent on and independent of the first: the birth of democratic citizenship and its illusions. According to Marx, it was not until 1830 that the French bourgeoisie regained the political role it had been able to play during the French Revolution only between Thermidor and 18 Brumaire. (Between 1815 and 1830, it found itself under the domination of the "counterrevolution.") And it regained this role only because it abdicated henceforth the pretension of incarnating a universal ideal of the state, charged with realizing the ultimate ends of humanity. The bourgeoisie finally accepted the state of 1830 "as the *official expression* of its own *exclusive* power and the *political* recognition of its own *special* interests" (see selection 7). By the time Marx was writing *The Holy Family*, French history had readopted the common law of the European states—a constitutional monarchy that was the product of civil society and nothing more.

Thus the history of the French Revolution according to the Marx of 1843–44 took place within a dialectic between the state and civil so-

22. In France this was the case not only with liberal tradition but with socialist or republican anti-Jacobin historiography as well (Proudhon and Quinet, for example).

23. In one of his journals that dated from his stay in Paris, Marx noted, under the general heading "Toward the abolition of the state and civil society," this first point, which is a good summary of his thinking at the time: The *History of the genesis of the modern state*, or the *French Revolution*. The arrogance of the political being—

ciety. The development of society was at the origin of the Revolution, which was itself born of the contrast between the bourgeoisie's exclusion from politics and its economic and social power. Moving away from Hegel, Marx is also close on this point to French historians of the Revolution, with whom he was very familiar. But the Revolution itself, once set in motion, was no prisoner of its origins. It was characterized by a provisional hypertrophy of politics that freed it from the conditions that produced it: a tendency expressed in its claim to represent a universal emancipation of humanity; in the belief in political voluntarism, which involved recourse to the Terror; and in the use of an anachronistic ideology borrowed from antiquity—characteristics revealing in three different forms the same disjunction between bourgeois society and the revolutionary state. After this period, the fall of Robespierre ushered in several years during which the bourgeoisie recovered the free play of its interests and its "prosaic" domination, only to lose them again on 18 Brumaire to a new version—this one administrative and all-conquering—of revolutionary Terror. Not until July 1830 did it recover its dominance—definitively, Marx in 1844 erroneously believed, sharing a widespread illusion on this point—and then under the form (finally admitted) of an explicit consent to the limits of its historical mission. These forty decisive years, between Sieyès and Guizot, are seen as the years of the bourgeoisie's education.

Taken in its chronological dimension from 1789 to 1830—at once its broadest dimension and the only one that ultimately discloses its real meaning—the French Revolution thus constituted both a historical triumph and a historical failure. The triumph was the establishment, against all odds, of a society in which bourgeois interests ended up being the sole beneficiaries of the immense transformation, in conformity with the truth of the event. These interests, indeed, "far from having been a *failure*," "won" everything, and had a "*most* effective success," surviving "*pathos*" and the rhetoric that surrounded their birth: "Interest was so powerful that it was victorious over the pen of Marat, the guillotine of the Terror, and sword of Napoleon, as well as the crucifix and the blue blood of the Bourbons."[24] In this way, in his own vocabulary, Marx imagines a history of the revolution quite similar to Guizot's: based on the ultimate primacy of the

---

confusion with the state of antiquity. Relationship of revolutionaries to civil society. Doubling of all elements into civil beings and political beings." See selection 8 and Rubel's note in Marx, *Oeuvres,* 3:1021–26.

24. Karl Marx, *The Holy Family,* trans. Dixon and Dutt (Moscow: Progress Publishers, 1975), 96.

social over the political and conceived as the inevitable reappropriation of the state by the bourgeoisie, in accordance with the reality of
civil society, after the interludes of the Terror, the Empire, and the
Restoration.

But if Guizot saw July 1830 as signaling the definitive victory of
the French Revolution, Marx viewed it as a mark of its failure, because it negated the universal aspects of the Revolution and its avowed
claim to emancipate the whole of society. The class war was Guizot's
legacy to Marx; but whereas Guizot considered it to have ended in
1830, Marx extended its benefits, against the bourgeoisie, to what he
sometimes called the "mass," that is, the most numerous portion of
the society. If the Revolution failed this disinherited people, it was because it had become alienated from its true interests at the birth of the
modern political state. It "did not have in the *political* 'idea' the idea
of its real *'interest,'* i.e., whose true life-principle did not coincide
with the life-principle of the Revolution, the mass whose real conditions for emancipation were essentially different from the conditions
within which the bourgeois could emancipate itself and society."[25]

Thus the opposition between the state and civil society underlies
the contradiction between real interest and political alienation. Curiously enough, this opposition also corresponds to a duality in the
types of historical analysis implicitly proposed. The origins or the
causes of the Revolution lay in civil society: the young Marx, who
never considered this problem in detail, contented himself with something he had always taken for granted: the knowledge that the development of bourgeois society was the root cause of the political
mutation of 1789. His thought already carries with it this notion that
the political is determined by the social (or rather, by the socioeconomic), a notion whose paradoxes he would justify all his life—
notably in his works on nineteenth-century France. But even if the
Revolution was provoked by the mutations of civil society, it remains
true that its entire course took place on another level, as though totally disconnected from its origins. This was the subsequent history
of the state's transformations, since the destruction of what Marx calls
"feudal society" was substantially accomplished as early as 1789 and
fully completed by 1793. The Revolution thus followed a course independent of its objective and necessarily determined historical function. Paradoxically, it is this very course that made it a historical event
of capital import: it manifested in all its violence both the birth of the
modern state and the illusion inseparable from it. Through the Revo-

25. Ibid.

lution, history revealed for the first time how, on the basis of a modern society transformed by egoism and money, politics harbors and manifests an entire panoply of communal mystifications characteristic of the modern era. By these means, Marx reintegrated the apparent contingency of this cascade of manifestations into the law that presided over the origins of the event.

In all these texts of 1843–44, which so frequently address the French Revolution, Marx is trying to construct a theory of politics primarily as the emergence of modern alienation. Just as he substitutes politics for religion as the dominant illusion of society, so he takes the baton from Feuerbach and proceeds to criticize the new mirage, a role that comes all the more naturally to him since democracy is but an avatar of Christianity. Marx would thus become the Feuerbach of secularized universalism. Politics, inasmuch as it incarnates this universalism, is simultaneously nothing, since it is civil society's illusion of itself, and everything, since history cuts its course by means of this representation, as shown precisely by the history of the Revolution from 1789 to its belated end in 1830.

To understand this history characterized by political hypostasis, it must therefore be recognized that it was produced by a dialectic of the real and the imaginary, and that the imaginary took precedence over the real, representation over interest, as long as the French were claiming to be founding a new society of free and equal men. In other words, this imaginary idea of community invented by the French Revolution also functioned as a real process of real history. The modern political state has fictive yet social existence; the working of the concept exposes the fiction but does not prevent the concurrent revelation of its role as a historical force. Although it is not an objective reality, it exists in history as if it were, for the same reason that religion does: because everyone believes in it. The "critique" must precisely allow its role to be conceived as both illusory and formidable.

If Marx nonetheless dwelled much more on the first aspect than on the second, it is because he was intellectually imprisoned in a radical combat on two fronts, as his polemic against Bruno Bauer makes clear. On the philosophical front, he had to eradicate the Hegelian and post-Hegelian religion of the concept, which he considered to be linked to the practical impotence of Germany: hence his emphasis on the construction of a historical reality absolutely distinct from the subject and operating as a pure given, exterior to consciousness. Reality is history revealed by philosophy quite independent of the intentions of the actors who, thenceforth, take a secondary position. On the political front, the young Marx wanted at any price to distinguish his position from the French and German Jacobin tradition: the critique of this tradition is the first imperative of his radicalism. This explains why Marx emphasized above all the mystifying and mystified character of the French Revolution in relation to its real significance: if only the latter is important, the successive forms of mystification of the democratic universal are reduced to a secondary role.

This twofold intellectual obsession may be perfectly illustrated by an analysis of the concept of the rights of man and of the citizen. Marx understood that this concept is inseparable from a philosophy of the subject as elaborated by the theories of natural law or by Kantianism. Just as he saw only the bourgeois individual in the Kantian subject, so he exposed the power of money and of the marketplace that underlies the citizen's liberties. Given over to his passion for hunting down the reality behind the concept—a passion that dominates his critique of Hegel via Feuerbach—he was entrenched in a system of opposition between apparent and real history: he fed his violent antispeculative and anti-German reaction with English political economy (the civil society defined by particular interests) and with an admiration for the realism of the French bourgeoisie of 1830. Interests are what is true in the rights of man; citizenship is what is false. This philosophico-political reduction kept Marx from having any concept of democracy other than one of illusion or mystification, and from perceiving what Tocqueville, during this same period, understood: that the illusion of democracy is its very truth.

Indeed, what Marx called the "democratic abstraction" translates into his own language the idea that also fascinated Tocqueville, namely, that democratic equality is the constant striving of individuals toward an inaccessible end. The democratic individual considers himself to be equal and similar to any other individual, while nature and society continually produce unequal individuals. Marx denounced this contradiction between the fact and its representation as typical of an illusion. Obsessed by the search for the reality behind the idea, he sought to define the historical conditions under which equality can finally become real. For Tocqueville, this was a meaningless ambition, because the abstract character of democratic equality is precisely its nature. The "illusion" of democracy is what comprises its reality and its strength. In the world he analyzed, equality is above all the manner in which the individual imagines his relation to others. It does not imply that all men are equal, but that all can and should be. It incites, simultaneously with the progress of equality, the sentiment of inequality: an unending dialectic that throws the whole social body

into a corpuscular agitation characteristic of modern societies. According to this analysis, both the search for the conditions of "real"
equality and the denunciation of inequality are constituent parts of the
democratic universe and in no way capable of going beyond it: what
pushes Marx into his critique of political economy is nothing other
than the incessant working of the egalitarian abstraction, whose very
principle is incessantly and unendingly to pursue its realization.

For if Marx threw himself into economics as though into the
true content of modern history, it was in search of the truth of the
illusion. Basically, it was enough for him to have defined and re-
defined the state as a communitarian lie to exhaust its whole history.
Since the reality is civil society where money is king, what good is it
to devote further analysis to its imaginary opposite, the equality of
men? This is an essential question and one that from this period on
directed the young Marx, as shown by the *1844 Manuscripts,* toward
another, more important "critique," a critique of economics.[26] Henceforth he would often return to the history of France and its political
revolutions, but as if, in passing, he was snagged by some current
event. His central work would be devoted to modern economics and
to its supreme laboratory, English history. His privileging of the reality of civil society over its diverse political forms very soon diverted
the young Marx from a systematic study of the modern state. Perhaps
this was why he never did write the book on the Convention that he
considered during his years in Paris. At any rate, it is what lends an
allusive and incomplete aspect to his historical analysis of the French
Revolution, in contrast to the very different systematic character of
his more general interpretative work, which itself issued from his critique of politics.

If the Revolution demonstrated the birth of the modern democratic state between 1789 and 1799 or (to use an alternative chronology that has no effect on the problem) between 1789 and 1830, the
question still remains why this birth was accompanied by such a multiplicity of political forms. For the history of the Revolution properly
speaking, if we accept the fundamental significance that Marx attributed to it, was a succession of political regimes that incarnated the
new state: the constitutional monarchy, the Jacobin Terror, the parliamentary republic, Bonaparte's dictatorship. How these different regimes manifested the spectacular blossoming of the same principle or
of the same collective illusion, and why they succeeded one another

26. In shifting from the state to civil society, from politics to society, Marx
simultaneously went from the French to the English example.

so rapidly within the space of ten years, are questions to which Marx never accorded the systematic treatment that nevertheless seems called for by the manner in which he posed them.

By means of the Revolution, bourgeois civil society freed itself from its feudal fetters and achieved the freedom of individuals and of the market; this was the "prosaic" side of the balance sheet. But in doing so, civil society replaced its former subjection to an absolute monarch with a political system founded on citizenship; this was the vital, enthusiastic aspect of the phenomenon, the aspect that lent the period what Marx termed its "tone." To the extent that the Revolution elaborated this hypostasis of the political—which had apparently become independent of its real basis—one can perceive between the lines of the young Marx's conception an interpretation of its course in terms of ideology and the false consciousness it had of its own mission, which in turn deflected actual history from that mission. In this respect, 1793 is an excellent symbol of the paroxysmal period of the revolutionary ideology of man's emancipation, which led to the idealization of the state and to its provisional emancipation from civil society. This may explain the particular interest it held for Marx, since it is the period on which he comments most, and around which he builds a particular interpretation of Robespierrist ideology in terms of its confusion of the ancient and the modern. Moreover, Marx may have had other reasons to admire 1793 besides its use for philosophical demonstration; similar in this respect to French socialists whose works he read or with whom he associated in Paris, he liked the radical extremism and the energy of the Convention, and even the historical poetry born of the voluntarist illusion.

Even so, Marx's vision, unlike that of Esquiros or Louis Blanc,[27] for example, does not contrast 1793 to 1789, the socialist annunciation to bourgeois reality. In his view, the Revolution was a homogeneous historical phenomenon: the illusion that dominated 1793 already characterized 1789, and Bonaparte recapitulated the Robespierrist Terror under a different form. It is this very homogeneity that Marx emphasized the most, the better to guard against the phenomenal diversity of the event. And if the period of the Terrorist dictatorship was able to draw upon the greatest revolutionary energy, it was because it also evinced the greatest blindness to what it was in the midst of accomplishing. From this perspective, Robespierre foretold not socialism, as Louis Blanc asserted, but the provisional emancipa-

---

27. Esquiros, *Histoire des Montagnards* (Paris: 1847); Louis Blanc, *Histoire de la Révolution française,* 12 vols. (Paris: 1847–62).

tion of the revolutionary state from its bourgeois sleeping partner, the Napoleonic dictatorship.

What remains totally unexplained is the series of chronological phases of the relationship between state and society that served as the weft of the whole revolutionary history. Though the process that led from 1789 to 1793 can be understood easily enough as the passage from monarchy to republic and the radicalization of ideology, it is difficult to understand how the system that returned in Thermidor '94 to its truth, that is, to the exercise of power by the bourgeoisie, slipped once more into the Bonapartist version of the dictatorial state. The first Bonaparte represented the same problem to the young Marx that the second would present to the mature Marx: that of a state instituted by the bourgeoisie, partially in its service and yet completely independent of it. Simultaneously bourgeois and nonbourgeois, what did Robespierre represent, and what does Napoleon represent? A prisoner to the idea of the subordination of politics to civil society, unable to conceive of the autonomy of politics under any other form than that of an illusion, the young Marx bequeathed to the future Marx a question he had not clearly resolved but that he had posed to its full extent, since he had made it the central mystery of the French Revolution.

2

The Marx of 1848 Confronts 1789

But then came *The German Ideology,* in which Marx freed himself both from Hegel and Feuerbach. Here, universal history—through its various epochs—is no longer the progressive unveiling of the rationality at work in its apparent disorder nor the successive manifestations of the Spirit as deciphered by the philosopher's concepts. Nothing other than the product of man's activity, it has become its own tribunal. By virtue of this famous reversal, which subordinates thought to being, Marx situated the dialectic of opposites in matter instead of making it an attribute of logic. At the same time, he rid himself of the concept of the "essence of man" so dear to Feuerbach. Man is defined solely by his historical existence, but the history that produces this existence also furnishes him with the means to understand its direction because it obeys laws immanent to its development. The "critical" rage of the young Marx found issue, in the end, in the transposition of Hegelian idealism into historical materialism. Dialectical reason exists in things before it exists in thought: it exists in thought because it exists in things.

From now on, the main task for the philosopher is to examine closely the real course of history and to reconstruct it as the sole repository of the meaning of man in his relations with nature and his fellow men. Hence the recycling—though in a materialistic sense—of the Hegelian concept of labor, with the accent placed on the division of labor as "one of the chief forces of history up till now" (see selection 9), and consequently on the central role of the notion of social class that Marx borrowed, as a matter of fact, from French historians of the ancien régime and the Revolution. Nevertheless, in order to show this idea in its fullest dimensions, Marx did not turn immediately to the history of France and resume his work on this subject. He treated the idea first in its general aspect, explaining that it sheds light not only on the social activity of individuals but also on their intellectual activity, since "the class which has the means of material production at its disposal, consequently also controls the means of mental production, so that the ideas of those who lack the means of mental production are on the whole subject to it."[1] Members of the class that dominates the process of the production of wealth also dominate the production of thought. Most often these are not the same individuals, since the division of labor also operates among those who dominate; but the phenomenon of total social ascendancy occurs through their common membership in a dominant class. Material power and spiritual power have the same origin.

It is thus in a climate very different from that of the works of his so-called youth that Marx addressed the problem of the relationship between society and the ideas it produces. In *On the Jewish Question,* or *The Holy Family,* society alienates itself in the representations— such as the democratic state—it constructs of itself, or in the learned ideas it appends to its representations—such as the Jacobin dictatorship's reference to antiquity. As we have seen, it is difficult to understand from these works how the communitarian illusion of the state takes such a varied succession of ideological forms; but Marx explains the production of ideas less in terms of domination than in terms of alienation. Man separates himself from his human essence by projecting it into the imaginary. In *The German Ideology,* on the other hand, there is no longer any "essence of man" but only the successive historical forms of humanity. Representations and ideas are an integral part of each of these historical forms, varying according to which classes dominate them. Hence Marx adapts Montesquieu to his new system: an aristocratic society will cherish honor, a bourgeois society liberty. Furthermore, in an implicit reference to the French ancien régime as analyzed by Restoration historians, he says that the idea of the separation of powers will prevail as an "eternal law" in a country where supremacy is divided between the king, the aristocracy, and the bourgeoisie.

These examples illustrate the extent to which the new theory remains ambiguous. Dominant ideas are the direct product of class domination, expressed by intellectuals or ideologists who belong to that class: while producing a new system of social relations, the bourgeoisie simultaneously produces ideas that justify that system and the men who give form to those ideas. But in the case of French absolutism, there is, by definition, no dominant class, since the absolute

1. Karl Marx, Friedrich Engels, *Collected Works,* (New York: International Publishers, 1976), 5:59.

monarchy represents, on the contrary, the provisional (but potentially long-term) impossibility of any real social supremacy, torn, as it is, between the interests of the nobility and those of the bourgeoisie. It is thus hard to know which role to accord to the ideologists of each of the three powers involved in this sort of reciprocal neutralization. Marx suggests rather the idea of a collective illusion born of an equilibrium. Since his examples mix morals, beliefs, law, ideas, and ideologies as exemplifying the spiritual production of a society or era, the force of this text comes less from its precision—which is nonexistent—than from a twofold sociological postulate: that the production of ideas cannot be detached from material production; and that it is therefore organically linked to the social conditions of that production—in other words, to classes. The Hegelian detour by way of the concept deploying itself in history is thus reduced by a materialist *coup de force* to the philosopher's illusion concerning his own practice, which he denies is determined. Now it is Germany's economic and social backwardness that feeds German speculative superstition.

Not that the illusion of universality was absent from the English and French revolutions. On the contrary, Marx develops the idea that if every revolutionary class must foster revolutionary ideas in order to prepare the overthrow of the class that preceded it, it must also imbue those ideas with a universalistic form and ambition so that it will appear to be the spokesman for the whole of society and will establish its domination on a broadened basis. Here Marx was thinking in particular of French Enlightenment philosophy, implicitly returning to the already classic problem of the intellectual origins of the Revolution. Like the German bourgeoisie, the French bourgeoisie spoke in the name of man in general, thus disguising its interests and the new domination it wished to establish over society in universalistic language. But the French bourgeoisie used this language to clothe a revolutionary project aimed at a radical transformation of society. The German bourgeoisie—fragmented, hesitant, poorly developed, and incapable of thinking in national terms—further mystified this language by carrying the universalistic abstraction to its extreme.

Marx thus found a new system of thought from within which to give theoretical form to the old obsession of his youth: German backwardness as an alternative on the one hand to English economics, and on the other to the French Revolution. In disengaging himself as violently as always from Hegelianism, he had done with the whole philosophic heritage of Germany, and notably with Kantianism, which would henceforth be thought of as philosophical mask for the impotence of the German bourgeoisie:

The state of affairs in Germany at the end of the last century is
fully reflected in Kant's *Kritik der praktischen Vernunft*. While the
French bourgeoisie, by means of the most colossal revolution
that history has ever known, was achieving domination and
conquering the continent of Europe, while the already politically emancipated English bourgeoisie was revolutionising
industry and subjugating India politically, and all the rest of the
world commercially, the impotent German burghers did not get
any further than "good will." Kant was satisfied with "good
will" alone, even if it remained entirely without result, and he
transferred the *realisation* of this good will, the harmony between it and the needs and impulses of individuals, to *the world
beyond*. Kant's good will fully corresponds to the impotence,
depression, and wretchedness of the German burghers. (See
selection 9)

This passage shows the extent to which Marx, when he was
constructing his theory of universal history, was capable of falling
into an extraordinary oversimplification, of the kind generally attributed only to his lesser disciples. It also makes one wonder as to the
reasons why he excepted his own thinking from the forces determining that of his unfortunate compatriots—introducing what is without
a doubt the central philosophical inconsistency of his doctrine. But
the French Revolution, even more than the rejection of the German
"philistine," offered him the perfect material from which to fashion
his new theories, this time in positive form. For here he found veritable classes, the antagonism between the Third Estate and the nobility, a national state, a liberal and revolutionary philosophy, and a
revolution—all the elements associated with a history already written
by French historians.

But this history, too, had to be set back on its feet, beginning with its central actor. What Marx admired about the French
bourgeoisie of the eighteenth century as opposed to the German
bourgeoisie, and about its philosophers as opposed to the German
philosophers, was the energy with which they defined and realized
their objectives, and the relative clarity of the ideas they fostered
or developed in relation to those objectives. Marx discerned in the
French eighteenth century a particularly clear image of historical necessity, working through the elaboration and implementation of liberalism as a doctrine expressing real class interests and even, at least in
part, affirming them as such. Although he never actually quotes
Guizot, one continually senses the influence exerted on Marx by the
historical works of this leader of the Doctrinaires, who, like Marx—

earlier than Marx—was persuaded that the key to interpreting the final century of the ancien régime was the bourgeoisie's victory over the nobility. The difference between the two authors is, of course, that for Guizot the bourgeoisie achieves the end of history by finding liberty, while for Marx it merely acts under the mask of universal values to inaugurate another historical period: that of its own class interests.

But in regard to the French bourgeoisie, Marx, its adversary, nonetheless shared some of the admiration more spontaneously felt for it by Guizot, its son. This reaction is less strange than it seems if we take into account its implicit critique of German philistinism and, above all, the purely intellectual joy of constructing a systematic embodiment of historical necessity in conformity with the general interpretation presented at the beginning of the book. But in this image of the French bourgeoisie energetically taking possession of its history, we can also see how far Marx has come since *The Holy Family*: in the analytical framework offered by *The German Ideology* there is no longer a place for the imaginary self-representations produced by bourgeois society, such as the Jacobin and the Napoleonic states. These last, products of the alienation of civil society, by virtue of this fact acquired at least a provisional status of autonomy in relation to civil society. But that is finished with, and the bourgeoisie reigns supreme over its own history. The idea of the priority of civil society over the state has taken the form of the determination of ideas and representations by bourgeois class interests, a conception which leaves infinitely less room for the infinite diversity of history's cultural products. Marx's subsequent work will make this quite clear.

Consider, for example, the treatment reserved in *The German Ideology* for French Enlightenment philosophy. Instead of the speculative form given by authors such as Kant and Hegel to liberal individualism or national claims, *The German Ideology* has the advantage of offering a version of bourgeois liberalism more closely linked to practice and more conscious of its real objectives. Marx made quick work, particularly, at the end of the book, of the utilitarian concept of society as elaborated in England and in France in parallel with the two great revolutions that brought the bourgeoisie into power in the two countries. He saw utilitarianism—the idea that social relations are founded upon what each individual perceives and takes as useful to himself—as the basis of bourgeois philosophy, the condition that makes political economy possible, and the transparent disguise for exploitation and market relations. That is why he suggests that utilitarianism has a history which is itself linked to the various stages of development of the English and French bourgeoisies. At the start, there is English manufacturing and commerce, the era of Hobbes and Locke. Marx summarily combined these two philosophers as the first theorists of bourgeois civil society, even though Hobbes is much more a theorist of politics than of society and has little in common with Locke beyond his recourse to the notion of a state of nature as a means of conceptualizing the modern individual. It is true that the idea of an original contract establishing society reveals, in the works of both authors, the precedence of the social over the political, as well as the founding value of the individual contracting wills. But since Marx, in this passage, had in mind the genealogy specific to *homo oeconomicus*—defined by his liberty, protected by his rights, cut out for competition and the marketplace—the reference to Locke seems more appropriate here than the evocation of *Leviathan*.

French philosophers, notably Helvétius and Holbach, gave this concept a more universalistic character. Interpreters, according to Marx, of the French bourgeoisie's battle for emancipation, Louis XV's *fermier général* and the German baron impoverish the conception by depriving it of its economic content, while making it into a symbol of universal philosophy conforming to the vocation of eighteenth-century Paris. But the economic content was retrieved, in another context, by the Physiocrats, even though they are unable—given "the underdeveloped economic relations of France" (see selection 9)—to overcome the constraints of an agrarian economy. Not until Godwin, and especially Bentham, in England at the very end of the century—in short, not until the bourgeoisie has "arrived"—does the fusion occur between utilitarian doctrine and its real content, political economy (which, for Marx, means liberal political economy).

This page of *The German Ideology* is one of the rare passages in which Marx attempts to illustrate concretely the materialist theory of history, the principles of which he expounded upon earlier. As we have seen, the result is not fully convincing. In his rapid overview of the history of ideas in France and England, Marx hardly does better than his lesser disciples of the twentieth century—which tends to prove that the method is flawed. Beyond characterizing so many great authors so vaguely, he also quite arbitrarily employs the notion of determination by means of what he calls "real conditions"—that is to say, the economic and social infrastructure. In what way, for example, is Helvétius more "universalistic" than Locke? And how, supposing he is, can this trait be explained by the respective states of development of English and French capitalism? Marx asserts rather than demonstrates. Moreover, his analysis of economic history properly speaking is just as preemptory: eighteenth-century France is characterized, in turn, by a frenzy of negotiations and speculations when Marx is explaining Helvétius and Holbach, and by an economy that is still "feudal" when he is describing the limits of physiocratic thought. The mechanistic use of Marxism as a theory of history begins with Marx.

Within this context, the meaning of the French Revolution is henceforth unequivocal: it is no longer the metamorphosis of the modern democratic state but the seizure of state power by the bourgeoisie. Marx still considers the Revolution a *political* event, but a political event determined by economic and social evolution, by the development of productive forces—the market economy and the bourgeoisie. This determinism, which explains Marx's shift to the side of material conditions as opposed to concepts, to the side of civil society as opposed to the state—in short, to Adam Smith's side as opposed to Hegel's—makes it impossible to conceive of the French Revolution as a manifestation of the polymorphic nature of the state or as the alienation of market society in an imaginary community of citizens. Indeed, within the materialist interpretation there is no longer—as there was in *The Holy Family* thanks to the concept of alienation—anything that allows the Revolution to be detached from its social determination, or the state from bourgeois society. The state is now merely "the form in which the individuals of a ruling class assert their common interests, and in which the whole civil society of an epoch is epitomized."[2] As a consequence, the question that *On the Jewish Question* or *The Holy Family* allowed him to pose, if not to resolve—What explains the extraordinary diversity of forms of state manifested by the French Revolution, if the civil society that supported it remained the same?—is henceforth formulated in such a way as to render it utterly insoluble. It becomes a matter of understanding why a project as determined as the government of the bourgeoisie, a project inscribed in the evolution of society, assumed such a chaotic and polymorphic course. If the Revolution was nothing more than the conquest of the state by a bourgeoisie that was already master of society—a conquest achieved in 1789—then interpretation of what followed 1789 is either impossible or arbitrary.

Indeed, if the whole revolutionary process and the abundance of its successive manifestations must be continually reduced to their common denominator—the bourgeoisie and its domination—it becomes impossible to conceive of them under an autonomous form, as Marx was able to do in *The Holy Family* with the concept of "poli-

2. Ibid., 5:90.

tics" as an illusory projection of society. The hypertrophy of the figure of the state, and its relative independence of society, is henceforth nothing but a residual phenomenon of backward Germany, since it is tied to the impotence of a bourgeoisie incapable of achieving a dominant position or even a national state. That, however, is what the French bourgeoisie did, first under the shadow of monarchical power, then, by the Revolution, to its own immediate benefit. Like French historians of the Restoration, Marx continued to associate 1789 with the antiquity of French national unity and the work of the monarchy; but behind this age-old labor he saw the gradual conquest of the bourgeoisie in search of total supremacy over society and the state. So much so that the whole revolutionary process can only be interpreted as the history of that takeover rather than, as in earlier works, a cascade of alienations. The already classic problem of revolutionary historiography—that of grasping the nature of the event as a totality in spite of such contradictory successive manifestations—no longer existed, because 1789, 1793, and Thermidor were all part of the single epic of bourgeois emancipation. This, for Marx, is what the German philistine is incapable of understanding, seized as he is with panic in the face of the conditions of real history and "recoiling in horror from the practice of this energetic bourgeois liberalism as soon as this practice showed itself, both in the Reign of Terror and its shameless bourgeois profit-making" (see selection 9).

Thus, for Marx as for his bourgeois predecessors of the Restoration, the Terror remained the great enigma of the Revolution. This makes perfect sense within the framework of a social interpretation based on a 1789 that unveils bourgeois dominance. But how then to explain the political radicalization and brutal intervention of the second revolutionary generation, supported by the lower orders of the cities? The Marx of these years was no longer the Marx of *The Holy Family,* but the question still remains with him. He no longer saw the Terror as born of the classical representation of the citizen, which contradicts modern bourgeois individualism. Nor did he see it, as liberal historians did, as the detestable but provisional means by which the bourgeoisie saved what it had gained since 1789 from the European coalition. Instead, just like money, and despite appearances to the contrary, the Terror was integral to the implementation of liberalism. Yet in another passage of *The German Ideology* devoted to criticizing Stirner's analysis of the sacerdotal character of Robespierre (see selection 9), Marx says exactly the opposite. There he portrays the opposition to Robespierre (the Girondins and the Thermidorians) as representatives of the propertied classes, and the Robespierrist dictatorship as emanating from the only "truly revolutionary class," the "innumerable masses." A little later, he reaffirms this interpretation in the same terms, reproaching "Saint Max" for having said nothing about "the actual, empirical grounds for the cutting off of heads—grounds which were based on extremely worldly interests—though not, of course, of the stockjobbers, but of the "innumerable masses" (see selection 9).

Thus we find ourselves faced with two contradictory analyses of the Terror, both of them incompatible with the analysis in *The Holy Family* because both are founded on class realities—faithful, in this respect, to the general theory of history developed by Marx. In the first, the Terror is an instrument for the realization of bourgeois interests and liberalism—all to the glory of the "energy" of the French revolutionary bourgeoisie. In the second, on the contrary, 1793 escapes from the bourgeoisie, and the Robespierrist and sans-culotte dictatorship (Marx does not distinguish between the two, following the example of the historians he had read) incarnates the interests of the "masses," since they are involved in pushing the revolution beyond liberalism. Here we rediscover—presented in a totally different and much clearer form, in terms of class—the idea that the French Revolution inspired attempts to go beyond the horizons of bourgeois society. But in the theoretical context of *The German Ideology* this idea comes up against the notion of an unequivocal—uniformly bourgeois—meaning of the French Revolution.

In an attempt to disengage ourselves from this contradiction, we might refer to one of Marx's slightly later texts, such as the long article that appeared in the *Deutsche Brüsseler Zeitung* in October–November 1847, consisting of a polemic with Karl Heinzen on the conditions for the German revolution. Here Marx came to Engels's aid in order to reaffirm the thesis of *The German Ideology,* notably the derivative, subordinate character of the state in relation to bourgeois society once this latter has reached maturity. The property relations constituting that society are far from being a result of the bourgeoisie's political domination; on the contrary, its political domination is the product of that social structure. And here Marx added:

> If therefore the proletariat overthrows the political rule of the bourgeoisie, its victory will only be temporary, only "an element in the service of the *bourgeois revolution* itself, as in the year 1794, as long as in the course of history, in its "movement," the material conditions have not yet been created which make nec-

essary the abolition of the bourgeois mode of production and
therefore also the definitive overthrow of the political rule of
the bourgeoisie. The terror in France could thus by its mighty
hammer-blows only serve to spirit away, as it were, the ruins of
feudalism from French soil. The timidly considerate bourgeoisie
would not have accomplished this task in decades. The bloody
action of the people thus only prepared the way for it. (See
selection 13)

From this frequently cited passage, commentators usually retain
only the phrase in which the Terror "objectively" accomplishes the
tasks of the bourgeois revolution by sweeping away the ruins of feudalism. And yet, even when considered alone, this idea scarcely resists analysis within the Marxist context as Marx himself presented it;
if it is true that the whole evolution of French society prepared the
bourgeoisie to seize power as it would a ripe piece of fruit, why did it
draw back when the time actually came to do so? Moreover, we have
seen that Marx often praised the French bourgeoisie's "energy" and
historical consciousness in contrast to its German counterpart. But
then, all at once, we find it as "timidly considerate" as the German
philistines, and reduced to a sort of common nature, shared inter-
nationally by the whole class. Finally, if we treat the notion of the
"hammer" of the Terror as vital to the bourgeois revolution, not in
terms of its coherence with what can already be called the Marxist
philosophy of history, but in relation to the known facts, it no longer
resists examination. It can indeed be said that the French bourgeoisie
needed the people in order to overthrow "feudal" institutions, but in
1789, not in 1793; and neither the fourteenth of July nor the peasant
movements of July and August can be subsumed under what Marx
terms "the regime of the Terror."

But the rest of the passage quoted harbors problems even more
redoubtable. For here Marx defines the dictatorship of 1794—the
Robespierrist dictatorship—as the "overthrow" of bourgeois political
domination by the proletariat, albeit a "temporary" overthrow since
the objective conditions for a proletarian revolution had yet to crys-
tallize. Finally, there is a third element: this overthrow would nevertheless serve what it had overthrown. This is a completely new thesis
for Marx. For although he had always written—from *The Holy Family* to the *Manifesto of the Communist Party*—that the bourgeois revolution was pregnant with an embryonic proletarian revolution, just as
bourgeois society was pregnant with the proletariat, it was Babeuf
who embodied the idea, the announcement, and not Robespierre who
embodied the reality, even provisionally.

Be that as it may, the accumulation of contradictions and extravagances in the work of a great mind are but a symptom of the limitations of the system in which it is enclosed. Compelled by his philosophy of history to reduce political forms to their class content, Marx attributes to the Robespierrist dictatorship (and to its most spectacular form, the Terror) a popular, antibourgeois, and, he goes so far as to say, proletarian reality. But obligated, by virtue of the same imperative, to define the whole French Revolution as the advent of the liberal bourgeoisie, he must also subordinate the "proletarian" episode to the realization of its opposite. As a result, two questions necessarily remain unanswered: first, the nature of this episode and of the historical situation that could have produced it; and second, the explanation for the enigma of a political "regime"—the Terror—that was not the product of the society that it nevertheless served. These inconsistencies are the inevitable price Marx pays for negating the autonomy of political history.

In the 1847 article we can find no solution to the contradiction raised in *The German Ideology* between a uniform conception of the French Revolution—bourgeois from start to finish in its actors and consequences—and a conception that acknowledges the exceptional character of the Jacobin dictatorship while subordinating it to the end result. Both share at least the same main point—the reduction of politics to civil society, which makes the French Revolution into the history of the conquest of state power by a bourgeoisie that has already taken over society. It must, furthermore, be noted that in everything he wrote on the Revolution during this period, Marx remained rigorously attached to this pure notion of historical necessity, without making the least allusion, for example, to the role that might have been played in the Revolution by external events such as revolutionary France's war against the European monarchs. This is a theme running through French historiography[3] as an explanation or justification of the Terror. Marx made no use of it. Having a deductive mind, he stuck to the elements of the conceptual framework he had at last found.

The revolutions of 1848, especially the Prussian and German revolution, would provide an essential testing ground for this conceptual framework. In the preceding years, Marx never stopped comparing

---

3. It was Mignet who, in his *Histoire de la Révolution française* published in 1824, gave this thesis the formulation destined to become a classic in French historiography.

the political revolution—of which the French example remained the outstanding model—to the social revolution, the revolution of the future. The first was fundamentally the conquest of state power by a bourgeoisie already dominant within society, and the subsequent juridical transformation of property relations. The second, which must abolish not feudal but bourgeois ownership, would, in contrast, bring about a general emancipation of society and thus the extinction of politics. Marx continually threw this contrast in the faces of the German democrats, whom he reproached for confusing the republican idea with the idea of social liberation. But he also emphasized that even though the two historical processes were quite distinct, being different and even contradictory in content, they were nevertheless doubly linked: first, because they appeared in an ordered succession; second, because the first facilitated the second by virtue of the organizational possibilities it offered to the proletariat. The hypothesis of a German proletarian revolution following a successful bourgeois revolution frequently recurred in the writings of 1847 and was an essential element of the *Communist Manifesto*. Thus the writings from the *Neue Rheinische Zeitung*—founded by Marx and Engels in Cologne in June 1848—tried to use the idea of a German republic to mobilize not only the militants linked to the Communist League, but all the democratic forces.[4]

But the German revolution was to be short-lived. The Prussian bourgeoisie, and the German bourgeoisie generally, preferred a compromise with the existing dynasties and aristocratic society to an alliance with the popular classes. In a brilliant page from his polemic against Karl Heinzen over the German situation, Marx predicted, a year in advance, the course of events:

> Germany . . . has it own Christian-Germanic brand of bad
> luck. Its bourgeoisie has got so very far behind the times that it
> is beginning its struggle against absolute monarchy and seeking
> to create the foundation for its own political power at the mo-

4. In this regard, see the preface written in 1895 by the aged Engels to *The Class Struggle in France:* "When the February revolution broke out, we were all, in the way in which we conceived of the conditions and course of revolutionary movements, under the spell of past historical experience and notably that of France. Was it not precisely this latter that, since 1789, having dominated all of European history, set off once again the signal of general upheaval? Thus it was obvious and inevitable, that our ideas about the nature and workings of the "social" revolution proclaimed in Paris in February 1848, the proletarian revolution, should be strongly colored by memories of the models of 1789–1830."

ment when in all the advanced countries the bourgeoisie is already engaged in the most violent struggle with the working class and when its political illusions are already antiquated in the European mind. In this country, where the political wretched-ness of the absolute monarchy still persists with its whole appendage of run-down, semi-feudal estates and relationships, there also already partially exist, on the other hand, as a conse-quence of industrial development and Germany's dependence on the world market, the modern contradictions between bour-geoisie and working class and the struggle that results from them. . . . The German bourgeoisie therefore already finds it-self in conflict with the proletariat even before being politically constituted as a class.[5]

For Marx, this advance diagnosis explained the failure of the 1848 revolution in Germany and revived two old sentiments which had never left him: disdain for the pusillanimity of the German bour-geoisie—trapped as it was between two eras, and incapable of facing up to its "historic" tasks—and admiration for the manner in which the French bourgeoisie, in contrast, had accomplished its political revolution at the end of the eighteenth century in the name of an en-tire people. From this view came some of Marx's important observa-tions on the French Revolution between 1848 and 1850.

These remarks are faithful to the spirit of *The German Ideology,* which they complete on certain points. More than ever, Marx em-phasized the uniform nature of the phenomenon, defined at once by its form—political—and by its content—bourgeois. He placed the accent on the audacious manner in which the French bourgeoisie broke with feudalism, and the radicalism of its attitude, which al-lowed it to incarnate the revolutionary nation. He had already cele-brated, in a passage in *The German Ideology,* the brutal seizure of power in June and July of 1789 by the Estates General, transformed under the direction of the Third Estate into the National Assembly—an act of revolutionary authority that established the concept of sov-ereignty and the modern doctrine of representation (see selection 9). In an article of July 1848 he reproaches a new German philistine—the Prussian minister of agriculture—for his actions or, rather, his tim-idity, by contrasting the minister's work to that of his French prede-cessors: "The French people finished with the feudal burdens in *one day,* the fourth of August 1789, three weeks after the storming of the

5. Marx and Engels, *Collected Works,* 6:332.

Bastille. On 11 July 1848, four months after the March barricades, the feudal burdens finished with the German people." And Marx then adds this essential sentence, which proves that he credits the French (as opposed to the German) bourgeoisie with having a real understanding of its actions and the conditions of its historic role: "The French bourgeoisie of 1789 did not leave its allies the peasants in the lurch for one moment. It knew that the basis of its rule was the destruction of feudalism on the land and the establishment of a class of free peasant landowners" (see selection 16). The French Revolution, although defined by the interests of the bourgeois class, was made by all the people, with the peasantry at the fore, since this latter also found a provisional advantage in the conditions of the bourgeoisie's ascendancy over the nobility.

The question of the class alliances indispensable to the success of the Revolution—a question that, after the failure of 1848, was to preoccupy Marx for the rest of his life—was the point of departure for his famous article in the *Neue Rheinische Zeitung* of December 1848, "The Bourgeoisie and the Counterrevolution" (selection 17). We must pause to consider this text at some length, first because of its profundity and intrinsic beauty, and second because it closes the 1845–48 period of Marx's life—the period between finding the method and question which would preoccupy him for life, and the moment when, at the age of thirty, he would analyze, in this light, his first great political setback: the failure of the German revolution.

Present at this melancholy rendezvous were Mark's three homelands—Germany, England, and France, the three nations whose histories he saw as the history of the world. The German revolution is brought before the tribunal of the French and English revolutions in an attempt to understand the reason for its defeat. For Marx, who here revives an earlier idea ever-present in his thoughts,[6] the English

---

6. See especially, in *Moralizing Criticism and Critical Morality,* in Marx and Engels, *Collected Works,* 6:322, this comparison: "In the English as well as the French revolution, the question of property presented itself in such a way that it was a matter of asserting free competition and of abolishing all feudal property relations, such as landed estates, guilds, monopolies, etc., which had been transformed into fetters for the industry which had developed from the sixteenth to the eighteenth century."

In this same text, on the preceeding page, we find the idea that the two revolutions are comparable to the extent that both allow "the first manifestation of a truly active Communist party . . . within the bourgeois revolution" (Marx and Engels, *Collected Works,* 6:321): levelers on one side, followers of Babeuf on the other.

and the French revolutions, the two great moments in European modernity, are fundamentally comparable in two respects: they accomplished the same historical task, the political accession of the bourgeoisie, and they did so with the same strategic disposition of collective actors—the bourgeoisie and the people on the one hand, the monarchy, the nobility, and the church on the other.

Such a claim assumes, of course, that we are speaking of the English revolution of 1648, not that of 1686: here lies the sum total of the misunderstanding between Marx and Guizot, as illuminated by a slightly later article by Marx (1850), which reviews a recent book of Guizot's: *Pourquoi la révolution d'Angleterre a-t-elle réussi? Discours sur l'histoire de la révolution d'Angleterre* (see selection 18). In speaking of the "success" of the English Revolution, Louis Philippe's former minister naturally meant its conservative outcome, as brought about in 1688 by the ruling circles' call for a new dynasty. For Marx, on the contrary, that "success" would have been a sign of failure, due, like the German failure of 1848, to the bourgeoisie's capitulation to the great landowners, if the Glorious Revolution had not been preceded by a *real* revolution—the revolution of 1648 whose radical action was exactly what saved the compromise of 1688 from being a retreat.

The English revolution, as far as Marx was concerned, was 1648 and Cromwell, the death of the king and the Navigation Act. It was a revolution led by the bourgeoisie, like the French Revolution, and similarly drawing support from a proletariat and other popular strata that had yet to develop a class existence—and hence, a fortiori, class

---

A systematic comparison of the two revolutions (1640–88, and 1789–1830) is made very early on by Engels, in an article in *Vorwärts* of 31 August 1844: "The seventeenth-century English revolution was the exact model of the French Revolution of 1789. In the Long Parliament we can easily distinguish the three phases that in France would be the Constituent Assembly, the Legislative Assembly, and the Convention. The passage from the Constitutional Monarchy to democracy, from military despotism to the restoration and to the revolution of the *juste milieu,* appeared much more markedly in the English revolution. Cromwell was Robespierre and Napoleon rolled into one. The Gironde, the Montagne, and the *hébertistes* and *babeuvistes* corresponded to the Presbyterians, the independents, and the levellers. The political outcome of both [of these revolutions] was relatively modest, and all the parallels that could be elaborated with the greatest abundance of details also demonstrate that the religious revolution and the irreligious revolution, to the extent that they remain political, tend; when all is said and done, to come to the same end."

On this same question, see Bruno Bongiovanni, "Marx e la rivoluzione inglese," *Quaderni di storia,* no. 18, July–December 1983.

consciousness—independent of the bourgeoisie. Thus "where [these social categories] stood in opposition to the bourgeoisie, as for example in 1793 and 1794 in France, they were in fact fighting for the implementation of the interests of the bourgeoisie, although not in the *manner* of the bourgeoisie. The *whole of the French terror* was nothing other than a *plebeian manner* of dealing with the *enemies of the bourgeoisie,* with absolutism, feudalism, and parochialism" (see selection 17). Since, within the framework of the French-English comparison, he cannot treat the peasant question, which is so radically different in the two countries, Marx illustrates the popular character of the two bourgeois revolutions by referring to the Levellers and the sans-culottes. In doing so, he gives a new version of the 1793–94 period in France: it is no longer the story of a proletariat carrying out a provisional seizure of power for its own benefit, but of a heterogeneous collection of social strata "which did not form a part of the bourgeoisie" and had no political independence; these strata opposed the bourgeoisie only the better to bring victory for its interests. Thus the provisional victory of this ill-defined coalition changed not the content of the Revolution but its method, which for a time became "plebeian."

This new interpretation, more refined than that of 1847, offers the advantage of maintaining the unity of content of the entire course of the Revolution. There is, to be sure, intervention by the proletariat and the popular masses. But since this proletariat lacks sufficient development, there is no political consciousness independent of that of the bourgeoisie, only a style, a particular form of intervention and of government, exemplified by the Terror. Now it is a matter of explaining how a poorly developed proletariat can participate in a dominant political coalition, why the bourgeoisie allows itself to be dispossessed—even provisionally—of a power it has only just won, and, finally, how the disparate coalition that succeeded it could carry out the purposes of the bourgeoisie while struggling against it. Unfortunately, Marx said nothing more about this, and never would. What is implicit in his analysis, however, is that having celebrated the audacity and historical intelligence of the bourgeoisie of 1789, he imputed to the bourgeoisie of 1793 a collective sentiment of dread when faced with the very consequence of its actions. In doing so, he rediscovered in this bourgeoisie the attributes of the German philistines: the timorous petit-bourgeois spirit he so despised. But Marx could not write about that, for the contrast between the French and German bourgeoisie lay at the heart of his analysis. On the other hand, since his aim was to explain the Jacobin and Robespierrist dictatorship, it was probably difficult for him to launch into a battle against the moderatism and "petit-bourgeois mentality" fostered by a government composed, socially, of petit-bourgeois. The uniformly bourgeois determination of the diverse political forms of the French Revolution continued to pose insurmountable problems for Marx.

In any case, Marx recovers the tone of a son of the Enlightenment in order to celebrate, in the rest of the article, 1648 and 1789 as dates marking the birth of a new European society. For at bottom he was of one mind with the great liberals, with whom he was bound in a love-hate relationship: when it came to discussing the French Revolution in terms of a final result, everything was clear; this Marx had learned from their books. To understand that the significance of the course of this event was virtually self-evident in his eyes, it is enough to listen to his combined eulogy of 1648 and 1789 at the barely sealed tomb of the German Revolution:

> The revolutions of 1648 and 1789 were not *English* and *French* revolutions; they were revolutions of a *European pattern*. They were not the victory of a *particular* class of society over the *old political order;* they were the *proclamation of the political order for the new European society.* In these revolutions the bourgeoisie gained the victory; but the *victory of the bourgeoisie* was at that time the *victory of a new social order,* the victory of bourgeois property over feudal property, of nationality over provincialism, of competition over the guild, of the partition of estates over primogeniture, of the owner's mastery of the land over the land's mastery of its owner, of enlightenment over superstition, of the family over the family name, of industry over heroic laziness, of civil law over privileges of medieval origin. The revolution of 1648 was the victory of the seventeenth century over the sixteenth century, the revolution of 1789 was the victory of the eighteenth century over the seventeenth century. Still more than expressing the needs of the parts of the world in which they took place, England and France, these revolutions expressed the needs of the whole world, as it existed then. (See selection 17)

In this admirable text Marx takes up in his own vocabulary a theme familiar to Benjamin Constant, Madame de Staël, Guizot, and the men of 1830: namely, that there is but a single history of Europe, and that the two modern nations in which this history can be traced by turns in the seventeenth and eighteenth centuries come from the same mold. Like Marx and in opposition to Burke, the French liberals viewed the two revolutions—the English and the French—as two acts from the same play: the advent of the "middle class," bearer of what they themselves called "civilization." Like Marx and prior to Marx, they had difficulty grafting onto this diagnosis an interpretation of the various episodes by which the victory of the bourgeoisie over the nobility and the old society took place: this was because, like him, and prior to him, their point of departure was the social determination of the political. But in his desire to turn the class struggle against them by elaborating a materialist theory of history, Marx made the difficulties of interpretation encountered by the French liberals into philosophical deadlocks. Now the French Revolution had a meaning, but its course was no longer intelligible.

• • •

If this was the case, it was because in setting the Hegelian dialectic "on its feet," Marx had profoundly modified the interpretation of the French Revolution that appeared in his first works, before the turning point of *The German Ideology*. *On the Jewish Question* and *The Holy Family* already treated the French Revolution as the victory of bourgeois society over feudal society, but without reducing its course to this advent or to this result. On the contrary, the Revolution—envisioned as a dramatic unfolding of the events that characterized it—was the product of a provisional disequilibrium between the society that brought it about (which it reveals more than it creates) and the revolutionary state, which was its manifestation. The space provided by Feuerbachian alienation allowed the young Marx to think of the Revolution, according to his own terms, as the "genesis of the modern democratic state" (see selection 8). But this history of the communitarian illusion of members of a mercantile society only makes sense in relation to a generic essence of man, of which it is the alienated representation. After Marx's break with Feuerbach, however, human history no longer refers to humanity in itself. It has nothing more than its immanent reality, and that alone can explain the range of manifestations it has produced. The materialism of *The German Ideology* no longer allows for any play between bourgeois civil society and the bourgeois political revolution. For all their diversity, each of the episodes that succeeded one another so rapidly from 1789 to 1799 have to be reduced not only to their common origin but to a single end: the production of bourgeois society, even in opposition to the bourgeoisie. The multiform theater of the Revolution has found its *deus ex machina*, which manipulates its strings.[7]

It is this rigidity that gives Marx's very concept of revolution the peculiarity of being both central and obscure. In his thinking, the Revolution is the principal—and necessary—expression of modern historical change: Marx never ceased to belong to a European political culture obsessed with the French example. All of his militant activity was directed toward a German revolution. Sometimes it was envisioned as going beyond the French precedent, sometimes as a mere updating of German history; but in both cases it was a matter of provoking or participating in a great event comparable to 1789, an event that would mark a decisive break between two eras. Evidence of this view is that Marx, during the German 1848, never ceases to have the French example in mind and to tally the German failure against the French precedent. This aspect of his thought and activity make revolution a privileged form of historical action, a new form of man's reconciliation with the world.

Nevertheless, Marx's theory of history, and, more particularly, the interpretation that this theory implied concerning the history of his own time through the concepts of the market and the modern individual, cast the revolution as a mere adjustment. It was the necessity for his adjustment, and not the human will, that determined when it would come to pass. Henceforth, subordinated to the development of productive forces and to the maturation of civil society, the Revolution exhibits two characteristics in contradiction to the implications of its very concept. On the one hand, it is less the result of men's political activity than of their acquiescence to the inevitable. On the other, it constitutes a ratification of what was produced before it; it is completely defined by its causes and contained in its origins; it derives its identity from—and takes as its function to manifest—what has preceded it. Masquerading as a break with the past, the Revolution is actually the consummation of the past. Marx thus rediscovers and recycles in the language of materialism a classic paradox of French liberal historiography of the 1820s, which was itself saturated with the idea of the inevitability of the revolutionary event: if 1789 was the crowning of the ancien régime, what then was the Revolution?

The historical necessity of the French liberals and that of Marx

---

7. The reader interested in reading the Marxist critique of my critique of Marx may refer to Raymond Huart, "Du jeune Marx au coup d'État du 2 décembre 1851," *Cahiers d'histoire de l'Institut de recherches marxistes* 21(1985): 5–27.

differ in the sequence of causes and effects: whereas Guizot presented the victory of the bourgeoisie as inscribed both in a providential design and in the work of the monarchy, Marx saw it as the product of a contradiction induced by the development of the forces of production. Nor does their belief in historical necessity lead them to similar predictions of the future: Guizot saw the victory of the bourgeoisie as an end to history that must be perfected by the foundation of durable representative institutions: Marx considered 1789 as but one stage in the final emancipation of humanity from the reign of exploitation. What both schools do share is the difficulty entailed in every attempt to conceive of the notion of revolution within a deterministic framework. One has only to observe how Marx, in considering the German revolution of 1848, constantly oscillated between a call to his compatriots to engage in revolutionary activity and a pessimistic view of the objective constraints which encumber their actions, the price of his nation's backwardness. After stating in *The German Ideology* that his country's bourgeoisie is "at the same point" as the French bourgeoisie in 1789—meaning that evolution has assigned them the same liberal and national tasks with half a century's delay— he raises the quite different possibility of a proletarian revolution succeeding a successful bourgeois revolution, only to return, in 1848 and after, to the reasons why Germany was not even capable of producing a 1789 (see selections 13–17).

The contradiction or incoherence in this use of the concept of revolution cannot be resolved by distinguishing objective and subjective factors of historical change. For this distinction can exist only up to a certain point within Marx's theory, which clearly gives precedence, in the unfolding of causes and effects, to the objective elements of development. This is a point driven home again and again in *The German Ideology,* because it marks and fuels the decisive break with idealism—so much so that it becomes difficult, taking this point of departure, to account for too great a gap between the objective situation and the disposition of forces, economic and social on one hand, political and ideological on the other. Thus, in the German case, Marx introduces first the hypothesis that a bourgeois revolution could eventually lead to a proletarian revolution, and then the idea that a bourgeois revolution misses its goal even though the conditions for it may be as advanced as those of 1789 in France. These two propositions, which illustrate the reversal of Marx's analysis of the German situation before and after 1848, both dissociate the idea of the revolution from that of historical necessity: in the first case, the proletarian revolution could take place even though the historical time was ripe only for the bourgeoisie. In the second, the bourgeois revolution did not take place even though it was inscribed in the evolution of society. Thus the revolution cannot be considered necessary, and bourgeois Germany must come into being in some other way.

The ambiguity of Marx's concept of revolution lies in the fact that it sometimes implies, and sometimes excludes, the concept of historical necessity. When a revolution has taken place, as it did in France at the end of the eighteenth century, Marx interprets it as having been produced entirely—in its results, its forms, its course— by the inevitable advent of bourgeois society. When a revolution has not taken place, as in Germany in 1848, he simply attributes the failure to the incapacity of the actors, to the pusillanimity of the German bourgeoisie—traditionally timid and henceforth threatened on the left by the working class. It follows that this failure has no effect on the prior existence of a fully developed bourgeois society, which will find means other than revolution to express itself. In the first case Marx reduces the revolution to the manifestation of its social content, while, in the second, he makes it only one of several possible, but not inevitable, paths to the affirmation of bourgeois society. In the first case, he subordinates politics. In the second, he emancipates politics, at least relatively—testimony to a contradiction written into his theory of history, one that will continue to haunt the political part of his work, notably his analysis of the French revolutions of the nineteenth century.

As to the French Revolution strictly speaking—the revolution constituting in his eyes, since his youth, the classic model of bourgeois revolutions—Marx does once in a while interpret it in terms of its historical actors: the great men of 1789 or of 1793, or even the victorious class as a whole. But these are secondary and, moreover, contradictory notations, since he most often celebrates the audacity, the firmness, and the breadth of vision of the French revolutionary bourgeoisie, though on occasion he explains 1793, conversely, in terms of the pusillanimity of this very bourgeoisie. The core of his interpretation of the French Revolution was closely tied to the necessity of the event, lodged in the prior existence of a socially dominant class. One of the paradoxes of this analysis is that the history of this class, and of the new social formation it engenders and incarnates, is never written or even sketched out by Marx. Philosophically, Marx gives civil society precedence over the state, and thus makes it the center of his explanation. But he never bothers to demonstrate his proposition. Everything proceeds as though the theoretical postulate were sufficient for him and authorized him to deduce the economic and social maturity of the eighteenth-century French bourgeoisie from its political performance in 1789, rather than adopting the opposite procedure of verifying his hypothesis. Marx used history more as a reservoir of illustrations for his theory than as an instrument of research possessed of its own intellectual constraints.

Indeed, what is striking about all the writing he devotes, between 1845 and 1850, to the history of modern France is the virtual nonexistence of empirical references to French economy and society in the period before 1789. Marx studied the French Revolution much more than he studied the ancien régime. For this earlier period of French history he never did the enormous amount of reading that would, a little later, nourish the years of impassioned labor on English social history that culminated in *Das Kapital*. Most of the notes he devoted to the French ancien régime concern the absolute monarchy as a provisional system of equilibrium between the nobility and the bourgeoisie. Few deal with the classes themselves, their evolution, or that of the economy, no doubt because, not having done his own research, Marx was prisoner to his readings, and notably to Guizot. But all this stems above all from an implicitly teleological conception of French history—another inheritance from liberal French historians—according to which 1789 represents such an obvious victory of the bourgeoisie that all prior history can be organized in relation to it. Throughout his life, moreover, Marx was interested only in *political* history—that of revolutions, more precisely—as if the transformations of civil society, which are supposed to be the key to that history, can, on the contrary, be legitimately deduced from it by a sort of magical intelligibility granted to revolutions by history.

The history of the bourgeoisie's development as a class since the Middle Ages is sketched out in the least summary fashion in *The German Ideology*. Once again, we are presented with a general picture, painted broadly on a European scale, in which Marx retraces the manner in which a merchant class provisionally detached itself from the medieval bourgeoisie, and from the craft guilds defined by their juridical status, to constitute a social group emancipated from the constraints of feudal society and finding its conditions for development in "free" commerce and industry. These merchants, initially specializing in international trade between the different urban centers, gradually took control of production, notably in the textile industry, because they supplied its capital: hence the development of cottage industry and factories. This celebrated analysis of the genesis of the bourgeoisie, which has been the object of numerous studies, notably by historians,[8] is not really a part of my subject to the extent that it is not specific to France. Let us say nonetheless that it allows us to elaborate concepts—such as the primitive accumulation of capital, the transitional phase between feudalism and capitalism, or the pre-capitalist bourgeoisie—which permit a more subtle and more exact analysis of the problem of the social origins of the French Revolution than does the fanciful postulate of a modern industrial bourgeoisie dominating French society from the end of the eighteenth century. But if, starting from Marx, we can accept the thesis nowadays adopted unanimously by historians—that of a French Revolution dominated by a bourgeoisie belonging to the ancien régime, with no relation to industrial capitalism and largely independent even of capitalism and largely independent even of capitalism plain and simple, except in terms of proprietary individualism[9]—it nevertheless remains the case that when Marx defines the conditions for the bourgeois revolution, he speaks most often of a bourgeoisie that has reached a sufficiently advanced stage of its development that it must, at any price, brutally break the relations of production inherited from feudal society. This is the meaning of the famous formula of the *Communist Manifesto*,[10] whose power of simplification explains its formidable success as well as a certain number of historical extravagances.

What, more precisely, did Marx think and say about the French bourgeoisie of 1789 and before? Not much, as we have seen. The most explicit text in this regard is the one cited earlier from *The German Ideology,* where, in considering utilitarian philosophy in England and in France, he contrasts the economic and social conditions of the two countries and what he calls "the struggling, still undeveloped bourgeoisie" with "the ruling, developed bourgeoisie" (see selection

8. This problem has indeed engendered an important discussion since the 1930s, particularly in English Marxist historiography. Essential elements of this discussion may be found in P. M. Sweezy, M. Dobb, H. D. Takahashi, R. Hilton, and C. Hill, *The Transition from Feudalism to Capitalism: A Symposium* (London, 1954).

9. If it is true that the individualist conception of ownership is a precondition for a capitalist economy, that conception is insufficient to launch the economy's development, as is illustrated by the French case.

10. "At à certain stage in the development of these means of production and of exchange, the conditions under which feudal society produced and exchanged, the feudal organization of agriculture and manufacturing industry, in one word the feudal relations of property, became no longer compatible with the already developed productive forces; they became so many fetters. They had to be burst asunder, they were burst asunder." Karl Marx, *The Revolutions of 1848,* ed. David Fernbach (New York, Vintage Books, 1974), 72.

9); a bit further on, discussing the Physiocrats, he seeks to push the contrast further by speaking of "the undeveloped economic relations of France whose feudalism, under which landownership plays the chief role, was still unshaken" (see selection 9). These are imprecise notations, their only interest being that they underline once more the teleological character of the Marxist analysis of French history, since its central event, the Revolution, is, in this instance, no longer simply the product of the bourgeoisie's struggle: here it is also credited in advance with having a radical effect on the economy by destroying feudalism—as if it must bring an end to the ascendancy of landed property.

It is thus clear that the Marx of 1845–50, that is, on either side of the revolution of 1848, saw in French history only the Revolution. The obsession with 1789—his old German obsession—persists, but under new forms. It is no longer, as it was in the Feuerbachian years, a question of fashioning a critique of the modern democratic state. Now he is striving, on the one hand, to integrate the French Revolution into the materialist theory of history as sketched out beginning in 1845 in *The German Ideology,* and on the other, to make a German revolution. The philosopher has become a militant revolutionary. He preserves from the earlier period his store of readings on the French Revolution—Benjamin Constant, Guizot, Mignet, Thiers, Buchez and Roux: in short, all the available literature of the time—but he rearranges his knowledge according to what he has become, and to the theoretical and practical tasks he has fixed for himself.

His conceptual system henceforth leads him to emphasize those aspects of the French Revolution most evidently in conformity with bourgeois civil society, which the Revolution is supposed to produce and to manifest from start to finish. On the other hand, Marx's militant activities lead him to study and to celebrate the deliberate aspect of the Revolution, in order to draw from it an example of energy to offer to German history. This brings him to write what are probably his best passages of this period on the French Revolution, on 1789, and on the role of the bourgeoisie during those few months—from April to August—during which what he calls feudal society (i.e., the structuring of society according to orders and organized bodies), is destroyed. During this crucial period, the historical actors play exactly the roles assigned to them by the philosopher: the bourgeoisie carries out the bourgeois revolution. The intelligence and energy of individuals match the importance of what they do, and their actions are nothing other than the objective accomplishment of the historical duties of their class—carried out, however, in the name of the nation. *The German Ideology* includes some brilliant pages on this theme, underlining the importance of the transfer of sovereignty from the king to the Estates General, in June, just as the old feudal institution was being transformed into the National Assembly: the birth of modern citizenship, which is at the same time the birth of bourgeois property, transforms the old notion of *représentation* from top to bottom. While wrapping the proprietors' new social domination in the flag of universalism, the bourgeoisie feels sure enough of itself to draw support against the aristocracy and the court from the urban and rural popular masses. After 14 July, the municipal revolution, and the peasant insurrection, the Assembly does not hesitate before the August decrees, which liquidate ancien régime society. Thus, in the events of 1789, Marx finds a perfect illustration of his doctrine; they give him the opportunity to integrate into a single account the meaning of a historical action, the energy and intelligence with which it is pursued, and the clarity of the change it brings about. All his life, Marx would consider the history of France to be the classic repertoire of revolutions: thus he would refer back not only to the redoubling of the revolutionary episode since the end of the eighteenth century, but also to the exemplary character of the original event.

But the sort of perfect intelligibility that 1789 presents to him makes the interpretation of all that follows that much more difficult. The young Marx had a good reason to be interested in the Jacobin terror, the Directory, and the Napoleonic dictatorship: to him, the genesis of the democratic state constituted, as he said, the essence of the Revolution. In contrast, the post-1845 Marx reduces the whole of the Revolution to the birth of bourgeois civil society—to which even the episodes that escaped the bourgeoisie contribute. In order to explain this contradiction, he does not, like the liberal historians, invoke "circumstances" (the war with Europe and the civil war, the constraint of the external and internal situation). The "hammer" of the Terror still finds its justification, just like 1789, in the necessity of realizing the bourgeois revolution—now betrayed by a bourgeoisie that has become "timid"—and of extirpating the last "feudal ruins" from French soil. Marx thus invokes the failure of the bourgeois actor in order to replace him with the popular actor, but this matters little since the revolutionary state appears as a secondary figure in the process, totally subordinated to its social determination. Moreover, the imperial period seems to have disappeared from his field of reflection, as if it were henceforth distinct from the history of the Revolution (the converse of the interpretation put forth in *The Holy Family*). The

whole range of political manifestations that, strictly speaking, constitute the French Revolution is henceforth brought under the vast um-
brella of bourgeois domination.

One can gauge the impoverishment of historical analysis entailed in this tyranny of the materialist interpretation by returning to
the review Marx wrote in 1850 of a recent essay by Guizot addressing
the English revolution (see selection 18). In this essay, Louis Philippe's
former prime minister had just reaffirmed the superiority of the English revolution over the French. Taking up again an old comparative
theme of his youth, Guizot was all the more inclined to tip the balance
toward the English in that February 1848 had sounded the death knell
of his historical ambition: to end the French Revolution by establishing representative government on a durable foundation. That is why
his essay consists of an inventory of the particular elements of the English success, as compared to the French failure. The optimism of this
initial comparison—which, in the 1820s, undergirded the confident
ambition to achieve a French 1688—has now given way to a pessimistic sense of difference in the former prime minister of an overthrown regime. And Guizot reserves a large place among the sources
of English liberty for political and cultural factors, such as the existence of a religious revolution anterior to the political revolution, the
slow constitution of representative tradition suited to brake the dynamic of the revolutionary spirit. It is with these arguments that
Marx takes issue, in the exact measure to which they appeal to a type
of historical explanation contradictory to his own.

His article on Guizot's little book is not one of his best written.
Perhaps he was relatively unfamiliar with seventeenth-century English history at the time; he had probably acquired what he did know
from books by Guizot—who had himself studied this period seriously in his earlier works.[11] But, above all, Marx despised the political
conservative in Guizot, the loser of 1848; and he no longer dissociated
the historian from the bourgeois. Not that the two were unrelated:
the Guizot, who, in 1850, wrote about the "success" of the English
revolution was obviously writing about himself also and his failure of
February 1848. But his book, which is exclusively historical, cannot
be regarded merely as a rationalization of that failure, even if the failure provides its starting point. Marx's prose, moreover, may—in the

11. Guizot was the author, under the Restoration, of the *Histoire des origines
du gouvernement représentatif* (1823), in which he treated England at great length, and
of the *Histoire de Charles 1er* (1826), which constituted the first part of his *Histoire de
la Révolution d'Angleterre*. He also published a bibliography of seventeenth-century
English history.

opposite sense—also be interpreted in relation to the stakes of the 1848 revolution. Very polemical, his essay offers an example of a form of Marxist "critique" destined for a great future: boxing up the adversary in ideological prejudice while assuming for itself, as if it were self-evident, the privilege of objectivity.

Marx was not interested in the question of representative government. In his eyes, this last is but the product of a class which has just come to power through the English revolution, as would its French equivalent, a century later, through the other revolution. While in Guizot the victory of the bourgeoisie derives its universal meaning from the establishment of free institutions—the true end of history— for Marx this victory is inseparable from the reign of interests—the ultimate reality, more or less directly disguised by regimes and ideas. Absorbed in his obsession to find the economic behind the political, Marx, when speaking of the English revolution, conceded to Guizot neither its religious character nor its paradoxical will to restore a tradition older than itself. Free thought, he replied, prior to being a French specialty, was an English invention, and in the beginning the French Revolution also thought to reestablish the ancient Constitution of the realm. These are weak responses when put beside the question posed, responses oblivious to the historical inventory of the differences that separate the two revolutions, the two countries, and the two eras. Marx ignored the differences because he believed that he possessed, on a superior level of interpretation, an explanatory scheme which would bring identity to diversity.

All that Guizot nostalgically listed as English particularities— notably Protestantism and representative institutions—Marx felt it sufficient to cast as so many products of bourgeois society in order to bring the English revolution back into the common mold. And if there is indeed a difference between the two revolutions, it is neither religious, nor political, nor institutional, but social: the seventeenth-century English bourgeoisie contracted an alliance with the large landowners, who for their part were engaged in developing a capitalist agriculture, whereas the French Revolution, to the contrary, had to destroy the great "feudal" landowners. The famous difference between the two histories thus comes down to two modalities of a single history: the history of capitalism. Marx believed, moreover, that the stability of English institutions so admired by Guizot would not make it through the nineteenth century. To his eyes, the Reform Bill of 1882 already prefigured the end of the social compromise established in the seventeenth century; the English industrial bourgeoisie appeared to him to be condemned to destroy the ancient constitution in the name of its interests, thus opening the way to unprecedented class conflicts. Like so many of his contemporaries, Marx saw England on the brink of political convulsions[12]—and thus reduced to the common fate exemplified by France.

The paradox of this discussion is that Guizot, twenty or thirty years earlier, would have agreed with Marx about the convergence of the two histories, for in the 1820s he made this convergence the substance and meaning of European history.[13] At that time, he too saw in the English Revolution, as Madame de Staël had done before him,[14] the same historical necessity that would engender the French Revolution in the following century; but this necessity, while spelling the victory of the commoners over the nobility, also implied the foundation of representative institutions, the last stretch that France had to cross in order to end its revolution. This is the source of Guizot's intellectual optimism during that era, when—as historian and politician at once—he explored the chances for a French 1688. But 1848 destroyed his faith by demonstrating that the French revolutionary tradition could not be converted to the English model: hence the contrast established in 1850 between the English success and the French failure, as though an identical necessity had ceased to reside in the two revolutions.

Marx did not have the same difficulty as Guizot in dealing with this comparison because he had never considered representative institutions to be an end of the history of the bourgeoisie. On the contrary, they appeared to him—in the English case—to be the product of a particular social compromise, fragile and provisional, condemned

12. On the eve of his first voyage to England on 5 July 1833, Tocqueville wrote to the Countess of Pisieux: "I for one would like to go and divert myself a little at our neighbors'. But now it is said that they will decidedly go into revolution and that one must hurry up if one would see them as they are. I am thus hastening to go to England the way one might rush to the last showing of a great play." Once there, Tocqueville abandoned the notion that England was in revolution. Alexis de Tocqueville, *Voyages en Angleterre, Irlande, Suisse et Algérie,* vol. 5 of *Oeuvres Complètes* (Paris, 1958), 2:36; but in August 1835, in his famous letter to Molé about the complexity of the English case, he spoke once again as if one of the objects of his second trip to England was to give himself "the view of a great people churning in the midst of a great revolution." And after this trip, in the following year, he wrote to his friend Reeve (Letter of 22 May 1836): "It seems to me that you have been in full revolution for five years."

13. This was the direction of his course at the Sorbonne on the history of representative institutions (1820–22).

14. The comparable character of the English and French revolutions was the central theme of Madame de Staël's posthumous *Considérations sur la Révolution française* (1818).

by the march of capitalism in the nineteenth century; it follows that England was bound shortly to reexperience the political instability inseparable from class struggle, along the lines of the French model. Where Guizot saw the irrevocable separation of the two histories he had wanted to unify—and believed to have done so—Marx found the proof of their imminent reunion by virtue of the inexorable effect of capitalism and the proletarian revolution. Marx's critique of Guizot follows a teleological logic, created in the name of a future revolution whose imminence was proclaimed by *The Communist Manifesto*. It offers a good example of the dichotomy never absent from his thought and work: he was to study the economic and social history of capitalism in England, but French history furnished him with the political model of the revolutionary rupture. Only the proletarian revolution of tomorrow allowed the two histories to be reconciled and comprehended as one.

With Marx's writings on the French Revolution between 1845 and 1850—that is, from either side of an 1848 that never ceased to remind him of the great Revolution that preceded it—we are in possession of his interpretation, and recognize what it owes both to circumstances (namely, 1848) and especially to the theory that gives it meaning even if it does not explain its course. In his intellectual life to follow, the French Revolution would play a less important role than it did during the two periods I have just covered on either side of *The German Ideology*: first, the period conventionally known as that of the "young Marx"; and then the period of the Marx whose every effort was directed toward setting back on its feet that history—so dear to German philosophy—that walked on its head. For this reason we can evaluate Marx's work on the French Revolution by comparing it with Hegel's, for during these two periods Marx never ceased to "critique" Hegel's work.

The paradox of this comparison is that the most "speculative" philosophy, to use Marx's vocabulary, is also the philosophy that devotes the most attention to historical detail. Hegelian idealism is infinitely more preoccupied with the concrete results of eighteenth-century French history than is Marx's materialism. It contrasts a chronology of the working of the Spirit infinitely more precise than the chronology of the development of productive forces.

There is indeed in Hegel, throughout his works, a systematic interpretation of the French Revolution and of modern France in terms of successive forms of self-consciousness. The outlines of this interpretation are shifted, and the relative weight of various events modified, from the *Phenomenology* to *The Philosophy of History* of his last years: this is the inevitable tribute paid by the Hegelian dialectic for the privilege given to the present in deciphering the work of the Spirit. But these modifications themselves bear witness to the conceptual imagination constantly at work in what is almost half a century's reflection, begun precisely with the French Revolution and bound to renew and enrich its meaning as history continues to reveal it. In this respect, Marx's dialectic cannot have the same integrative capacity in this permanent labor of absorption of the real by historical reason: by substituting the contradictions of the modes and relations of production for the constantly open-ended succession of forms of self-consciousness, his dialectic renders the conceptualization of history at once more rigid and less rich. Simplification of the past is the price paid for claiming to know the future.

This is easy to understand if we compare, for example, Marx's treatment of the French ancien régime with the way it is treated in the *Phenomenology*. Marx, as we have seen, never addressed this period in a systematic fashion; but, because it contains the question of the origins of the Revolution, he often resorted to two ideas that came, incidentally, from both Guizot and Hegel: namely, that French absolutism, as a power arbitrating between the nobility and the bourgeoisie, derived its provisional authority from the reciprocal neutralization of those two classes; and that it collapsed in 1789 because the bourgeoisie had already won the game in the domain of society and culture before taking on the sphere of political power. But Marx never developed these two ideas by systematically relating them to the fabric of historical facts. He never wrote a history of the French ancien régime which would explain how this latter gave birth to the Revolution.

In contrast, the Hegel of the *Phenomenology* wrote, in extraordinarily abstract language, a veritable history of that same period, a narrative account cast in a speculative mode. If the irresistible march of the "spirit of the times" voids the different representations of the past of their content even before the past has been conceived of as such, it does not preempt philosophy from reconstituting the intelligibility of the process after the fact. In the *Phenomenology* we find a definition of the ancien régime characterized by an opposition between noble consciousness and base consciousness, a crisis of an ancien régime in which a consciousness torn apart testified that a civilization was in the process of dying, a revolution of the *Aufklärung* by which the universal man of social utility triumphed over religion. The end of the aristocratic world was the work of Louis XIV, who privatized the monarchy and destroyed the nobility by means of the Court. The ancien régime that fell in 1789 was dead long before the official date of its disappearance; when the Revolution broke out, there were no longer either villeins or lords, but only bourgeois. In this famous reconstruction, Hegel, in his own manner, reconsidered all the questions related to the problems of the origins of the Revolution: the political ambiguity of the absolute monarchy, the role of the increase of wealth in ending the principle of nobility, the precocity of the crisis of the ancien régime in the eighteenth century, the anti-religious radicalism of French Enlightenment philosophy, the cultural unification of elites in the bourgeois conception of the world.

That the slow erosion of the old edifice was accomplished before 1789 did not stop Hegel from hailing the "unprecedented" and "prodigious" character of the Revolution: it is the event in the history of humanity that provides the most food for thought, to the extent that the destruction of the ancien régime in the name a notion of liberty links it with philosophical thinking. Hegel profoundly grasped the dual nature of 1789 as at once an accomplishment of what has occurred and an absolute novelty—an affirmation and a negation of liberty.

As to the course of the Revolution itself, the *Phenomenology* elaborates at great length the contrast it presents between the two successive periods of 1789 and 1793. In attempting to reconcile the idea of a French Revolution as bearer of an internal contradiction with the idea of a French Revolution that obeys a single logic from start to finish, it renews the sort of questioning already classic among the survivors and observers of the French events. Indeed, for Hegel, 1789 and 1793 pertained to different but nonetheless interrelated concepts. 1789 manifests the *Aufklärung*'s termite work by revealing, in the ruins of the wormeaten old order, the triumph of utility as a principle of society. But institutions founded on utility rest only upon the particularity of individual desires, while the truth of the French Revolution, beneath the surface of social utility, is founded on the fulfillment of the old Christian promise of freedom to man as man, not merely as citizen of the city of antiquity. Manifesting thus the long labor of the Spirit in history, the Revolution constituted the affirmation of self-consciousness as free will, coextensive with the universal, transparent to itself, reconciled with being. The Terror was the preeminent manifestation of this pull toward absolute liberty, "this self-conscious actuality raised to the level of pure thought or abstract matter . . . [which] shows itself . . . to be what cancels and does away with self-thinking or self-consciousness." [15] A logical paradox condemned to failure, whose impasses Hegel analyzes in the Rousseauian democracy of the Year II.

The vision of the French Revolution proposed by the *Phenomenology* is thus completely different from the one proposed by Marx, although he conserved some of its elements, simply transposing them within his materialist conception. For example, the role Hegel attributed to the *Aufklärung* in the dissolution of the ancien régime and the advent of the modern universality of man is, in Marx, played by the extended efforts of the bourgeoisie within the bounds of feudal relations of production: in the subterranean activity of history that the Revolution of 1789 merely brought to light, like delivering a child, Marx's real society is substituted for Hegel's self-consciousness. But this "real" society derives its "reality" from a mere philosophical postulate; deduced from a materialist theory of history, it simultaneously deprives Marx of the freedom to think about the "reality" of the events of the Revolution that came about without it, or in opposition to it, as in 1793. This is why Marx never stopped bringing 1793 back into the orbit of 1789: in order, at any price, to fix the Terror and the dictatorship of the sans-culottes within the bourgeois identity of revolutionary history. Hegel, on the other hand, saw 1789 as a manifestation of an anthropology of the Enlightenment according to which it is social utility that founds truth: an inevitably provisional episode whose inconsistency quickly gave way to the fundamental ambition of the Revolution—absolute liberty of consciousness and its immediate realization in the world. Thus, in the *Phenomenology,* the Terror is the key period of the whole process.

Thus Hegel did not have to separate 1793 and 1789 as if it were a deplorable episode in the wake of a happy event. His isolation of the Jacobin period as a particular phase of self-consciousness was not meant to amputate it from the course of the Revolution, according to the most common tendency of liberal thought. True to the formidable acceptance of history that animates all of his work, Hegel thought of 1793 in terms of the ultimate unveiling of the abstract universal man of 1789, while Marx, similar in this respect to the Restoration historians, could see it only as a phenomenon secondary to the bourgeois nature of the Revolution as manifested by 1789 and, consequently, subordinate to it. Marx inverted the interpretation of Guizot or Mignet since he celebrated 1793 instead of deploring it, but he shared their historico-philosophical presuppositions: class struggle

15. Hegel, *The Phenomenology of Mind,* 606.

and the victory of the bourgeoisie were seen to constitute the essence of the Revolution, of which 1789 represents the central manifestation and 1793 a sort of circumstantial accompaniment—necessary, but secondary.

Once again, on this point, the young Marx's "critique" of the Hegelian concept of the state lies at the root of what separates Marx and Hegel. In making the state both a product and a disguise of civil society, as we have seen, Marx had difficulty accounting for the plurality of its revolutionary modalities: and the difficulty deepens with *The German Ideology*. In contrast, the dialectic that, for Hegel, constitutes the history of the French Revolution places him right at the heart of the problem of the various forms of the revolutionary state, for it is a dialectic of the relationship between the universal man of the *Aufklärung* and the historical conditions of his existence. It follows that, just as there is a Marxist "critique" of Hegel, one can also conceive of an *a posteriori* Hegelian "critique" of Marx, suggesting that Marx based his famous conceptual reversal on an illusory idea of a civil society independent of the state, a civil society such as the principles of 1789 claimed to be its radical affirmation.

Indeed, if (to move from the *Phenomenology* to the *Philosophy of Right*) the Revolution manifested the appearance of liberty as the foundation of the social, this extraordinary attempt at a concrete political realization of man's "being in itself"—his existing for himself and no other—was itself conditional upon the emancipation of society from its historical conditions of existence. This emancipation was that of the natural, universal man, independent of the relations and ties woven for him by history, defined solely by his needs, as in English political economy. Such is the foundation of the abstract, nonhistorical character of man as put forth by the Revolution. The precondition of civil society is, in effect, liberty for all, since liberty has as its object individuals considered in light of the equality of their nature, affected by needs, and at the same time freed of all the institutions that limit them in fact and by law. It is this axiom of political economy—the modern principle of work as the source of liberty— that became, during the French Revolution, the social foundation of politics. The private individual who pursued his own interest necessarily became, by virtue of his work, the citizen of modern society.

But in order to affirm the abstract universality of liberty, the Revolution had to proceed by a schism between civil society and the state and to deduce, so to speak, the political from the social. This was its error, its failure; and this was also the failure of contractual theories, notably that of Rousseau. Rousseau was quite correct in searching for and locating the "thought concept" of the state in the will and not in utility, but he was wrong to consider the general will only in terms of particular wills, and consequently in terms of the antecedence of the social to the state. This conception limits the products of the union of individuals to arbitrary decisions, taken in the name of an illusion of rationality and ignorant of the work of reason in history. The civil society of needs that defines the universality of man can find historical reality only as a state.

Left to itself, indeed, civil society is only capable of defining a political end consisting of the protection of liberty and property—a sort of optional citizenship according to individuals' expectations. But nothing is further from Hegelian thought than the reduction of institutions to psychological particulars, as protected by Enlightenment philosophy in terms of natural law, innateness, the arithmetic of interests, or the harmony of egoistic interests. Hegel's state transcends proprietary individualism. It alone allows for the reconciliation of the constitutive abstraction of modern society—that which defines need, labor, classes—with historicity. It is society in its history, in its relationship with universal history. It alone reveals the historical character of the idea of a nonhistorical nature of social man, because its reality subsumes and supersedes this idea. It is only through the state, this superior form of history, that society is organized according to reason.

For Hegel, the error of the French Revolution lies in the ignorance of this truth, just as its course can also be explained by it. Thus the Hegelian theory of the modern state opens up a space for the interpretation of the revolutionary events neglected by the majority of liberal historians,[16] and even more so by Marx, locked, as they were, inside the idea of civil society's precedence over the state, and of 1789's precedence over 1793. Hegel locates the failure of the French Revolution, that "majestic sunrise" that brought modern liberty to light, in terms of its incapacity to conceive of the state; the extent of this incompetence is best gauged by the Terror, by its rejection of any mediation between the pure liberty of individuals and their collective, historical existence. For Hegel, the dictatorship of the Year II thus expressed the truth of the French Revolution precisely to the extent that it incarnated its error and failure—which also had a name, Rousseau. It was the general will, cast in a secondary fashion as the product of

16. On condition, of course, that we do not include such historians as Michelet or Quinet in this definition.

a contract, that gave rise both to the endless conflicts between factions and to the Terror, the ultimate avatar of "absolute liberty" deprived of historical mediation. In this way, Hegel constructed a theory of the political development of the Revolution exactly where Marx, seeking to reverse Hegel's terms, created the blind spot of his interpretation.

3

Marx and the French Enigma (1851–1871)

By 1850, Marx had written essentially all he would ever write about the French Revolution as such— its origins, its history, its interpretation. Part 2 of this book testifies to the great scarcity of commentary and reflection on this subject during what can be considered the second half of his intellectual life, starting from the middle of the century.

This is because after 1850, he was the man of *Capital,* the great work of his life on the great subject of his life. Here we find him finally at the heart of "civil society," face to face with the mechanism of the capitalist economy, unencumbered by the enigmas of the "political revolution" and the state, immersed in English history, of which he would become simultaneously the historian, the economist, the sociologist, and the philosopher. A logical continuation of the reversal of the Hegelian dialectic, this agenda provided him with a field consonant with the object of research he had defined, which was capitalism itself. Abruptly, the mysteries of French history dropped to a secondary position among his preoccupations.

Yet current events unceasingly brought these mysteries back to the London exile's attention. France, though not the premier nation of capitalist economics, remained the preferred terrain of political tremors: the Revolution would not come to an end. It reappeared at the fall of the July Monarchy to engender a cycle bitterly comparable to the cycle of the First Republic, with its own Girondins, Jacobins, and Thermidorians and even a second Bonaparte to round out the caricature. Twenty years later, when the Second Empire fell, it was the Revolution that again decked out the new Republic with its parade of souvenirs and insurrections, from 4 September to the Commune. On both these occasions, Marx returned to the elements of the extraordinary power of constraint and repetition that the Revolution never ceased to exercise over the French nineteenth century, seeking to integrate them into his general system of interpretation. This was a difficult task insofar as it involved dealing with repetitive political events that illustrated the force of traditions more than they matched the interests of social classes—events periodically breaking the continuity of the forms of the state without any corresponding transformation of civil society. In this respect, the nineteenth-century revolutions in France renewed the problem that the French Revolution posed for Marx from the start. Thus his analyses of the Second Republic, 2 December, and the Commune are particularly interesting. Even though they are not directly concerned with the French Revolution but with its aftermath, they allow us to grasp, by a kind of magnification, the full extent of the difficulties posed for his thinking, from beginning to end, by the interpretation of the birth and metamorphoses of French democratic culture.

Understanding the Revolution's continually renascent character was a problem classic to nineteenth-century political thought. It was the problem posed, above all, by the liberals from Royer-Collard to Tocqueville[1]; and it gave Guizot's intellectual and political activity its entire meaning. For Marx, the terms of this problem appeared in reverse: it was not a question of ending the Revolution but of beginning another, perhaps similar in form, but certainly new insofar as its content would no longer be political but social. The year 1789 marked the victory of the middle class; the task of the following century would be to assure the victory of the proletariat. The modern conflict is no longer the opposition between the bourgeoisie and the nobility, but the clash between the working class and the bourgeoisie, the two great collective actors of the capitalist economy. Whereas the liberals most often—at least after 1830—viewed the return of insurrections and coups d'état as so many deplorable renewals of the Revolution, Marx hailed them as the promise of the real revolution to come. Nevertheless, in his meticulous and almost anxious investigation into nineteenth-century French politics, there is something very comparable to the question indefatigably posed by the Doctrinaires[2] and liberal politicians. For even as he wished passionately, at each Par-

1. In fact, the theme of "terminating the French Revolution" is inseparable from the Revolution itself, and it occurred to each of the successive actors once they gained positions of influence or power, from 1789 to 1794, from the Monarchists to Robespierre and his friends, passing through the Feuillants, the Girondins, and the Dantonists. It became all but an obsession of Thermidorian thought before reappearing, a generation later, at the center of Doctrinaire reflection.

2. That is, the men grouped around Royer-Collard and Guizot, theoreticians of the monarchy according to the Charter, who shifted to the opposition in 1820, and became the fathers of Orléanism from 1830 on.

isian insurrection, for the victory of the "true" emancipation of man brought about by the proletariat of the barricades, Marx discerned in each the weight of the traditions bequeathed by the events of the end of the eighteenth century and the repetition of the great Revolution. He continued to nurse the melancholy idea, already expressed during his youth in terms of the comparison of Germany's ancien régime with France's ancien régime, that history repeats itself as a parody of the past—farce following tragedy, as he remarked of the French 1848. His formula evokes precisely the same question raised by Tocqueville's observation in his *Souvenirs* that the French Revolution was continually being reborn from its ashes.[3]

Thus, for Marx, nineteenth-century France continually displayed both the proletarian revolution of the future and the bourgeois revolution of the past. These two ideas are not incompatible, provided there is a readiness to see the revolution as a form of historical action that can be given a variety of contents; a tradition through which the French are particularly inclined to experience all of their political conflicts, since these last find their origin—and almost their matrix—in the French Revolution. Indeed, Marx indicated at several points just how sensitive he was to this spectacular particularity of modern French history. On the other hand, the idea of the repetition of the same revolution is completely alien to his conceptual system, imprisoned as it is within the bourgeois revolution/proletarian revolution opposition. For if, as in nineteenth-century France, the bourgeois revolution has already taken place, delivering civil society once and for all from its "feudal" bonds, there is only one real revolution that can succeed it, and that is the social revolution of the proletariat. Hence Marx's state of perpetual anticipation of this revolution to come; hence his contempt for "bourgeois" revolutionaries, who are by definition condemned to parody.

The French revolutions of the nineteenth century were therefore either abortive or parodic. The failure of the revolutions of the first sort—June 1848 and March 1871—was the failure of a heroic attempt

3. "The constitutional monarchy was successor to the ancien régime; the Republic to the monarchy; to the Republic, the Empire; to the Empire, the Restoration; then came the July Monarchy. After each of its successive mutations, it was said that the French Revolution, having achieved what was presumptuously called its work, was finished: it was said and believed. Alas! I myself had hoped for this under the Restoration, and again since the fall of the Restoration government; and now, here is the French Revolution starting up again, for it is still the same one." Alexis de Tocqueville, *Souvenirs* (Paris: Folio Gallimard, 1978), 117–18.

condemned in advance by the objective conditions of society. As to those of the second sort, it is difficult to speak of them in terms of success or failure since bourgeois domination was complete, both before and after. Hence the parodic character—at once repetitive and ridiculous—of the insurrectional spectacle mounted, for example, by the revolution of February 1848. The Republic, the Gironde, the Montagne, and the second Bonaparte appeared there only as a particular French form of the false consciousness of historical actors in relation to their own actions—the rhetoric of imitation.

It remains true that July 1830, February 1848, and the coup d'état of 2 December changed the form of the state under which the bourgeoisie's domination was both exercised and concealed. These events cannot simply be seen as useless or grotesque repetitions. They substituted a constitutional monarchy for a king surviving from the ancien régime, a successively revolutionary and conservative republic for the constitutional monarchy, and then a new imperial despotism for the republic. In considering these changing forms of the French state, Marx returned to the old problem about the French Revolution that had never ceased to intrigue him and continued to manifest its unalterable mystery throughout the following century: how to make sense of a bourgeois society so precociously formed and yet so incapable of mastering its political history. The only advantage that the French Revolution of the eighteenth century had over its nineteenth-century successors was anteriority—an important advantage, certainly, since it implies a superiority of historical invention. But in constantly replaying its history, the succeeding revolutions only renewed its mystery, a mystery which Marx confronted again and again without ever coming any closer to unraveling it.

Nevertheless, he never stopped considering and reconsidering this mystery, as he did during his youth, whether his point of departure was 1830, 1848, or 1871 rather than 1789 or 1793. But he did not simply change centuries. He had also quit using the example of 1789 to refute the Hegelian theory of the state by means of the Feuerbachian critique of religion. Henceforth he had to do battle with his own theory of history and of the state in order to account for what was occurring before his eyes in France. At once a historian and a witness to these events, he was too familiar with their details to be able to subject them to the arbitrary abstractions of historical materialism on the model of the treatment he reserved between 1845 and 1850 for the French Revolution. And, in any case, the present offered a much more urgent challenge to the objectives of his doctrine than the past,

since the intelligibility of that present is inseparable from revolutionary action. This is what gives his three books on the French events a
tension that has no equivalent in the rest of his works.

In these books he does not resolve the problem posed for his
theory by the multiplicity of French regimes and revolutions. But the
ambiguities and subtleties he multiples to this end make these "French"
historical analyses—in their very contradictions—brilliant texts. Marx
did not leave to others the task of exploring the impasses of Marxist
political history, and no one since has done it so dazzlingly.[4]

Since he earlier shared Guizot's illusion that the 1830 revolution
had terminated the revolutionary cycle in the English manner by finally bringing the bourgeoisie of 1789 to power, more than forty
years later, through its sons,[5] 1848 constituted for Marx—just as for
Guizot, Tocqueville, and many others—the reopening of the French
political enigma. A twofold enigma, really, because it involves, first,
ascertaining whether or not 1848 possessed a radically new character
in relation to the French Revolution, and second, understanding why
resumption prevailed over novelty—why, indeed, there was a resumption at all. On the first point, Marx was all ready with his diagnosis, since it lay close to the very heart of his doctrine: a little more
than one-half century after 1789 put its signature to the advent of
bourgeois society, the 1848 revolution was pregnant with a proletarian revolution. This last did occur, but it failed: Marx saw a modern proletariat at work on the Parisian barricades of June, and the real
revolution of 1848 springing from the mendacious cradles of republican rhetoric. The crushing of this real though premature revolution
however, brought Marx back to his analysis of the other revolution,
the one by means of which the bourgeoisie—ever the bourgeoisie—

4. Among the vast literature of commentaries on Marx's theory (or, according to these authors, the lack of theory) of the state, and notably with regard to his
analyses of the French nineteenth century, I would recommend Jon Elster's *Making
Sense of Marx* (Cambridge University Press, 1985), especially chapter 7, "Politics and
the State."

5. There is a particularly vivid testimony to this "English" obsession of the
men of 1830 in Rémusat's *Mémoires*: "Thiers and Mignet envisaged the course of the
French Revolution as a curve whose points had all been predetermined by the course
of the English revolution. With an almost mathematical precision, they calculated
the direction events were to follow. Thus they accepted without hesitation that
which appeared inevitable, and even desired that which they held to be necessary—a
change of dynasties. Hence, rational and non-absolute Orleanism . . . we had one
thought in common, the French Revolution, to be brought to an end by the reality
of representative government." (vol. 3, 286–87)

reaffirmed its class power over society after believing it had lost it between February and June.

What is absurd is that February 1848 was no longer accomplishing a necessary historical task, unlike the famous precedent it was imitating. It was a caricature of the great events of the late eighteenth century to the precise extent that, instead of accepting and giving life to this culmination of history, the Second Republic turned it away in the name of the past. The revolutionary or Bonapartist parody was the French version of reaction. Having become a tradition, even the Montagne was transformed into its opposite. But if the French revolutions of the nineteenth century found themselves thus condemned by the dialectic of history, their reason for existence still remains to be explained.

To what were these revolutions due—to what could they be due—if their sole object was unflaggingly to reaffirm, through successive regimes, the bourgeoisie's domination over society? What was the significance of the political instability within this immutably bourgeois social order? This was the French question par excellence in the nineteenth century. Guizot and Tocqueville, for once in agreement, sought the beginning of a response in the long survival of revolutionary passions—a survival resulting from the violence inscribed in the originating event—which continued independently of the social state to which it gave birth, and constantly threatened its harmony by arousing hatred between classes. But Marx did not leave himself the liberty of thus separating the political and the ideological from the social, still less the liberty of casting them as the determining factors in historical interpretation. So he had, as always, to find in the French revolutions—even if they were false revolutions, incapable of giving birth to a new society—the class interests that constituted them at least as political mutations. A single bourgeoisie, but diverse and short-lived constitutions: how was this peculiar French situation to be understood?

Marx suggested two types of responses, one tied to the structure of the French bourgeoisie, the other tied to the nature of the modern state.

Since there were several regimes, there must have been several bourgeoisies, or at least several parts to the bourgeoisie. Beginning with 1848, this idea becomes essential to an understanding of Marx's analysis of France. In light of the fact that the July Monarchy—a supremely bourgeois government—was overthrown by the Parisian insurrection of February 1848, it was no longer sufficient simply to contrast the Restoration, which was in the hands of the great land-owning proprietors, to the monarchy of the finance and industry after 1830. This opposition between landed interests and financial or indus-trial interests, the classic illustration of which Marx found in the En-glish debates over the abolition of the customs tariff on wheat,[6] no longer explains anything about 1848 and the extraordinary series of political reversals inaugurated by February 1848. In the series of ar-ticles he published on the Second Republic in the *Neue Rheinische Zeitung* of 1850,[7] Marx reorganized the internal structure of the bour-geoisie according to the succession of political phenomena manifested by the 1848 revolution. The July Monarchy becomes nothing more than the regime of the financial aristocracy. One part of the opposi-tion to Guizot was made up of the industrial bourgeoisie; the other (that of *Le National*), of the *capicités*;[8] the petite bourgeoisie and the peasantry had no political existence. The objective of the Second Re-public was to bring all the parts of the bourgeoisie within the sphere of political power, but the February insurrection introduced a new arrival, the proletariat. And so June became necessary to bring the February Republic back to its true objective—domination by the bourgeoisie as a whole.

This domination was in fact, in its republican form, only the "dictatorship of the sword" exercised by General Cavaignac: Marx retained the "critical" obsession of his youth, his passion for hunting down the truth behind the veil of illusion, and the bourgeois state re-mained one of the privileged domains of that quest. To him, history thus remained, by definition, dominated by what it made: the class interests for which the state is proxy. However, universal suffrage, that great republican novelty, introduces an unprecedented margin of play by offering the exploited classes—the working class, the peasan-try, the petite bourgeoisie—periodic occasions to manifest their inde-pendence or rebelliousness. Is this what occurred on 10 December 1848 when the French vote brought Louis Napoleon Bonaparte to the

6. In 1846, the English parliament voted to abolish the Corn Laws that pro-tected the English agricultural market, a defeat that remained a symbol of the landed interests so long under attack by the pressure group of industrial interests.

7. These are the articles Engels would gather together, adding his own pref-ace, in 1895 under the title, *The Class Struggles in France*.

8. *Le National* was a moderate republican newspaper published during the July Monarchy. *Les capacités* was Guizot's term for men whose eligibility for suffrage came not from the fact that they owned land but from their educational accomplish-ments. For a brief discussion, see Marx's *Surveys From Exile,* ed. David Fernbach (New York: Vintage Press, 1974), 63.—Trans.

presidency of the Republic? Yes and no. On the one hand, Marx does in fact analyze this vote as a "peasant insurrection" against the bourgeois republic, with its rich, its taxes, its politicians, in the name of the Napoleonic legend.[9] But this electoral "insurrection" drew along with it not only the majority of the popular vote, both proletariat and petit bourgeois, but also the majority of the vote to the grande bourgeoisie; in this respect, then, far from constituting a chance of history, it was, on the contrary, an expression of its mainspring—the interests of the dominant class. After its brief recourse to Cavaignac to break the revolutionary proletariat, this bourgeoisie finally found a better guarantee in Louis Napoleon than in the republicans, even the conservative ones. The nephew's presidency thus constituted, after the republic, the second institutional form of the unification of bourgeois interests.[10]

In these infinite variations on the theme of the political being reduced to the social, we rediscover the eternal Marx, avidly seeking to lay bare the illusion of democracy. Indeed, the idea of a bourgeoisie divided into fractions by varied but not contradictory interests, while lending Marx's "French" analyses more subtlety than in the preceding period, still suffers from the infirmity typical of this type of interpretation: it is deduced from observation of the very political conflicts it purports to explain. Marx, moreover, manipulated this idea with a certain arbitrariness, as needed. For example, although he most often defined the industrial bourgeoisie as excluded from the July regime, he also occasionally made it one of the sections that supported that regime.[11] His analysis of the interests underlying what he calls "bourgeois republicanism"—the quintessential men of 1848—is never explicit, probably because this fraction of the bourgeoisie is more easily defined in political or ideological terms than in purely social terms. One might criticize in the same manner his application of the concept of the proletariat to the June insurgents: the lower orders of the Pari-

9. See Marx, *Surveys,* 72.

10. Ibid., 73.

11. Indeed, while Marx always characterized the July Monarchy as the reign of the "financial aristocracy" and the "industrial bourgeoisie" as one of the forces of opposition, he wrote a little further on (*Surveys,* 88): "The bourgeois class was divided into two great fractions which had alternately maintained a monopoly of power—*big landed property* under the *Restoration,* the *financial aristocracy* and the *industrial bourgeoisie* under the *July monarchy.*" The same idea appeared in the *Civil War in France* twenty years later: "The July revolution transferred power from the hands of the landowning proprietors to those of the big industrialists." In the second draft of *La Guerre civile en France* (Paris: Editions Sociales, 1972), 258.

sian barricades have little to do with the modern working class. In many respects, in all these analyses Marx is much more a prisoner to the political illusions of his time—even including those he himself has helped to create—than he is a discoverer of truths hidden from his contemporaries.

Indeed, he was constantly tempted by an ideological analysis of French politics executed in terms of conflicting traditions. He understood better than anyone that French politics presented such spectacular confrontations and diverse regimes because it was constrained to do so by the heritage of the French Revolution; for not only did the Revolution prohibit any national consensus regarding the form of the state, but, more specifically, it fragmented the loyalties of the dominant class while yet bequeathing to it the specter of a republic inseparable from the Terror. The French bourgeoisie had a retrospective fear of its own revolution, which was, nevertheless, what entitled it to govern France. This accounts for its rifts and its conflicts. On occasion, Marx abandons his obsession with the social to explore this contradiction in and of itself, and to gauge the weight of traditions and representations in the battles for power. For example, he described, in strictly historical and institutional terms, the elements of the political crisis that clinches, within the dominant bourgeoisie, the accession of a Bonaparte to the presidency of the Republic.[12] But this sort of analysis, which, moreover, he handles admirably, remains exceptional. Marx always lapsed into an interpretation in terms of the interests of classes or "fractions of classes."

Apart from its artificial character, the problem with this system of interpretation based on the class interests of political actors is that it contradicts the other type of response Marx suggests to the enigma of French political instability, which is related to the nature of the modern democratic state and its (at least relative) independence of civil society. This is an idea Marx used frequently in his pre-1850 works, but one that he reserved for the absolutist state, conceived as a product of the rivalry between the nobility and the Third Estate during the long period when the bourgeoisie was not yet sufficiently developed to make its revolution—an idea current elsewhere in French historiography during the Restoration,[13] which is where Marx found it. Until 1850 he never extended the idea to the modern, postrevolutionary state of the bourgeoisie. But this is what he now suggests in his

12. Marx, *Surveys*, 82.
13. Especially in the works of Augustin Thierry and Guizot.

analyses of the French nineteenth century, notably in *The Eighteenth Brumaire*.

The problem posed in that work is no longer one of interpreting the series of political battles that wove the history of the Second Republic, but of understanding Louis Napoleon Bonaparte's confiscation of the state. What an unprecedented, scandalous, but nevertheless expected event, this coup d'état of 2 December, by which a mediocre and despised adventurer, bearing a magical name, appropriated absolute authority over a great nation with relative ease, taking control of the most powerful administrative machine of the era! Anyone who finds it difficult today to imagine the indignation aroused by the event need only read Victor Hugo's *Histoire d'un crime*. While the country let things take their course, a great portion of the political class went into internal exile, and the great republican intellectuals took the route of exile plain and simple. Beyond the contempt in which the new head of France was held, the circumstances of his success added to the shame felt by the friends of liberty. For the coup d'état of 2 December was not the product of a dramatic political conjuncture like the one that allegedly explains 18 Brumaire—a combination of a civil and a foreign war—but the cynical capture of a great country, immobilized and demoralized. It was a ruthless caricature, which robbed the French of what was unique in their history—the Revolution, that national and international epic, and the hero that imbued them with the image of his genius.

But if the February revolution replayed the great original spectacle in a derisory fashion, it was because it gave cruel expression to the mystery of the event when stripped of the excuse of "circumstances" and of the festoons of the national rhetoric—the link that united, in the history of France, the revolutionary phenomenon and the despotism of the administrative state. Tocqueville and Quinet, each in his own manner, made this melancholy fact the center of their analyses.[14] And the question Marx posed in *The Eighteenth Brumaire* belongs to the same type of questioning because it considers the nature of the state born of the putsch of 2 December and its relation to society.

Louis Napoleon had to imprison, if only for a few days, the parliamentary representatives of the propertied classes. He took power against them and would exercise it without them, drawing support

---

14. Tocqueville in *L'Ancien Régime et la Révolution* (1856), Quinet in *La Révolution française* (1865).

from the silent majority that had elected him three years earlier. Sym-
bolizing the dissociation of the masses from the nation's traditional
elites, his power could no longer be defined as that of the bourgeoisie
or even of a fraction of the bourgeoisie. He thus revived, in its most
extreme form, the enigma of France's postrevolutionary history for
Marxist theory, and Marx addresses this enigma once again and more
extensively than ever: it forms the entire subject of his *Eighteenth Brumaire,* the best of his books on the history of France.

In his preceding work, Marx had portrayed the election of December 1846 not only as a present plebiscite but as an action willed by
the "majority of the grande bourgeoisie:[15] the dictatorship of General
Cavaignac, indispensable for only a moment in order to smash the
proletarian insurrection in the name of unified bourgeois interests,
was rapidly replaced by Louis Napoleon's presidency, which was assumed to offer a better guarantee of these same interests. But that interpretation did not survive the coup d'état of 2 December, since this
latter clearly manifested a conflict between the president and the representatives of the party of Order. *The Eighteenth Brumaire* analyzed
the Napoleonic state of the Second Empire at once as independent of
the social support of the bourgeoisie and as the combined product of
peasant nostalgia and bureaucratic development.

The second Bonaparte's dictatorship was, above all, a power
geared to the wishes of the most numerous class of the nation, the
peasantry. We need not, in the present context, go into the details of
Marx's celebrated analysis of this adjustment—the conditions of production of the small landowning peasantry, the isolation of each unit
from all others, the transfer to an all–powerful state of its incapacity to
act as a class for itself, its attachment to the Napoleonic version of the
French Revolution. It is more important to note that he mixed two
different orders of reality in this analysis, since he has recourse both to
a structural interpretation, linked to the conditions of the peasant
economy, and to a historical explanation, drawn from the existence of
an ideological tradition. But this tradition itself ultimately obeys the
imperatives of the infrastructure, for progressive as it was at birth,
when the French peasant, freed from feudal servitude, acceded to
total ownership of his parcel of land, a half-century later the tradition
had become an impediment to economic and social development.
Marx falls back upon the theme of parody, inseparable from his historical thinking since its function was to express the survival of an
ideology in a situation that has changed. This disjunction makes it

15. Marx, *Surveys,* 73.

possible to understand how the Napoleonic state, brought to power by the peasantry—the rural electoral "insurrection"—could not but betray the hopes placed in it: these hopes were illusions. The bourgeoisie, which in 1789 was allied with the peasants against the aristocrats, had become their usurer.

Here we rediscover, in a new form, the interpretation of the French state in terms of an anachronism—an interpretation that the young Marx put forward in *The Holy Family* with regard to the Terror and the Jacobin dictatorship. Taking up an idea of Constant's (see above, p. 21), he had seen the Robespierrist Terror as the product of a confusion between the nature of modern society and the nature of ancient society. Several years later, he utilized anew this idea of a false consciousness of historical reality to explain the second appearance of the Napoleonic state. But this time the peasants are its bearers and victims, and it is less a matter of a false consciousness of reality than of consciousness lagging behind reality.

While Robespierre knew Sparta and Rome only through books, the French peasantry had contact with Bonaparte only through their memories. In both cases, ideology was born of ignorance of the laws of history; but in the first case, ideology seized upon the principle actors and dictated to them a kind of politics quite alien to the objective demands of the French Revolution, hence necessarily provisional. In the second case, ideology constitutes the collective memory of a class, a memory born of recent experience, and constituting a public opinion capable of determining the form but not the content of the state.

Moreover, this state possesses another characteristic that renders it relatively independent of the dominant class in civil society: composed as it is of a civil servant "army" of a half-million men, as well as a real army, which is just as large, it possesses its own principle of growth, as illustrated by the history of France from the old monarchy to the Revolution. It extends and develops itself like a "frightful parasitic body," substituting itself for the activity of society to the degree that it destroys and assumes powers constituted within the feudal organization of society, that is, linked to corporate bodies and traditional collective privileges. Never was Marx closer to Tocqueville than in studying this sapping of the old society by a state external to it, which invaded like a cancer by virtue of a sort of necessity: "the seignorial privileges of the landowners and towns were transformed into attributes of the state power, the feudal dignitaries became paid officials, and the variegated medieval pattern of conflicting plenary authorities became the regulated plan of a state authority characterized by a centralization and division of labour reminiscent of a factory" (see selection 22).

Marx pursued this analysis with an observation even closer to what was to be the great Tocquevillian paradox: "The task of the first French revolution was to destroy all separate local, territorial, urban and provincial powers in order to create the civil unity of the nation. It had to carry further the centralization that the absolute monarchy had begun, but at the same time it had to develop the extent, the attributes and the number of underlings of the governmental power. Napoleon perfected this state machinery" (see selection 22). In this way, for Marx as for Tocqueville, the French Revolution continued the work of the monarchy. It was linked not only to the political advent of the bourgeoisie, but also to the perfecting of the centralized administrative state whose foundations had been laid by the French kings. Marx stops confusing these two sets of results, as he did in so many of his earlier texts: the modern state is not a mere instrument in the hands of the dominant class but possesses its own autonomy from society, as did the monarchical state from which it issued.

But the monarchical state drew its independence from the reciprocal neutralization of two classes—the nobility and the bourgeoisie. The postrevolutionary situation is, on the contrary, characterized by the undivided domination of the bourgeoisie. The reason the modern state is not simply a bourgeois state—as would be predicted from the balance of social forces—has to do with the manner in which it recycles the interests it must guarantee as so many administrative abstractions defined by the general interest. The increasing plurality of these interests, which goes along with the division of labor, is no longer taken care of by society itself but by a state whose intervention endows them with a universal content: the Marx of *The Eighteenth Brumaire* thus falls back on the Marx of *On the Jewish Question* to analyze the modern state as an "abstraction" of society. But this abstraction ceases to be a pure illusion; to the contrary, it constitutes the state's margin of maneuver vis-à-vis society—and makes possible its autonomy and the constant enlargement of this autonomy. Witness the nineteenth century: "Every *common* interest was immediately detached from society, opposed to it as a higher, *general* interest, torn away from the self-activity of the individual members of society and made a subject for governmental activity, whether it was a bridge, a schoolhouse, the communal property of a village community, or the railways, the national wealth and the national university of France" (see selection 22). If we add the demands of social and political repression to this tentacular administrative activity, we can understand the formidable sphere of power separated from society constituted by the postrevolutionary French state—the prize sought in so many battles: "All political upheavals perfected this machine instead of smashing it. The parties that strove in turn for mastery regarded possession of this immense state edifice as the main booty for the victor" (see selection 22).

In these pages, Marx goes to the heart of a paradox he had ignored up to this point: namely, that the bourgeoisie is the first dominant class not to be a governing class. Reigning over civil society, which it has turned into a marketplace composed of isolated individuals defined by their work alone, it is incapable of establishing its title to exercise political power in terms of this equality among individuals; and this is true even when the bourgeoisie, by the division of labor and the increase of wealth, has vastly increased the opportunities for state intervention in society. The possibility of a nonbourgeois state in the service of the bourgeoisie—of which the Second Empire offers the classic example—is rooted in this double reality.

What are the implications of this idea? First of all, it means that the situation of transparency between the bourgeoisie and the state is exceptional: 1789 offered a fleeting example of such transparency before the revolution became involved in the interminable ballet of representations of the modern state. But it also implies that the political dispossession of the bourgeoisie has no effect on the social domination of bourgeois interests; quite to the contrary, these interests can be better protected by a government whose agents are not directly drawn from the dominant class. That class gains the advantage of being able to devote all of its time to its economic role. Even more important, by these means it can better mask, in the eyes of the classes it exploits, the fact that this allegedly nonbourgeois state is, in reality, at the service of the bourgeoisie.

Not that it deliberately chooses such a deception: in speaking of 2 December 1851, Marx refers to the bourgeoisie's "abdication." By resorting to a savior, the bourgeoisie abandons its political prerogatives to save its material interests. This relinquishment is an accident of history to the extent that it derives from an ideological tradition specific to French peasants and eludes the consent of the political representatives of the dominant class. It is, nevertheless, an expression of historical necessity because it has become the indispensable means of saving bourgeois interests, which are increasingly threatened by the proletariat. There is thus an "abdication" in the sense that in the preceding period—the period of the Republic—the bourgeoisie governed directly (even though Louis Bonaparte was already chief executive), and that it must now cede power completely to a group of people it does not control. But this "abdication" brings to its culmination an evolution inherent in the nature of the modern state and visible with the emergence of the state during the French Revolution: to wit, it is simultaneously a bourgeois state and a state independent of the bourgeoisie. "Only under the second Bonaparte does the state seem to have attained a completely autonomous position" (see selection 22). The French bourgeoisie continues more than ever to reign over civil society, but under the cover of a gang of adventurers brought to power by the peasants' memories. History has brought its demonstration full circle.

This paradoxical and parodic state, which manifests and heightens the contradictions in bourgeois society, is also the last of the series. To understand it, we need only read Marx's last basic writings on nineteenth-century France, those about the Paris Commune, written in 1871. There we find him once more on the lookout for any new developments in the French political crisis. And, as always, he again takes up the entire period of postrevolutionary history since 1789, in order to reinterpret it in the light of its most recent events. In these writings the 1789–1871 cycle is considered in terms of a history of the state in which Marx repeats almost verbatim the analyses of *The Eighteenth Brumaire*,[16] but the Paris Commune in the end represents the antithesis of the secular movement that produced the bourgeois state in the caricatural form of the Second Empire. The French Revolution accomplishes the work of the monarchy by its "gigantic cleansweep," ridding the central state of the vestiges of feudalism that are its final obstacles; the Empire is its final form. After this, the parliamentary regime established in 1815 brings this state under the "direct control" of the dominant classes, which are both unified and divided— unified in the increasingly repressive exercise of power against the proletarian revolution, divided by the interests of the different fractions of which they are composed, until the conservative republic of 1848 embodies the unified form of their domination. But 2 December demonstrates the fragility and even the impossibility of this bourgeois ecumenicism: the Empire "was the only form of government possible at a time when the bourgeoisie had already lost, and the working class had not yet acquired, the faculty of ruling the nation" (see selection 30). Thus, in analyzing the latter-day Bonapartist state, Marx falls back upon the interpretation he had always applied to absolute mon-

16. K. Marx, F. Engels, *Commune de Paris* (Paris: Editions Sociales, 1972), 39–41.

archy: namely, that it expresses a provisional point of equilibrium between two classes, one rising, one declining, whose reciprocal neutralization explains this state's independence of civil society. Proof of this interpretation is that the Commune, which brings an end to the Empire, is its "direct antithesis," a proletarian revolution set not only against bourgeois domination but also against the central state produced by that domination.

The last Parisian revolution of the nineteenth century thus allows Marx to introduce a new explanation of the strange fate of Napoleon III. The Second Empire illustrates not only a sort of structural incapacity on the part of the bourgoisie to become a governing class, but also a historical evolution constituting the supreme form— which is also the last form (in the sense that Lenin would later refer to imperialism as the supreme stage of capitalism)—of the state of bourgeois interests. Nevertheless, this final addition made in the light of the events of the Commune adds a further obscurity to Marx's concept of the bourgeois state, rather than removing its contradictions. To be convinced of this, one need only consult the different versions of his final text (see selection 30).

Here Marx returns to the idea that the bourgeois state in nineteenth-century France, especially in its republican form, is only an "instrument of class domination" and that, in order to combat the threat of proletarian revolution, it has to give way to the more effective despotism of the Bonapartist gang (see selection 30). On the other hand, he later retains the idea of a French state that is "parasitical" upon a society increasingly independent of it, a state that attains its "final" development with Napoleon III:

> The governmental power with its standing army, its all-directing bureaucracy, its stultifying clergy and its servile tribunal hierarchy had grown so independent of society itself that a grotesquely mediocre adventurer with a hungry band of desperadoes behind him sufficed to wield it. It did no longer want the pretext of an armed coalition of old Europe against the modern world founded by the revolution of 1789. It appeared no longer as a means of class domination, subordinate to its parliamentary ministry or legislature. [It humbled] under its sway even the interests of the ruling classes, whose parliamentary show work it supplanted by self-elected Corps Législatifs and self-paid Senates. (See selection 30, first draft)

Nonetheless, the state itself, which escapes the control of the traditional, parliamentary representatives of the bourgeoisie, so much the better embodies and protects the reign of money, which remains its mainspring, as illustrated by the imperial regime's penchant for speculation. Its "independence" of the politically organized aspect of bourgeois society masks its true nature, which is still defined by this society in its ultimate stage of decomposition. This power,

> cloaking under the tatters of a masquerade of the past, the orgies of the corruption of the present and the victory of the most parasite fraction, the financial swindler, the *debauchery* of all the reactionary influences of the past let loose—the pandemonium of infamies—the state power had received its last and supreme expression in the Second Empire. Apparently the final victory of this governmental power over society, it was in fact the orgy of all the corrupt elements of that society. To the eye of the uninitiated it appeared only as the victory of the executive over the legislative, of the final defeat of the form of class rule pretending to be a superior power to society. But in fact it was only the last degraded and the only possible form of that class ruling, as humiliating as to the working classes which they kept fettered by it. (Ibid.)

Thus, in the space of a few lines, Marx writes successively that the modern state in its final stage, under the form of the Second Empire, has become wholly independent of society, and nevertheless represents the "last degraded and the only possible form" of bourgeois domination. The idea of a terminal stage of the history of this state has not really altered the contradictory character of his thinking about the bourgeois state. It simply adds an illusion and some supplementary ambiguities, owing to the necessity of situating the Commune in a dialectic antithesis with the Second Empire.

The illusion is of course that Napoleon III's state represents the "last" form of the bourgeoisie's class domination. Here Marx yields not only to the revolutionary impatience characteristic of his political temperament, but also to the logic of his doctrine: since the Commune has taken place and become a necessary part of the liquidation of the bourgeois state, the state it has overthrown must necessarily be the last in the series. Marx badly needed to endow the three-month-long Parisian revolution—for which he had not wished,[17] and which

---

17. Since 9 September 1870, Marx had alerted the French militants to an uprising in his second address to the International, in these very meaningful words: "Any attempt to overthrow the new government when the enemy is all but knocking at the gates of Paris would be desperate folly. The French workers must fulfill their duty as citizens, but at the same time they must not let themselves be led astray

was not led by his friends[18]—with a "Marxist" meaning. We thus find it invested with the mission of the completion-destruction of the history of the bourgeois state that began in 1789 and ended with this revolution, since it announced the beginning of the reappropriation of the state by the society of producers—a new political form of social emancipation for the proletariat. Hence the role that devolved upon the Second Empire of representing the last form of the cycle begun in 1789—the final appearance of the bourgeois state contrived by historical reason, not only its parody and caricature, but the exacerbation of its lies and vices.

As in 1848, Marx was again the victim of the revolutionary illusion inseparable from his intellectual and moral life. It is quite true that the great historical cycle opened up by the French Revolution would come to a close in the 1870s. Its end, however, resulted not from the proletarian revolution and the destruction of the centralized state, but from the founding of the Third Republic, the political form, finally discovered, of a consensus between the bourgeois, the petit bourgeois, and the peasant. This new regime, which would owe a great deal of its social base of support to the failure of the Commune and the disappearance of the Parisian insurrection threat, could not appreciably modify the Napoleonic structure of the administrative state. What was extinguished at Sedan was not the modern French state as it emerged from the French Revolution, but the magical power of a name over the French people.

It is not difficult to reconstitute the mechanism of Marx's historical illusion. It is always the same: it consists in contradicting the spirit of his doctrine in order to save the letter of it, and in deducing economic and social evolution from political history. Since the Commune did take place, the Second Empire, which preceded it, must necessarily have been a sort of Late Empire in the hands of crooks and parasites, the last manifestation of what had been a conquering bourgeoisie. This type of reasoning is all the more interesting because it leads Marx to a radical misinterpretation, for the regime of Napoleon III was not merely one of financial speculation but of the industrial and commercial expansion of French capitalism. The role in this ex-

by national *memories* of 1792, the way the French peasants let themselves be duped by national *memories* of the First Empire." Document cited in Marx, *La Guerre civile en France,* 11.

18. The Paris Commune never ceased to be in the hands of militants belonging to the various "French" traditions (neo-Jacobins, Blanquists, Proudhommians, etc.) elsewhere in conflict but all opposed to Marx.

pansion attributable to the state and to the emperor, as opposed to the historical conjunction, matters little here. This debate has no bearing on Marx's misinterpretation, which consists of mistaking the most brilliant years of the nineteenth-century French bourgeoisie for the years of its decadence, and the imperial state for its funeral procession when it was really its cradle. For such a great mind to arrive at such an extravagant conclusion, it must have been led astray by political passion or impatience—which was exactly the case: the Commune cannot be conceived of as the first proletarian revolution, no matter how brief, unless the state preceding it was the most decadent form of the bourgeois state. To remain true to his vision of historical evolution, Marx had to sacrifice the obvious facts of the economic and social history of the Second Empire by subordinating them to a hypothesis implicit in his political diagnosis.

These illusions of a doctrinaire thinker are similar in their peremptory character to many others punctuating the subsequent history of Marxism. But Marx nevertheless offers an infinitely richer example than that of his twentieth-century successors because he never stopped reworking these illusions. He could be wrong-headed, but never superficial. He understood that the coup d'état of 2 December and the "remake" of the Napoleonic state presented an interpretative challenge to his historical thinking; this episode epitomizes during his later years the same problems that the French Revolution itself posed during his youth, which is why he devoted to it such an accumulation of often mutually incompatible analyses. A reading of this series of analyses, dating from 1849 to 1871, from *The Class Struggles* to *The Civil War,* testifies to their continual enrichment, but this sedimentation removes none of their ambiguous or contradictory character, more obvious than ever in the writings of 1871.

The principle contradiction arises from Marx's analysis of the imperial state both as a mere product of bourgeois domination, at the service of its interests, and as something entirely independent of society, endowed with a reality and a history sui generis. The two conceptions are not necessarily incompatible, provided they are used in a partial form so that their respective elements are balanced according to each circumstance and to each regime. Marx, on the contrary, uses them alternately, in their fullest philosophical sense. On the one hand, civil society is the only historical reality and the bourgeoisie is the deus ex machina of the modern world. On the other, the bourgeoisie's privileged field of action is the marketplace and not the state; it is a dominant, not a governing class, and it has realized a radical separation between the social and the political. These two propositions are arranged hierarchically in Marx, with the priority given to the former—according to which the social is the truth of the political. But it is precisely this hierarchical link that the history of France, and of the Second Empire in particular, bring into question; so Marx used his two lines of analysis in succession without ever joining them logically: hence the contradiction.

The problem posed by 2 December is the break between the state and the bourgeoisie. Marx does not simply write off this break as an illusion from the very outset, as would be his usual inclination, but sketches a theory of it, again involving all of French history, before and after 1789. He suggests that there is indeed a history of the state that is independent of the history of society—that the Second Empire is but its latest expression. Heir of the monarchical state both in its autonomy and its functions, the state born of the French Revolution and completed by Napoleon I possessed its own internal dynamic. It perfected the work of its predecessor by creating the conditions for a national market, in this respect obeying the demands of bourgeois society; but it loomed over that society, dominating it through the centrality of its authority, the multiplication of its functions, and the obeisance in which it held the army and the bureaucracy.

Marx thus suggests a capital distinction between the history of the centralized administrative state and the history of political regimes. The centralized state, according to this view, is the end result of a long-term project, extended over several centuries, and pursued with perseverance by very diverse and even contradictory types of governments. Absolutism began what the "gigantic clean-sweep of the Revolution" completed, thereby creating the social conditions necessary to the building of the modern state, which was the work of the First Empire: this is a surprising anticipation of the central thesis of Tocqueville's book, but originates in other premises and is couched in another vocabulary. In Marx, it is not "democracy" but the development of bourgeois society that is the key to the process. Similarly, the rise of the state in the nineteenth century is linked to the needs of this same society: economic and social needs inherent in the division of labor, political needs inseparable from anti-worker repression. Nevertheless, in the final analysis this rise resulted in the creation of a vast body independent of society and eventually imposing its law on society, on 2 December 1851—here Marx meets the Tocquevillian question underlying *The Old Regime and the Revolution*. Moreover, this question resonates with one of his favorite images, that of parody, insofar as the two most spectacular periods of the history of the modern French state were the two empires of Napoleon I and Napoleon III: the first the liberator from the feudal past, and the symbol of bourgeois emancipation; the second the product of capitalist oppression, and the parasite of a decadent class. From one Napoleon to the other, the French Revolution completes its cycle, which is that of the modern state.

Nonetheless, if Marx, contrary to Tocqueville, never systematically explored this idea (or intuition), it was because it did not mesh with, and even contradicted, his system of interpretation. As we have seen, since his youth, he never ceased to track the illusions linked to the conception of a state independent of society, first in the form of a critique of Hegel, then through the elaboration of his materialist theory of history. Marx of the period of *Capital* remained completely true to this mission, which was more easily accomplished with respect to the English example than to the successive French revolutions. We have seen the price in intelligibility he had to pay in order to remain true to himself when it came to the events of 1848. The Second Empire is an even better illustration of this sort of consistency.

Indeed, at the same time he advanced his idea of the independence of the state in order to explain the Second Empire, Marx continually incorporated other, contradictory interpretations. His interpretations are varied and not always easily reconciled, but they share an emphasis on the illusion of the independent state as an arbiter between the classes, and on the reality of the modern state as an instrument of the dominant interests in civil society, and thus of the bourgeoisie.

In order to understand this idea, we may start from the famous thesis in *The Eighteenth Brumaire* that the Napoleonic state was the state of the small land-holding peasantry. This thesis appears to support the notion of this state's independence—vis-à-vis the bourgeoisie, at least—to the extent that Napoleon III's dictatorship found its principal support in another class, which thereby wreaked a sort of revenge upon capitalist domination. This revenge was really a fiction, however, for the imperial regime would subjugate the peasant increasingly to the usurer instead of emancipating him. If the rural population really did bring Napoleon III to power, it was in the name of an illusion that, once unmasked by historians, would reveal the truth of the Bonapartist dictatorship, namely, the interests of the bourgeoisie. Instead of aligning themselves with the urban proletariat, which was, like them, exploited, the peasants, by an apparently antibourgeois vote, involuntarily sealed a reactionary alliance with a declining dominant class. The future Napoleon III's manipulation, to his own advantage, of a petit bourgeois and rural political tradition concealed his dependence with regard to the world of money and bourgeois society.

Through an analysis of the massive vote of the French peasantry in favor of the emperor's nephew, Marx pursued his quest for the long series of illusions inseparable from the modern state. Put the other way around, the state's truth has never ceased (and never does cease) to be located in the dominant class of civil society, and not in any neutrality or independence belonging to its bureaucracy.

In bringing Louis Napoleon to the presidency of the Republic, the vote of December 1848 was a surprise only in appearance; in reality, it obeyed social determinants all the more constraining because they were masked. Marx remained indifferent, or blind, to the factor of unpredictability introduced into French politics by universal suffrage in 1848. Even a major modification of the procedures for the devolution of power such as this, demanded as it was by the whole republican and democratic Left under the July regime, did not in itself interest him, since it changed only in appearance—formally but not substantially—the dependence of the political upon the social. Indeed, Marx's whole analysis presupposes the prior existence of a determination of the state by society; it is the interests of different classes, and the way the classes represent those interests, that allow him to account for the nature and form of the state. The implementation of universal suffrage changed nothing in regard to this rule: its principal interest was that it brought out more clearly the only fundamental reality—the divisions and relations of force in civil society.

In this sense, Marx never abandoned the theses and works of his youth. Theoretically constituted, like the market, of free and equal individuals, political democracy is, like the market, a lie. The truth of the market is the division of labor and classes, the exploitation of the weak by the strong and the poor by the rich. Democratic citizenship simultaneously disguises and expresses this truth because it is incapable of modifying its constraints; it maintains the political supremacy of the dominant class under the appearance of a sovereignty shared equally by each member of the social body. Far from being a possible threat to the bourgeois order, universal suffrage is, on the contrary, the political translation of a society defined as a marketplace. The uncertainties it appears to introduce remain, in the final analysis, subject to the iron law of civil society. Even the vote of December 1848, an object of surprise and scandal for many contemporary observers, is for Marx but a ruse of the history of the bourgeois state.

Thus Marx never dreams of supporting his intuitions about a

French state that has become independent and a parasite of society with the implementation of political democracy and the introduction of universal suffrage. Yet the surprise that emerged from the ballot boxes in December 1848, in contrast to the expectations of the bourgeois elites, constituted a perfect illustration of this novelty, namely, that the democratic devolution of sovereignty systematically dissociated political power from the existence of the state—a supplementary reason, and more likely to be essential, for the particular, autonomous, and impersonal development of the state. But Marx never extensively analyzes the impact of democratic procedures on the political sphere, quite simply because it does not interest him, obsessed as he never ceased to be with the reduction of the political sphere to the opposing interests in civil society.

Thus the vote of 10 December, even with its peasant joke, remains a joke, an apparent accident whose role in historical necessity is revealed by analysis to be that of letting the bourgeoisie shoot its last fireworks, sheltered by a power abandoned to the hands of its most corrupt elements. Up to the Second Empire, Marx explained the French revolutions of the nineteenth century by resorting to the vague notion of "class fractions" without ever clarifying why the bourgeoisie found itself successively divided, reunified, and then divided again. From 1851 on, it is no longer the "class fractions" that are in power but the shady financiers and "crooks": an image no longer economic, but moral, of the irremediable decadence of a class at the moment of its greatest apparent triumph. For lack of a definition, this image serves to give a Late Empire air to a bourgeois society that has become almost transparent to itself, since it finally manifests, unreservedly and openly, its true nature—money.

Without a mask, but for the last time: for upon the idea of the bourgeoisie's unbridled power Marx bizarrely superimposes the idea of its impending disappearance. The final form of the bourgeois state, the Second Empire is simultaneously heir to the revolutionary state and the product of a posterior historical situation. Comparable in this latter respect to the old absolute monarchy, it arises from a provisional equilibrium between two classes in conflict, neither of which is strong enough to reign alone or at least without having indirect recourse to a netural authority. The comparison with the absolute monarchy is nevertheless misleading, because the locus of social conflict has shifted and is henceforth no longer located between the nobility and the bourgeoisie but between the bourgeoisie and the proletariat. And it is all the more misleading in that, for Marx, the monarchy served as a veritable arbiter state for several centuries—preserving the nobility as a class, but accomplishing, in place of an insufficiently developed bourgeoisie, a certain number of the latter's "historical" tasks—while recourse to Napoleon III was merely a means for the bourgeoisie to trick the working class without sacrificing any of its supremacy. Marx was referring not to the social neutrality of the second imperial state but to the political ambiguities that surrounded its birth, certain of its orientations, and the very personality of Napoleon III. The fact that the bourgeoisie was obliged, at least in his eyes, to resort to this ex-Saint-Simonian adventurer, and was despised and hated by its parliamentary representatives, was a sign of its incapacity to exercise power directly, for fear of awakening the proletarian revolution. That is why the Second Empire, the forced hand of bourgeois interests, was also their last trump card, since it constituted the only form of government possible at a time when the working classes were threatening their hegemony.

With this new thesis, Marx found yet another means of reaffirming the idea of a fundamental link between the bourgeoisie and the modern state, for the new form of this state—the Empire—is resented both as a ruse of the bourgeoisie to dupe the proletariat and as a deception indispensable to parry its threat: another way of saying, in fact, that behind the scenes in the theater of ambiguities in which Napoleon was strutting, the dominant class was still pulling the strings. The necessary character of the new disguise this class has assumed only adds to its formidable tactical dexterity. It controls circumstances by adjusting to them—master, as ever, of the social and political arena. To this degree, the idea of a power maintained and even perfected by tactical skill constituted a new version for Marx of the illusion of the state. But this time it is an illusion voluntarily created by the dominant class, adding its effects to those of what we might call the spontaneous illusion, which concerned the communitarian character of the state.

The fact remains that this Promethean vision of a bourgeoisie both dynamic in the market and Machiavellian in political intrigues does not tally well with the notion of an "abdication" into the hands of an uncontrollable gang of adventurers. Marx constantly oscillated between the idea of the bourgeoisie's supremacy and that of its impending disappearance. Both ideas are inseparable from his conception of historical necessity. The first allows him to expose, under the apparent chaos of events, the unflagging activity of a social class that invents modern society. The second results from the contradiction inseparable from this activity, and from the maturing of the proletarian revolution. But this belief in historical determinism did not bring to

Marx, as would be normal, any particular talent for prediction: depending on events, he emphasized sometimes the sovereignty of the bourgeoisie, and sometimes its weakness. These circumstantial hesitations only add the weight of their uncertainty to the diversity of the interpretations he presents.

All the interpretations of the French Revolution that can be drawn from Marx's writings are thus organized around a dialectic between civil society and the state, and orbit the same paradox. On the one hand, the Revolution is but the grand presentation of what occurred prior to it and does not therefore really belong to it—the bourgeoisie's victory over society. On the other, defined as the bourgeoisie's victory over the state, it leads, according to Marx's 1847 definition, to "the genesis of the modern state." These two propositions are difficult to articulate together, insofar as this "genesis"—which is the history, strictly speaking, of the French Revolution—opens a flood of events so out of control and a series of regimes so diverse that their common origin explains next to nothing about them.

Marx did not invent this contradiction, which is characteristic of all the "social" interpretations of the French Revolution. He found it, as he found the class struggle, in French Restoration historiography. But he took it to its limit, following the twofold penchant—polemical and philosophical—of his genius. His intellectual superiority over the liberal historians, as over so many later "Marxist" historians,[19] lies in the fact that he never ceased exploring the different aspects of this contradiction or accumulating commentaries upon it that are themselves contradictory. In the place of the history of the Convention that he dreamed of but never wrote, he unwittingly left us an inventory of the reasons preventing him from undertaking it, in that he never succeeded in resolving the difficulties they placed in its way.

His work on the French Revolution can be divided into three great chronological groups, corresponding to three successive modes of treating the same problem and reusing the same materials; but they obey a systematic logic, which varies in accordance with the evolution of his thought and the circumstances of history. First came the Feuerbachian Marx, who during the apparent stability of the July Monarchy treated the modern bourgeois state according to the model of religious alienation. He is followed, during the years that witnessed a rekindling of the revolutionary phenomenon, by the materialist Marx, who envisioned this state as a mere product of the social domi-

19. See Appendix to this chapter.

nation of bourgeois interests. Finally, there is the Marx of the *Capital,* who constantly interrupted his meditations on English history and on the secrets of capitalism to interpret and reinterpret the instability of the forms of the state in bourgeois France, from 1789 to 1871.

Nevertheless, throughout his reflections on the Revolution, we find again and again the same problem posed since his youth, which might be called the problem of the "illusion" of the state in relation to civil society. And his various interpretations can be defined in terms of the solutions he brought to the problem. In the works of his youth, this illusion is the most recent product of historical man's alienation from his essence: this post-Hegelian concept allows him simultaneously to conceive of the modern democratic state as the imaginary locus of the equality of citizens, and to conceive of the multiplicity of its forms as so many successive metamorphoses, until 1789 finally finds its stopping point, with Louis-Philippe, in a truly, fully "bourgeois" state. Inherent in this interpretation is a theory of the Revolution as manifestation of this "political" illusion and the possibility of a history of the Revolution composed of the successive metamorphoses of that illusion. Hence, it seems, the particular attention paid by Marx to Revolutionary history during this period of his intellectual life.

In the following period, by contrast, the commentaries become scarcer, and, furthermore, the conception of the French Revolution as a history of the metamorphoses of the modern state disappears. The "illusion" of the state has ceased to be a philosophical concept and has become a mere product of historical necessity. Now the Revolution has only one meaning and no development; it consists entirely in the bourgeoisie's conquest of power and the establishment of a bourgeois state in each of its periods—1789, 1793, Thermidor, the Empire. Marx remains more fascinated than ever by the French events, which offer him the indispensable precedent to the proletarian revolution. But the tools he has at his disposal in order to understand these events are so inadequate that they allowed him to say virtually anything about them, thus advancing, for example, two contradictory interpretations of 1793, namely, that the Terror accomplished the tasks of the bourgeois revolution, and that it constituted a provisional overthrow of the power of the bourgeoisie.

But, contrary to what Marx and many others believed, the French Revolution did not end in 1830. At the same time as 1848 sealed the failure of the proletarian revolution, it reopened the parodic cycle of the bourgeois revolution. With the Republic and the Empire, history brought back to Marx the questions of his youth, to be considered in his maturity with the use of another vocabulary: if the "illusion" of the modern state was but the fraudulent means by which the bourgeoisie disguises its undivided reign, why this flood of revolutions and coups d'état serving the same power? Marx's most interesting response was the one that allowed him—at times—to reintroduce the idea of the state's independence in relation to society, in a chronological cycle that no longer goes from 1789 to 1830, as it did during his youth, but from 1789 to 1871. In some remarkable pages in *The Eighteenth Brumaire* and *The Civil War,* he analyzes the French Revolution both as the end of the process of the formation of the modern state begun by the monarchy, and as its veritable creation, crowned by the work of Napoleon. He sees the subsequent revolutions of the nineteenth century as so many successive modifications of this state, whose role and functions never stop increasing; the battles for control over it are all the more interminable because it has become a parasitic entity independent of society—until the Commune of 1871 proclaims its end, terminating the cycle begun by the Revolution.

In these brilliant summaries, which form something akin to a synthesis of his writings on France, Marx understands and underscores an essential trait of modern French history: that only the revolution of 1789 shook the very foundation and structure of the state, whereas the various regimes of the nineteenth century merely altered the organizational forms of power and the political equilibriums. Between the two Napoleons, there were many constitutions but only one administrative constitution, unchanged in its essential elements, situated outside of political conflicts by national consensus. Nevertheless, although this insight suggests to Marx the relative independence and autonomous history of the state in relation to society and even to bourgeois politics, he never really explores its fecundity because he constantly obscures it with the opposing idea of the "illusion" of the bourgeois state, the mere instrument of the dominant class, linked to the rise and decline of that class, conquering and condemned with it. This is the source of his absurd conviction as to the impending end of the bourgeois state, in 1871—evidence of his resurgent incapacity to conceive of its history as anything other than a reflection of the supposed evolution of society.

Marx was one of the greatest historians of England, and an intermittent, brilliant, and uneven observer of France, full of profound intuitions and peremptory prejudices. England offered him a history almost tailor-made to his doctrine, since it was the history that nourished his ideas: a precocious and dynamic capitalism, a homogeneous and powerful dominant class, a state constantly under its control. In France, by contrast, it was the democratic revolution that was precocious and capitalism that was tardy: its history was in the hands of a bourgeoisie of proprietors lacking an enterprising spirit, a bourgeoisie politically divided over its own experiences and incapable of mastering its past and the successive regimes produced by that past. Nevertheless, comparable in this respect to the French liberals of 1830, Marx belonged to an intelligentsia that was convinced that the two great European histories were cast from the same mold and were responsive to the same type of explanation. His own explanation, elaborated and developed at great length in the case of England, takes as its key the development of capitalism and of a class that was at once dominant and ruling, master of capital, of Parliament, and of the state. Couched in this Procrustean bed, the France of the Revolution and of the nineteenth century is not easily understood or even recognizable.

In defining France, during his youth, as the country of "politics," Marx certainly perceived its specific character with great accuracy: he saw its history slowly prepared by a monarchical state independent of classes, which was finally replaced by the sovereignty of individuals as citizens through the Revolution's invention of the democratic state. But he virtually obliterated the significance of this idea by reducing modern "politics"—democracy—to a communitarian lie of market society: even though it was at the heart of French history, the history of this democratic representation was henceforth condemned to exist only at the margin of real history, like an illusion, a fraud, or an imitation. Marx retained a weakness for 1789 but abhorred the bourgeois and petit bourgeois France born of the French Revolution, a society condemned to parody and even to farce under the invocation of *grands souvenirs*.[20]

This sentiment is an echo of Marx's old mistrust of the French *phrase,* the old Jacobin rhetoric, a mistrust visible throughout his life in all of his writings. But above all it expressed his inability to separate the concept of the democratic state from the concept of capitalist and bourgeois society, or to understand Tocqueville's obsession of the same period, namely, the implications of equality for the future of modern society. In what constituted for Tocqueville the very nature

20. This abhorrence was particularly acute during the years 1860–70, when Marx was fighting the influence of French ideologies—notably Proudhommism, Blanquism, and neo-Jacobinism—from within the First International. See, for instance, the following extract from his letter to César de Paepe (selection 29) of 14 September 1870: "The drama of the French, as for the workers, are their *grands souvenirs*. It is necessary that events put an end for once and for all to this reactionary cult of the past."

of democracy and its most profound truth, Marx on the contrary saw the illusion he never stopped denouncing and demystifying: modern individuals' representation of themselves as equals. It is no accident that Tocqueville, starting from the question he posed, abandoned English history—the privileged history of Guizot and Marx—for the American example: if the French Revolution constituted the advent of the democratic idea, it could only be compared to another history characterized by the same idea. If, on the other hand, the French Revolution was merely the advent of the bourgeoisie, then it is the English reference that counts; Guizot elaborated it under the angle of representative institutions, and Marx analyzed it as the first, and archtypical, example of the development of capitalist society. All three authors wrote their historical works as a function of their philosophies.

The surprising thing about Marx is that from time to time he had a vision quite close to Tocqueville's of modern French history and of the role the monarchical state and the democratic state had played and were still playing in it. There are moments when he escaped the dominant notion of the social and bourgeois determination of the course of events and ideas. The way in which an episode like the 2 December 1851 intrigued Marx was not far, as we have seen, from the questions that the future author of *The Old Regime and the Revolution* would pose for himself. But we have also seen that Marx's approach rather curiously mingles these questions with a completely different and even contradictory approach, which, for good reason, always ends by obscuring them, since it is the approach entailed in his philosophy of history.

It remains true that this periodic hesitation in Marx's thought, and the sort of remorse it reveals for the simplifications into which his leanings drew him, are never more visible than in his lifetime writings on the French Revolution and contemporary France. For this unending and ambiguous meditation on an enigma never ceased to be an implicit debate he carried on simultaneously with himself and with his works. As a result, he left not only Marxism to his commentators, but the elements of a critique of Marxism as well. The book he never wrote on the French Revolution bears witness in its own way to what is left unexplained in his magnum opus on English capitalism.

APPENDIX

Many Marxists have since written for Marx, or believed they have written, the book he never wrote. This is one way of returning to the statement that opened the present book, in an attempt to understand the extraordinary posthumous fortune of a dilemma he never resolved.

Marx never had a theory of the state; his successors drew one from the analytical elements he left behind, placing the accent on the dependency of the state—any state—on civil society. In so doing, they are not untrue to the spirit of Marx's doctrine, since this dependency—the secondary character—of the state in the historical dialectic never ceased to be emphasized by Marx, especially when opposing Hegel. Nevertheless, they tend to make this idea into a universal dogma, everywhere and always valid, whereas Marx, as we have seen, never stopped perceiving its difficulties and disputing, through the French example, its interpretative value. This simplification is particularly visible in Lenin, who made the idea into a cornerstone of Bolshevism, a subjectivist variant of Marxism: in his conception, the state is at once magnified as the locale of revolution and power, a privileged instrument of historical change, and reduced purely and simply to its class content according to the nature of its possessor, whether an aristocratic state, a bourgeois state, or a workers' state. Thus political thought in Bolshevism offers the characteristic contrast of being tactically rich and philosophically nonexistent.

In the twentieth century, Marxist historiography of the French Revolution was subjected to the backlash of this derivation of Marx's Marxism. It is more marked in its obsession with 1917 than in the meditation of *The Holy Family* or *The Eighteenth Brumaire*. That it is more Leninist than Marxist is evident in two instances: the first is the repudiation of Marx's theory about French absolutism. While Marx remained true throughout his works to the Restoration historians' idea that French absolutism was a power autonomous from society, arbiter between the nobility and bourgeoisie, the thesis that has become current in Marxist historiography in the twentieth century is that of an aristocratic state, governing the realm to the benefit of what was formerly the feudal class, politically dispossessed but still socially dominant throughout the period of the absolute monarchy. This is a way to extrapolate the Leninist intransigence about the class content of the modern capitalist state, instrument of monopolies, whatever may be the constitutional procedures. But it also presents a different vision of the French Revolution from that of the founding father, not only because its version of the monarchical state differs from Marx's, but also because, for Marxist historiography, eighteenth-century society was not dominated by the bourgeoisie as Marx believed.

By the same token, neither is the French Revolution the same. If the Revolution remains, in the last analysis, the product of the devel-

opment of capitalism, in the Leninist version it picks up a sort of supplementary necessity and brilliance from the fact that it must reverse
and uproot a society and an aristocratic state that defended itself tooth
and claw. In this domain as elsewhere, Leninism favors the voluntarist
side of Marxism: even more than the advent of the bourgeoisie, the
Revolution is the dramatic epic through which the bourgeoisie produces itself, a flood of violence and regimes whereby the inevitable
conflict with this powerful counterrevolution was manifest. In contrast to Marx, the Leninist historian of the Revolution celebrates its
course more than its outcome. Thus can be explained the accent
placed on 1793 rather than on 1789 and the fact that the Leninist historian prefers Jacobins to Constituants, to say nothing of Thermidorians. With the men of 1793, the Leninist historian finds himself in
familiar surroundings, since the Soviet experience also illustrated the
necessity for dictatorship and terror. He shares with the Jacobins and
Bolsheviks the belief that revolutionary action can and must change
society; it was precisely this belief that Marx analyzed as a characteristic illusion of politics.

P·A·R·T T·W·O
SELECTIONS FROM KARL MARX

1

The Philosophical Manifesto of the Historical School of Law

This article, drafted by Marx from April to early August 1842, appeared in the *Rheinische Zeitung* on 9 August 1842. In the articles he submitted to the *Rheinische Zeitung* from April 1842 on, Marx appeared as a liberal polemicist highly critical of the Prussian state (the Rhineland had been Prussian since 1815, having been French during the revolutionary and Napoleonic eras). He also criticized the ideologies and doctrines that supported Prussia's romantic-reactionary evolution since Friedrich Wilhelm IV's accession to the throne of Berlin in 1840, and especially the so-called historical school of law represented principally by Friedrich Carl von Savigny (1779–1861), who was a disciple of Gustav Hugo (1764–1844), professor of law at the University of Göttingen. From 1842 to March of 1848, Savigny was a minister in the Prussian government. The historical school of law, linked in part to reactionary romanticism and, on that account, fought by Hegel and by his liberal disciple Edouard Gans, stood in opposition to the universalism of the Enlightenment and to the doctrines of natural law. For Savigny as for Hugo, only a historically constituted and established tradition could found law; positive law was thus opposed to natural or traditional law. It was with the proponents of positive law—and so of the French Revolution—that Marx aligns himself here.

· · ·

. . . Hugo stands in a relationship to the *Other Enlightenment figures* of the eighteenth century similar to the one in which *the dissolution of the French state* during the immoral *court of the Regent* stood to the dissolution of the French state during the National Assembly. Dissolution on both sides! There it appears as *licentious frivolity,* which comprehends

Karl Marx and Friedrich Engels, *Werke* (East Berlin: Dietz, 1956–), 1:80–81. This edition will hereafter be cited MEW.

and ridicules the empty lack of ideas of the existent conditions, but only in order—all reasonable and moral bonds aside—to pursue *their game* with the crumbling ruins and to become itself driven and dissolved by that game. It is the *decay of the world of that time, celebrating itself.* In the *National Assembly* the *dissolution* seemed, in contrast, a *liberation of the new spirit* from the *old forms,* which were no longer *valid* and no longer *capable* of grasping that new spirit. It is the *self-consciousness of the new life* that *destruction destroys,* that *depravity depraves.* If *Kant's Philosophy* can justifiably be considered the *German theory* of the French Revolution, then *Hugo's natural law* could be considered to the *German theory* of the French ancien régime. In him we encounter once again all the frivolity of those *roués,* the *vulgar skepticism* that, contemptuous of ideas, totally respectful of the empirical, only senses its cleverness when it has killed the *Spirit* of the positive, in order then to possess the pure positive in its residual form and to be comfortable in this *animal* state. Even if Hugo measures the weight of reasons, he will with an unfailingly certain instinct regard what is reasonable and moral in institutions as something *dangerous* to reason. Only what is *animal* seems to *his reason* to be something *without danger. . . . ·*

2

Letters to Arnold Ruge in the *Franco-German Yearbooks*

These two letters were written by Marx to the young Hegelian Arnold Ruge in March and May 1843 and appeared in Paris in the single issue of the *Deutsch-französische Jahrbücher* (*Franco-German Yearbooks*) that appeared in February 1844. The *Deutsch-französische Jahrbücher* were a continuation of the *Hallesche Jahrbücher für Wissenschaft und Kunst* and the *Deutsche Jahrbücher für Wissenschaft und Kunst* and were run principally by Ruge, first from the university town of Halle and then, from 1841 on, because of censorship, from Dresden. The correspondence published in February 1844 also contained letters from Ruge to Marx, from Bakunin to Ruge, from Ruge to Bakunin, and from Feuerbach to Ruge. The pivot of discussion was the possibility—or, rather, the sad impossibility—of a political (bourgeois) revolution in Germany. In order to describe Germany's "miserable" political situation in his letter to Marx, Ruge quoted from the famous letter at the end of Hölderlin's novel *Hyperion:* "It is hard saying, and yet I speak it because it is the truth: I can think of no people more at odds with themselves than the Germans. You see artisans, but no men, thinkers, but no men, priests, but no men, masters and servants, but no men, minors and adults, but no men—is this not like a battlefield on which hacked-off hands and arms and every other member lie pell-mell, while the life-blood flows from them to vanish in the sand?" (*Hyperion,* trans. Willard R. Trask [New York: Frederick Ungar, 1965], 16. Ruge omits the word "priests" from his quotation.)

In October 1843, Marx settled in Paris with his wife Jenny von

MEW 1:337–39. Karl Marx, *Early Writings,* edited by Quintin Hoare, translated by Gregor Benton and Rodney Livingstone (Pelican Marx Library, 1975; New York: Vintage Books, 1975), 199–201. ©1975 by New Left Review. Reproduced by permission of Penguin Books, Ltd., and Random House, Inc. All further excerpts from this work are also reproduced by permission of these publishers. This selection translated by Rodney Livingstone.

Westphalen; there he rediscovered, among others, Ruge, the democratic poet Herwegh, and Heinrich Heine, another critic of the
"miserable" German political situation of 1830–48.

• • •

I

From a barge on the way to D., March 1843

I am now travelling in Holland. From both the French papers and the
local ones I see that Germany has ridden deeply into the mire and will
sink into it even further. I assure you that even if one can feel no national pride one does feel national shame, even in Holland. In comparison with the greatest Germans even the least Dutchman is still a
citizen. And the opinions of foreigners about the Prussian government! There is a frightening agreement, no one is deceived any longer
about the system and its simple nature. So the new school has been of
some use after all. The glorious robes of liberalism have fallen away
and the most repulsive despotism stands revealed for all the world
to see.

This too is a revelation, albeit a negative one. It is a truth which
at the very least teaches us to see the hollowness of our patriotism, the
perverted nature of our state and to hide our faces in shame. I can see
you smile and say: what good will that do? Revolutions are not made
by shame. And my answer is that shame is a revolution in itself; it
really is the victory of the French Revolution over the German patriotism which defeated it in 1813. Shame is a kind of anger turned in on
itself. And if a whole nation were to feel ashamed it would be like a
lion recoiling in order to spring. I admit that even this shame is not
yet to be found in Germany; on the contrary the wretches are still
patriots. But if the ridiculous system of our new knight[1] does not dis-
abuse them of their patriotism, then what will? The comedy of despotism in which we are being forced to act is as dangerous for him as
tragedy was once for the Stuarts and the Bourbons. And even if the
comedy will not be seen in its true light for a long time yet it will still
be a revolution.

The state is too serious a business to be subjected to such buf-
foonery. A Ship of Fools can perhaps be allowed to drift before the
wind for a good while; but it will still drift to its doom precisely because the fools refuse to believe it possible. This doom is the approaching revolution.

II

Cologne, May 1843

Your letter, my friend, is a fine elegy, a breath-taking funeral dirge; but it is utterly unpolitical. No people despairs and if stupidity induces it to live on hopes for many years a sudden burst of cleverness will eventually enable it to fulfil its dearest wishes.

However, you have stimulated me. Your theme is by no means exhausted. I am tempted to add a finale and when all is at an end give me your hand and we can start all over again. Let the dead bury the dead and mourn them. In contrast, it is enviable to be the first to enter upon a new life: this shall be our lot.

It is true that the old world belongs to the philistines. But we must not treat them as bogeymen and shrink from them in terror. On the contrary, we must take a closer look at them. It is rewarding to study these lords of the world.

Of course, they are lords of the world only in the sense that they fill it with their presence, as worms fill a corpse. They require nothing more than a number of slaves to complete their society and slave-owners do not need to be free. If their ownership of land and people entitles them to be called lords and master *par excellence* this does not make them any less philistine than their servants.

Human beings—that means men of intellect, free men—that means republicans. The philistines wish to be neither. What is left for them to be and to wish?

What they wish is to live and to procreate (and Goethe says that no one achieves more). And this they have in common with animals. The only thing a German politician might wish to add is that man *knows* this is what he wants and that the Germans are determined to want nothing more.

Man's self-esteem, his sense of freedom, must be re-awakened in the breast of these people. This sense vanished from the world with the Greeks, and with Christianity it took up residence in the blue mists of heaven, but only with its aid can society ever again become a community of men that can fulfil their highest needs, a democratic state.

By contrast, men who do not feel themselves to be men accumulate for their masters like a breed of slaves or a stud of horses. The hereditary masters are the aim and goal of the entire society. The world belongs to them. They take possession of it as it is and feels itself to be. They accept themselves as they are and place their feet where they naturally belong, viz. on the necks of these political animals who have no other vocation than to be their "loyal, attentive subjects."

The philistine world is the *animal kingdom of politics* and if we must needs acknowledge its existence we have no choice but to accept the *status quo*. Centuries of barbarism have produced it and given it shape, and now it stands before us as a complete system based on the principle of the *dehumanized world*. Our Germany, the philistine world at its most perfect, must necessarily lag far behind the French Revolution which restored man to his estate. A German Aristotle who wished to construct his *Politics* on the basis of our society would begin by writing "Man is a social but wholly unpolitical animal." . . .

NOTE

1. Frederick William IV of Prussia came to the throne in 1840.

3

Critique of Hegel's Doctrine of the State

This manuscript, first published in 1927, was written by Marx in Kreuznach during the summer of 1843 and thus after the Prussian government suppressed the *Rheinische Zeitung*. In his articles in the *Rheinische Zeitung*, Marx, as did Ruge in the *Hallesche Jahrbücher* and then in the *Deutsche Jahrbücher*, still held a position on the question of the state quite close to Hegel's: the state was seen to represent and defend the universal as opposed to the particular, the general interest (or the "public good") as opposed to the contradictory interests of the social groups and individuals that make up civil society. Marx still sometimes appeared to believe, with certain young Hegelians, that it was possible for the Prussian state to have a progressive and liberal role in Restoration Germany; the critique of the Prussian state, though sharp, presupposed the possibility of an internal amelioration of this same state. The manuscript of the summer of 1843 marks a break with this concept in a detailed commentary on paragraphs 261–313 of Hegel's *Philosophy of Right,* which were devoted to the state. Marx particularly attacks Hegel's praise for constitutional monarchy: the political form (republic or monarchy) carried less weight for him at this moment than did economic and social content (inequality, private property).

It was in Kreuznach that Marx read with great care—as testified by his notebooks—eighteenth-century texts in political philosophy (Rousseau's *Social Contract* and Montesquieu's *Spirit of the Laws*) and works by German and French historians on the history of France and the revolution of 1789 (see K. Marx, F. Engels, *Gesamtausgabe* [East Berlin: Dietz, 1975–], section 4, vol. 2).

• • •

MEW 1:260, 283–84. *Early Writings* (see source note to selection 2), 119–20, 146. Translated by Rodney Livingstone.

. . . The legislature made the French Revolution; in fact, wherever it has emerged as the dominant factor it has brought forth great, organic, universal revolutions. It has not attacked the constitution as such but only a particular antiquated constitution; this is because the legislature acted as the representative of the people, of the species–will [*Gattungswillen*]. In contrast to this, the executive has made all the petty revolutions, the retrograde revolutions, the reactions. Its revolutions were not fought against an old institution and on behalf of a new one; they were fought against the constitution itself, simply because the executive was the representative of the particular will, subjective caprice, the magical aspect of the will.

If the question is to make any sense at all, it can only mean: does the people have the right to make a new constitution? And this question can only be answered unreservedly in the affirmative, for a constitution that has ceased to be the real expression of the will of the people has become a practical illusion.

The contradiction between the constitution and the legislature is nothing but the *conflict within the constitution itself,* a contradiction in the concept of the constitution.

The constitution is nothing but an accommodation between the political and the unpolitical state; inevitably, therefore, it is itself a synthesis of essentially heterogeneous powers. Hence it is impossible for the law to proclaim that one of these powers, a part of the constitution, should have the right to modify the whole, the constitution itself. . . .

Let us now consider the *Estate* and *representative* systems. It was a definite advance in history when the *Estates* were transformed into social classes so that, just as the Christians are equal in heaven though unequal on earth, the individual members of the people became *equal* in the heaven of their political world, though unequal in their earthly existence in *society*. The actual transformation of the Estates into *classes* took place under the *absolute monarchy*. Thanks to the bureaucracy the idea of unity was made to prevail over the various states within the state. Nevertheless, alongside the bureaucracy of the absolutist government, the *social distinctions* between the classes remained political and the *political difference* persisted *within* and alongside the bureaucracy of the absolute government. Not until the French Revolution was the process completed in which the *Estates* were transformed into *social* classes, i.e., the *class distinctions* in civil society became merely *social* differences in private life of no significance in political life. This accomplished the separation of political life and civil society. . . .

4

On the Jewish Question

This article was a critical response to two articles by the young Hegelian Bruno Bauer, which appeared in 1843 and addressed the possibility—or rather, the impossibility—of the civil and political emancipation of the Jews in Germany. This question was topical at the start of the 1840s, particularly in Prussia because of Friedrich Wilhelm IV's "German-Christian" state projects. The German liberals were generally—with some nuances—favorable toward the emancipation of the Jews. Without being truly anti-Semitic, Bruno Bauer regarded the Jews, because of their religious nature, as unfit for emancipation; emancipation could thus come about only through the Jew's rejection of the Jewish religion and then of the Christian religion and the Christian state. Marx seems to have drafted his article during his stay at Kreuznach and at the beginning of his stay in Paris—thus at the end of the summer and during the autumn of 1843. He published it in the *Deutsche-französische Jahrbücher* in February 1844. Marx's argument rests on a twofold distinction: between the state and civil society, on the one hand, and between political emancipation and human emancipation on the other. Marx criticized the ideology of bourgeois liberalism, which separated the "rights of man" from those of the "citizen," as well as the economic foundations of this liberalism—egoism, money, and private property. It is wrong to see Marx's article as an anti-Semitic tract (see, for example, R. Misrahi, *Marx et la question juive* [Paris, 1972], who entitled one of his chapters "L'antisémitisme implicite et manifeste de *La Question juive*"). Like Moses Hess, who influenced him in Paris, Marx demonstrates that egoism and the love of money are not specifically Jewish characteristics but are characteristics of modern and Christian bourgeois society. The French Revolution certainly

MEW 1:361–70. *Early Writings* (see source note to selection 2), 226–34. Translated by Gregor Benton.

emancipated the Jews, and it was this emancipation that was brought once more into question in Germany after 1815; but for all that, neither real nor generic man had been emancipated.

• • •

. . . We have therefore shown that political emancipation from religion allows religion—but not privileged religion—to continue in existence. The contradiction in which the adherent of a particular religion finds himself in relation to his citizenship is only *one aspect* of the general *secular contradiction between the political state and civil society*. The final form of the Christian state is one which recognizes itself as state and disregards the religion of its members. The emancipation of the state from religion is not the emancipation of actual man from religion.

Therefore we do not tell the Jews that they cannot be emancipated politically without radically emancipating themselves from Judaism, which is what Bauer tells them. We say instead: the fact that you can be politically emancipated without completely and absolutely renouncing Judaism shows that *political emancipation* by itself is not *human* emancipation. If you Jews want to be politically emancipated without emancipating yourselves as humans, the incompleteness and the contradiction lies not only in you but in the *nature* and the *category* of political emancipation. If you are ensnared within this category, then your experience is a universal one. In the same way as the state *evangelizes* when, although a state, it adopts the attitude of a Christian towards the Jew, the Jew *acts politically* when, although a Jew, he demands civil rights.

But if man, although a Jew, can be politically emancipated and acquire civil rights, can he claim and acquire the *rights of man?* In Bauer's view he cannot.

> The question is whether the Jew as such, i.e. the Jew who himself admits that he is compelled by his true nature to live in eternal separation from others, is capable of acquiring and granting to others the *universal rights of man.*
> The idea of the rights of man was not discovered in the Christian world until the last century. It is not innate in man. On the contrary, it can only be won in a struggle against the historical traditions in which man has up to now been educated. Therefore the rights of man are not a gift of nature or a legacy of previous history, but the prize of the struggle against the accident of birth and the privileges which history has handed

down from generation to generation. They are the product of culture, and only he can possess them who has earned them and deserved them.

But can the Jew really take possession of them? As long as he is a Jew the restricted nature that makes him a Jew will inevitably gain the ascendancy over the human nature which should join him as a man to other men; the effect will be to separate him fron non-Jews. He declares through this separation that the particular nature which makes him a Jew is his true and highest nature in the face of which human nature is forced to yield.

In the same way the Christian as Christian cannot grant the rights of man.[1]

According to Bauer man must sacrifice the *"privilege of faith"* in order to be in a position to receive the universal rights of man. Let us consider for one moment these so-called rights of man. Let us consider them in their most authentic form—the form they have among those who *discovered* them, the North Americans and the French! These rights of man are partly *political* rights, rights which are only exercised in community with others. What constitutes their content is *participation* in the *community,* in the *political* community or *state.* They come under the category of *political freedom,* of *civil rights,* which as we have seen by no means presupposes the consistent and positive abolition of religion and therefore of Judaism. It remains for us to consider the other aspect, the *droits de l'homme* as distinct from the *droits du citoyen.*

Among them we find freedom of conscience, the right to practise one's chosen religion. The *privilege of faith* is expressly recognized, either as one of the *rights of man* or as a consequence of one of these rights, namely freedom.

Declaration of the Rights of Man and of the Citizen, 1791, Article 10: "No one is to be molested on account of his convictions, even his religious convictions." In Title I of the Constitution of 1791 the following is guaranteed as one of the rights of man: "the liberty of every man to practise the religion he professes."

The Declaration of the Rights of Man etc., 1793, counts among the rights of man, Article 7: "Liberty of worship." What is more, it even says, in connection with the right to publish views and opinions, to assemble and to practise religion, that "the need to enunciate these rights supposes either the presence or the recent memory of despotism." Compare the Constitution of 1795, Title XIV, Article 354.

Constitution of Pennsylvania, Article 9, §3: "All men have received from nature the imprescriptible *right* to worship the Almighty according to the dictates of their consciences and no one can of right be compelled to follow, to institute or to support against his will any religion or religious ministry. No human authority can under any circumstances whatsoever intervene in questions of conscience and control the powers of the soul."

Constitution of New Hampshire, Articles 5 and 6: "Among the natural rights, some are by their very nature inalienable because they cannot be replaced by anything equivalent. The *rights* of conscience are of this sort."[2]

The incompatibility of religion with the rights of man is so alien to the concept of the rights of man that the *right to be religious*—to be religious in whatever way one chooses and to practise one's chosen religion—is expressly enumerated among the rights of man. The *privilege of faith* is a *universal right of man*.

The rights of man as *such* are distinguished from the rights of the citizen. Who is this man who is distinct from the citizen? None other than the *member of civil society*. Why is the member of civil society simply called "man" and why are his rights called the rights of man? How can we explain this fact? By the relationship of the political state to civil society, by the nature of political emancipation.

The first point we should note is that the so-called *rights of man,* as distinct from the *rights of the citizen,* are quite simply the rights of the *member of civil society,* i.e. of egoistic man, of man separated from other men and from the community. Consider the most radical constitution, the Constitution of 1793:

Declaration of the Rights of Man and of the Citizen.

Article 2. "These rights, etc. (the natural and imprescriptible rights) are: equality, liberty, security, property."

What is liberty?

Article 6. "Liberty is the power which belongs to man to do anything that does not harm the rights of others," or according to the Declaration of the Rights of Man of 1791: "Liberty consists in being able to do anything which does not harm others."

Liberty is therefore the right to do and perform everything which does not harm others. The limits within which each individual can move *without* harming others are determined by law, just as the boundary between two fields is determined by a stake. The liberty we are here dealing with is that of man as an isolated monad who is withdrawn into himself. Why does Bauer say that the Jew is incapable of acquiring the rights of man?

"As long as he is a Jew the restricted nature which makes him a

Jew will inevitably gain the ascendancy over the human nature which should join him as a man to other men; the effect will be to separate him from non-Jews."

But the right of man to freedom is not based on the association of man with man but rather on the separation of man from man. It is the *right* of this separation, the right of the *restricted* individual, restricted to himself.

The practical application of the right of man to freedom is the right of man to *private property*.

What is the right of man to private property?

Article 16 (Constitution of 1793): "The right of *property* is that right which belongs to each citizen to enjoy and dispose *at will* of his goods, his revenues and the fruit of his work and industry."

The right to private property is therefore the right to enjoy and dispose of one's resources as one wills, without regard for other men and independently of society: the right of self-interest. The individual freedom mentioned above, together with this application of it, forms the foundation of civil society. It leads each man to see in other men not the *realization* but the *limitation* of his own freedom. But above all it proclaims the right of man "to enjoy and dispose *at will* of his goods, his revenues and the fruit of his work and industry."

There remain the other rights of man, equality and security.

Equality, here in its non-political sense, simply means equal access to liberty as described above, namely that each man is equally considered to be a self-sufficient monad. The Constitution of 1795 defines the concept of this equality, in keeping with this meaning, as follows:

Article 3 (Constitution of 1795): "Equality consists in the fact that the law is the same for everyone, whether it protects or whether it punishes."

And security?

Article 8 (Constitution of 1793): "Security consists in the protection accorded by society to each of its members for the conservation of his person, his rights and his property."

Security is the supreme social concept of civil society, the concept of *police,* the concept that the whole of society is there only to guarantee each of its members the conservation of his person, his rights and his property. In this sense Hegel calls civil society "the state of need and of reason."

The concept of security does not enable civil society to rise above its egoism. On the contrary, security is the *guarantee* of its egoism.

Therefore not one of the so-called rights of man goes beyond egoistic man, man as a member of civil society, namely an individual withdrawn into himself, his private interest and his private desires and separated from the community. In the rights of man it is not man who appears as a species-being; on the contrary, species-life itself, society, appears as a framework extraneous to the individuals, as a limitation of their original independence. The only bond which holds them together is natural necessity, need and private interest, the conservation of their property and their egoistic persons.

It is a curious thing that a people which is just beginning to free itself, to tear down all the barriers between the different sections of the people and to found a political community, that such a people should solemnly proclaim the rights of egoistic man, separated from his fellow men and from the community (Declaration of 1791), and even repeat this proclamation at a time when only the most heroic devotion can save the nation and is for that reason pressingly required, at a time when the sacrifice of all the interests of civil society becomes the order of the day and egoism must be punished as crime. (*Declaration of the Rights of Man,* etc., 1793). This fact appears even more curious when we observe that citizenship, the *political community,* is reduced by the political emancipators to a mere *means* for the conservation of these so-called rights of man and that the citizen is therefore proclaimed the servant of egoistic man; that the sphere in which man behaves as a communal being [*Gemeinwesen*] is degraded to a level below the sphere in which he behaves as a partial being, and finally that it is man as *bourgeois,* i.e. as a member of civil society, and not man as citizen who is taken as the *real* and *authentic* man.

"The *goal* of all *political association* is the *conservatism* of the natural and imprescriptible rights of man" (*Declaration of the Rights of Man* etc., 1791, Article 2). "*Government* is instituted in order to guarantee man the enjoyment of his natural and imprescriptible rights" (*Declaration* etc., 1793, Article 1).

Thus even during the ardour of its youth, urged on to new heights by the pressure of circumstances, political life declares itself to be a mere *means* whose goal is the life of civil society. True, revolutionary practice is in flagrant contradiction with its theory. While, for example, security is declared to be one of the rights of man, the violation of the privacy of letters openly becomes the order of the day. While the "*unlimited* freedom of the press" (Constitution of 1793, Article 122) is guaranteed as a consequence of the right to individual freedom, the freedom of the press is completely destroyed, for "the freedom of the press should not be permitted when it compromises public freedom."[3] This therefore means that the right to freedom ceases to be a right as soon as it comes into conflict with *political* life, whereas in theory political life is simply the guarantee of the rights of man, the rights of individual man, and should be abandoned as soon as it contradicts its *goal,* these rights of man. But practice is only the exception and theory is the rule. Even if we were to assume that the relationship is properly expressed in revolutionary practice, the problem still remains to be solved as to why the relationship is set upon its head in the minds of the political emancipators so that the end appears as the means and the means as the end. This optical illusion present in their minds would continue to pose the same problem, though in a psychological and theoretical form.

But there is a straightforward solution.

Political emancipation is at the same time the *dissolution* of the old society on which there rested the power of the sovereign, the political system [*Staatswesen*] as estranged from the people. The political revolution is the revolution of civil society. What was the character of the old society? It can be characterized in one word: *feudalism.* The old civil society had a *directly political* character, i.e. the elements of civil life such as property, family and the mode and manner of work were elevated in the form of seignory, estate and guild to the level of elements of political life. In this form they defined the relationship of the single individual to the *state as a whole,* i.e. his *political* relationship, his relationship of separation and exclusion from the other components of society. For the feudal organization of the life of the people did not elevate property or labour to the level of social elements but rather completed their *separation* from the state as a whole and constituted them as *separate* societies within society. But the functions and conditions of life in civil society were still political, even though political in the feudal sense, i.e. they excluded the individual from the state as a whole, they transformed the *particular* relationship of his guild to the whole state into his own general relationship to the life of the people, just as they transformed his specific civil activity and situation into his general activity and situation. As a consequence of this organization, the unity of the state, together with the consciousness, the will and the activity of the unity of the state, the universal political power, likewise inevitably appears as the *special* concern of a ruler and his servants, separated from the people.

The political revolution which overthrew this rule and turned the affairs of the state into the affairs of the people, which constituted the political state as a concern of the whole people, i.e. as a real state, inevitably destroyed all the estates, corporations, guilds and privileges which expressed the separation of the people from its community. The political revolution thereby *abolished* the *political character of civil society*. It shattered civil society into its simple components—on the one hand *individuals* and on the other the *material* and *spiritual elements* which constitute the vital content and civil situation of these individuals. It unleashed the political spirit which had, as it were, been dissolved, dissected and dispersed in the various cul-de-sacs of feudal society; it gathered together this spirit from its state of dispersion, liberated it from the adulteration of civil life and constituted it as the sphere of the community, the *universal* concern of the people ideally independent of those *particular* elements of civil life. A person's *particular* activity and situation in life sank to the level of a purely individual significance. They no longer constituted the relationship of the individual to the state as a whole. Public affairs as such became the universal affair of each individual and the political function his universal function.

But the perfection of the idealism of the state was at the same time the perfection of the materialism of civil society. The shaking-off of the political yoke was at the same time the shaking-off of the bonds which had held in check the egoistic spirit of civil society. Political emancipation was at the same time the emancipation of civil society from politics, from even the *appearance* of a universal content.

Feudal society was dissolved into its foundation [*Grund*], into *man*. But into man as he really was its foundation—into *egoistic* man.

This *man,* the member of civil society, is now the foundation, the presupposition of the *political* state. In the rights of man the state acknowledged him as such.

But the freedom of egoistic man and the acknowledgment of this freedom is rather the acknowledgment of the *unbridled* movement of the spiritual and material elements which form the content of his life.

Hence man was not freed from religion—he received the freedom of religion. He was not freed from property—he received the freedom of property. He was not freed from the egoism of trade—he received the freedom to engage in trade.

The *constitution* of the *political state* and the dissolution of civil society into independent *individuals*—who are related by *law* just as men in the estates and guilds were related by *privilege*—are achieved in *one and the same act*. But man, as member of civil society, inevitably appears as *unpolitical* man, as *natural* man. The rights of man appear as natural rights, for *self-conscious activity* is concentrated upon the *politi-*

cal act. *Egoistic* man is the *passive* and merely *given* result of the society which has been dissolved, an object of *immediate certainty,* and for that reason a *natural* object. The *political revolution* dissolves civil society into its component parts without *revolutionizing* these parts and subjecting them to criticism. It regards civil society, the world of needs, of labour, of private interests and of civil law, as the *foundation of its existence,* as a *presupposition* which needs no further grounding, and therefore as its *natural basis.* Finally, man as he is a member of civil society is taken to be the *real* man, *man* as distinct from *citizen,* since he is man in his sensuous, individual and *immediate* existence, whereas *political* man is simply abstract, artificial man, man as an *allegorical, moral* person. Actual man is acknowledged only in the form of the *egoistic* individual and *true* man only in the form of the *abstract citizen.*

Rousseau's description of the abstraction of the political man is a good one:

> Whoever dares to undertake the founding of a people's institutions must feel himself capable of *changing,* so to speak, *human nature,* of *transforming* each individual, who in himself is a complete and solitary whole, into a *part* of a greater whole from which he somehow receives his life and his being, of substituting a *partial* and *moral existence* for physical and independent existence. He must take *man's own powers away from him* and substitute for them alien ones which he can only use with the assistance of others.[4]

All emancipation is *reduction* of the human world and of relationships to *man himself.*

Political emancipation is the reduction of man on the one hand to the member of civil society, the *egoistic, independent* individual, and on the other to the *citizen,* the moral person.

Only when real, individual man resumes the abstract citizen into himself and as an individual man has become a *species-being* in his empirical life, his individual work and his individual relationships, only when man has recognized and organized his *forces propres* as *social forces* so that social force is no longer separated from him in the form of *political* force, only then will human emancipation be completed. . . .

NOTES

1. Bauer, *The Jewish Question,* 19–20.
2. See Beaumont, *Marie ou l'esclavage aux Etats-Unis* (Paris, 1835), 213–14.
3. "Robespierre Jeune," *Histoire parlementaire de la révolution française,* by Buchez and Roux, vol. 28, 159.
4. J.-J. Rousseau, *Du contrat social,* book II (London, 1782), 67.

5

Critique of Hegel's Philosophy of Right: Introduction

This article was written by Marx at the end of 1843 and published in the *Deutsch-französische Jahrbücher* in February 1844. The subtitle "Introduction" signals that the piece was the introduction to his *Critique of Hegel's Philosophy of Right* (a manuscript of 1843)—at least this is what Marx maintained in 1859 (see E. Bottigelli, *Genèse du socialisme scientifique* [Paris, 1967], 108). In fact, this piece forms an autonomous whole, a sort of manifesto independent and different in its orientation from earlier writings. Marx returns, it is true, to a description of Germany's historical and political "misery," and counters the position of the Hegelian left (the young Hegelians) and of Feuerbach particularly with regard to the critique of religion as an "illusion" of happiness, a substitute for earthly happiness. But for the first time the term "proletariat" appears in Marx's texts, a term absent from the manuscript of the summer of 1843 and from *On the Jewish Question,* where Marx spoke only of "real" or "generic" man as opposed to the bourgeois and liberal abstractions of the "citizen" and "the Rights of Man". Here appears also the idea of a union, a sort of community of interests between the proletariat—suffering humanity—on one side, and the revolutionary intellectuals—thinking humanity born of the critique of Hegelianism—on the other: a union appearing as a basis for the future German revolution, a revolution that would be not only bourgeois and political like that of 1789, but also universally human, and thus social.

In spite of this explicit reference to the proletariat, Marx's thought is still typical of a Hegelian of the Left—an idealist, if you will—to the extent that the active element (the "head") of the revolutionary movement is constituted by critical intelligence, while the masses, the proletariat, constitute its passive and material element

MEW 1:378–80, 385–91. *Early Writings* (see source note to selection 2), 244–45, 251–57. Translated by Gregor Benton.

(its "heart" or "body"), spawned by intellectual activity. Here Marx is very close to another great critic of German "misery," the poet Heinrich Heine, who in 1844, in his epic-satiric poem *Deutschland: Ein Wintermärchen* and in his posthumous *Briefe über Deutschland,* emphasized on the one hand the dialectical relations between thought and action, between theory and practice, between critical philosophy and the proletariat, the "lightning flashes of thought" come to fecundate the masses, and, on the other hand, the necessity of a definition of a specifically German revolutionary pathway surpassing the political (or bourgeois) revolution of the French type.

Also to be noted in this piece is the obsessive presence of what one could call, in Marx, the political (or revolutionary) French model (see, for example, the "crowing of the Gallic cock" at the end of the article). Here too, Marx is close to Heine and Ruge: the reference to the French Revolution and its imagery appeared quite frequently in the work of Heine when he wrote of a possible German revolution. As to Ruge, does he not conclude an 1843 article on "the intellectual alliance between the German and the French"—which contains a commentary on Louis Blanc's *Historie de Dix Ans*—with the Latin phrase: *Nulla salus sine Gallis,* "No salvation without the French" (A. Ruge, *Sämtliche Werke,* 2d ed., vol. 2 [Mannheim, 1848], 353). From this point of view, the young Marx, Heine, Ruge, and the majority of young Hegelians were opposed to the Germanophilia and Francophobia, and indeed, to the *Französenfresserei,* prevalent in Germany, particularly in Prussia, from the end of the Napoleonic epoch and reinforced by the nationalist crisis at the beginning of the 1840s in connection with the "German Rhine."

• • •

. . . *Religious* suffering is at one and the same time the *expression* of real suffering and protest against real suffering. Religion is the sigh of the oppressed creature, the heart of a heartless world and the soul of soulless conditions. It is the *opium* of the people.

The abolition of religion as the *illusory* happiness of the people is the demand for their *real* happiness. To call on them to give up their illusions about their condition is to *call of them to give up a condition that requires illusions*. The criticism of religion is therefore in *embryo* the *criticism of that vale of tears* of which religion is the *halo*.

Criticism has plucked the imaginary flowers on the chain not in order that man shall continue to bear that chain without fantasy or consolation but so that he shall throw off the chain and pluck the living flower. The criticism of religion disillusions man, so that he will think, act and fashion his reality like a man who has discarded his illusions and regained his senses, so that he will move around himself as his own true sun. Religion is only the illusory sun which revolves around man as long as he does not revolve around himself.

It is therefore the *task of history,* once the *other-world of truth* has vanished, to establish the *truth of this world.* It is the immediate *task of philosophy,* which is in the service of history, to unmask self-estrangement in its *unholy forms* once the *holy form* of human self-estrangement has been unmasked. Thus the criticism of heaven turns into the criticism of earth, the *criticism of religion* into the *criticism of law* and the *criticisms of theology* into the *criticism of politics*.

The following exposition—a contribution to this undertaking—concerns itself not directly with the original but with a copy, with the German *philosophy* of the state and of law. The only reason for this is that it is concerned with *Germany.*

If we were to begin with the German *status quo* itself, the result—even if we were to do it in the only appropriate way, i.e. negatively—would still be an *anachronism.* Even the negation of our present political situation is a dusty fact in the historical junk room of modern nations. If I negate powdered wigs, I am still left with unpowdered wigs. If I negate the situation in Germany in 1843, then according to the French calendar I have barely reached 1789, much less the vital centre of our present age.

Indeed, German history prides itself on having travelled a road which no other nation in the whole of history has ever travelled before, or ever will again. We have shared the restorations of modern nations without ever having shared their revolutions. We have been restored firstly because other nations dared to make revolutions and secondly because other nations suffered counterrevolutions: on the one hand, because our masters were afraid, and on the other, because they were not afraid. With our shepherds to the fore, we only once kept company with freedom, on the *day of its interment. . . .*

For Germany, theoretical emancipation has a specific practical significance even from a historical point of view. For Germany's *revolutionary* past, in the form of the *Reformation,* is also theoretical. Just as it was then the *monk,* so it is now the *philosopher* in whose brain the revolution begins.

Luther certainly conquered servitude based on *devotion,* but only by replacing it with servitude based on *conviction.* He destroyed faith in authority, but only by restoring the authority of faith. He transformed the priests into laymen, but only by transforming the laymen into priests. He freed mankind from external religiosity, but only by making religiosity the inner man. He freed the body from its chains, but only by putting the heart in chains.

But even if Protestantism was not the true solution, it did pose the problem correctly. It was now no longer a question of the struggle of the layman with the *priest outside himself,* but rather of the struggle with his *own inner priest,* with his *priestly nature.* And if the Protestant transformation of the German laymen into priests emancipated the lay priests—the *princes* together with their clergy, the privileged and the philistines—the philosophical transformation of the priestly Germans into men will emancipate the *people.* But just as emancipation did not stop with the princes, so will secularization of property not stop with the *dispossession of the churches,* which was set going above all by hypocritical Prussia. At that time the Peasants' War, the most radical episode in German history, suffered defeat because of theology. Today, when theology itself has failed, the most unfree episode in German history, our *status quo,* will founder on philosophy. On the eve of the Reformation official Germany was Rome's most unquestioning vassal. On the eve of its revolution Germany is the unquestioning vassal of lesser powers than Rome—of Prussia and Austria, of clod-hopping squires and philistines.

But a major difficulty appears to stand in the way of a *radical* German revolution.

The point is that revolutions need a *passive* element, a *material* basis. Theory is realized in a people only in so far as it is a realization of the people's needs. But will the enormous gap that exists between the demands of German thought and the responses of German reality now correspond to the same gap both between civil society and the state and civil society and itself? Will the theoretical needs be directly practical needs? It is not enough that thought should strive to realize itself; reality must itself strive towards thought.

But Germany did not pass through the intermediate stages of political emancipation at the same time as modern nations. Even the stages that it has left behind in theory it has not yet reached in practice. How is Germany, in one *salto mortale,* to override not only its own limitations but also those of the modern nations, to override limitations which in point of fact it ought to experience and strive for as liberation from its real limitations? A radical revolution can only be the revolution of radical needs, but the preconditions and seedbeds for such needs appear to be lacking.

Yet, even if Germany has only kept company with the development of the modern nations through the abstract activity of thought,

without taking an active part in the real struggles of this development, it has nevertheless shared in the *sufferings* of this development
without sharing in its pleasures and its partial satisfaction. Abstract
activity on the one hand corresponds to abstract suffering on the
other. Germany will therefore one day find itself at the level of European emancipation. It will be like a fetish-worshipper suffering from
the diseases of Christianity.

If we examine the *German governments,* we find that as a result of
the circumstances of the time, the situation in Germany, the stand-
point of German education and finally their own happy instincts they
are driven to combine the *civilized defects* of the *modern political world,*
whose advantages we lack, with the *barbaric defects* of the *ancien régime,* of which we have our full measure. In this way Germany must
participate more and more, if not in the reason then at least in the
unreason even of those state forms which have progressed beyond its
own *status quo.* For example, is there any country in the world which
shares as naïvely as so-called constitutional Germany all the illusions
of the constitutional state without sharing any of the realities? Or was
it just an accident that the idea of combining the torments of censorship with the torments of the French September laws, which presuppose freedom of the press, was the invention of a German government?
Just as the *gods* of all nations could be found in the Roman Pantheon,
so the *sins* of all state forms will be found in the Holy Roman German
Empire. That this eclecticism will take on unheard-of proportions is
assured in particular by the *politico-aesthetic gourmandise* of a German
king,[1] who proposes to play all the roles of royalty—feudal and bureaucratic, absolute and constitutional, autocratic and democratic—if
not in the person of the people then at least in his *own* person, and if
not for the people, then at least for *himself. Germany, as a world of its
own embodying all the deficiencies of the present political age,* will not be
able to overcome the specifically German limitations without over-
coming the universal limitation of the present political age.

It is not *radical* revolution of *universal human* emancipation which
is a utopian dream for Germany; it is the partial, *merely* political revolution, the revolution which leaves the pillars of the building standing. What is the basis of a partial and merely political revolution? Its
basis is the fact that one *part of civil society* emancipates itself and attains *universal* domination, that one particular class undertakes from
its *particular situation* the universal emancipation of society. This class
liberates the whole of society, but only on condition that the whole of
society finds itself in the same situation as this class, e.g., possesses or
can easily acquire money and education.

No class of civil society can play this role without awakening a moment of enthusiasm in itself and in the masses; a moment in which this class fraternizes and fuses with society in general, becomes identified with it and is experienced and acknowledged as its *universal representative;* a moment in which its claims and rights are truly the rights and claims of society itself and in which it is in reality the heart and head of society. Only in the name of the universal rights of society can a particular class lay claim to universal domination. Revolutionary energy and spiritual self-confidence are not enough to storm this position of liberator and to ensure thereby the political exploitation of all the other spheres of society in the interests of one's own sphere. If the *revolution of a people* and the *emancipation of a particular class* [*Klasse*] of civil society are to coincide, if *one* class is to stand for the whole of society, then all the deficiencies of society must be concentrated in another class [*Stand*], one particular class must be the class which gives universal offence, the embodiment of a general limitation; one particular sphere of society must appear as the *notorious crime* of the whole of society, so that the liberation of this sphere appears as universal self-liberation. If one class [*Stand*] is to be the class of liberation *par excellence,* then another class must be the class of overt oppression. The negative general significance of the French nobility and the French clergy determined the positive general significance of the class which stood nearest to and opposed to them—the *bourgeoisie.*

But in Germany every particular class lacks not only the consistency, acuteness, courage and ruthlessness which would stamp it as the negative representative of society; equally, all classes lack that breadth of spirit which identifies itself, if only for a moment, with the spirit of the people, that genius which can raise material force to the level of political power, that revolutionary boldness which flings into the face of its adversary the defiant words: *I am nothing and I should be everything.* The main feature of German morality and honour, not only in individuals but in classes, is that *modest egoism* which asserts its narrowness and allows that narrowness to be used against it. The relationship of the different spheres of German society is therefore epic rather than dramatic. Each begins to experience itself and to set up camp alongside the others with its own particular claims, not as soon as it is oppressed but as soon as circumstances, without any contribution from the sphere concerned, create an inferior social stratum which it in its turn can oppress. Even the *moral self-confidence of the German middle class* is based simply on an awareness of being the general representative of the philistine mediocrity of all the other classes. It is therefore not only the German kings who mount the throne *mal-*

à-propos, but every sphere of civil society which experiences defeat before it celebrates victory, develops its own limitations before it overcomes the limitations confronting it, and asserts its narrow-mindedness before it has had a chance to assert its generosity. As a result, even the opportunity of playing a great role has always passed by before it was ever really available and every class, as soon as it takes up the struggle against the class above it, is involved in a struggle with the class beneath it. Thus princes struggle against kings, bureaucrats against aristocrats, and the bourgeoisie against all of these, while the proletariat is already beginning to struggle against the bourgeoisie. The middle class scarcely dares to conceive of the idea of emancipation from its own point of view, and already the development of social conditions and the progress of political theory have demonstrated this point of view to be antiquated or at least problematical.

In France it is enough to be something for one to want to be everything. In Germany no one may be anything unless he renounces everything. In France partial emancipation is the basis of universal emancipation. In Germany universal emancipation is the *conditio sine qua non* of any partial emancipation. In France it is the reality, in Germany the impossibility, of emancipation in stages that must give birth to complete freedom. In France each class of the people is a *political idealist* and experiences itself first and foremost not as a particular class but as the representative of social needs in general. The role of *emancipator* therefore passes in a dramatic movement from one class of the French people to the next, until it finally reaches that class which no longer realizes social freedom by assuming certain conditions external to man and yet created by human society, but rather by organizing all the conditions of human existence on the basis of social freedom. In Germany, however, where practical life is as devoid of intellect as intellectual life is of practical activity, no class of civil society has the need and the capacity for universal emancipation unless under the compulsion of its *immediate* situation, of *material* necessity and of its *chains themselves.*

So where is the *positive* possibility of German emancipation?

This is our answer. In the formation of a class with *radical chains,* a class of civil society which is not a class of civil society, a class [*Stand*] which is the dissolution of all classes, a sphere which has a universal character because of its universal suffering and which lays claim to no *particular right* because the wrong it suffers is not a *particular wrong* but *wrong in general;* a sphere of society which can no longer lay claim to a *historical* title, but merely to a *human* one, which does not stand in one-sided opposition to the consequences but in all-sided opposition to the premises of the German political system; and finally a sphere which cannot emancipate itself without emancipating itself from—and thereby emancipating—all the other spheres of society, which is, in a word, the *total loss* of humanity and which can therefore redeem itself only through the *total redemption of humanity*. This dissolution of society as a particular class is the *proletariat*.

The proletariat is only beginning to appear in Germany as a result of the emergent *industrial* movement. For the proletariat is not formed by *natural* poverty but by *artificially produced* poverty; it is formed not from the mass of people mechanically oppressed by the weight of society but from the mass of people issuing from society's *acute disintegration* and in particular from the dissolution of the middle class. (Clearly, however, the ranks of the proletariat are also gradually swelled by natural poverty and Christian-Germanic serfdom.)

When the proletariat proclaims the *dissolution of the existing world order,* it is only declaring the secret of its own existence, for it *is* the *actual* dissolution of that order. When the proletariat demands the *negation of private property,* it is only elevating to a *principle for society* what society has already made a principle *for the proletariat,* what is embodied in the proletariat, without its consent, as the negative result of society. The proletarian then finds that he has the same right, in relation to the world which is coming into being, as the *German King* in relation to the world as it is at present when he calls the people *his* people just as he calls his horse *his* horse. By calling the people his private property, the king is merely declaring that the owner of private property is king.

Just as philosophy finds its *material* weapons in the proletariat, so the proletariat finds its *intellectual* weapons in philosophy; and once the lightning of thought has struck deeply into this virgin soil of the people, emancipation will transform the *Germans* into *men*.

Let us sum up the result:

The only liberation of Germany which is *practically* possible is liberation from the point of view of *that* theory which declares man to be the supreme being for man. Germany can emancipate itself from the *Middle Ages* only if it emancipates itself at the same time from the *partial* victories over the Middle Ages. In Germany *no* form of bondage can be broken without breaking *all* forms of bondage. Germany, which is renowned for its *thoroughness,* cannot make a revolution unless it is a *thorough* one. The *emancipation of the German* is the *emancipation of man*. The *head* of this emancipation is *philosophy,* its *heart* the *proletariat*. Philosophy cannot realize itself without the transcendence

[*Aufhebung*] of the proletariat, and the proletariat cannot transcend itself without the realization [*Verwirklichung*] of philosophy.

When all the inner conditions are met, the *day of the German resurrection* will be heralded by the *crowing of the Gallic cock*.

NOTE

1. Frederick William IV.

6

Marginal Notes on "The King of Prussia and Social Reform"

These "marginal notes" appeared in *Vorwärts!*, 7–10 August 1844; Marx had written them at the end of July. *Vorwärts!*, created at the end of 1843, had become, especially under the influence of Ruge and of Marx himself, a rallying point for the German radical and revolutionary émigrés in Paris. In June 1844, the revolt of the home-industry weavers in the Prussian province of Silesia, and their subsequent repression by the army, had produced a certain outcry in Germany and among the émigré milieux. The question of "pauperism" was suddenly presented in an immediate manner in Germany, echoing the same phenomenon in England and France.

In the *Vorwärts!* of 27 July 1844, Arnold Ruge had published an article entitled, "The King of Prussia and Social Reform" and signed it "a Prussian." Ruge was responding to an article published in Louis Blanc's journal *La Réforme* on 19 July 1844 that presented a Prussian royal ordinance on the war against "pauperism" as the result of the political power's fear of the weavers' movement (see A. Cornu, *K. Marx et F. Engels,* vol. 3, *Marx à Paris* [Paris, 1962], 71). Ruge thought that the Prussian ordinance was simply an administrative measure and that the uprising of the weavers was incapable of awakening any revolutionary hope as long as the social and material revolt at hand remained combined with a more general movement of a political nature: in the "misery" of German politics, a movement such as the Silesian weavers' was, at best, an industrial *jacquerie* and the King of Prussia had no reason to be afraid.

Against Ruge, and in a direct line from his theoretical "discovery" of the proletariat, in his *Contribution to the Critique of Hegel's Philosophy of Right* (see selection 5), Marx affirmed the importance of the Silesian movement for the future and the superiority of the social

MEW 1:399–403, 407–8. *Early Writings* (see source note to selection 2), 409–13, 418–19. Translated by Rodney Livingstone.

revolution over the political revolution. The state—whether the revolutionary Convention, the Napoleonic state, the English state, or as at that moment, the Prussian state—was, at any rate, incapable of finding a political solution to the social question of "pauperism." The change in Marx from the *Contribution* to the *Critique* of Hegel's philosophy of Right was that henceforth the proletariat had an active and no longer a passive role in the revolutionary process.

The rupture between Ruge and Marx that is evident here was in fact foretold in the correspondence of 1843 published in the *Deutsche-französische Jahrbücher* in early 1844 (see selection 2). There Marx already stood opposed to Ruge's political pessimism in the face of the German bourgeoisie's political nonexistence, a revolutionary hope at least in theory ("the approaching revolution"); this hope would be confirmed first by the theoretical "discovery" of the proletariat as the revolutionary class of the future and, second, by the revelation of the German proletariat's practices in Silesia. Still, fundamentally at issue was the question of a "German revolution": Marx, in his article of 7–10 August, having praised Weitling, writes that the German proletariat was the "theoretician" of the European proletariat and that Germany had the "vocation" for social revolution, thus compensating for the political nonexistence of the German bourgeoisie and for Germany's ineptitude for political revolution (see MEW 1:405).

• • •

. . . *Napoleon* wished to do away with begging at a single stroke. He instructed his officials to prepare plans for the abolition of beggary throughout the whole of France. The project was subject to delay; Napoleon became impatient, he wrote to Crétet, his Minister of the Interior; he commanded him to get rid of begging within a month. He said, "One should not depart this life without leaving traces which commend our memory to posterity. Do not ask me for another three or four months to obtain information; you have young advocates, clever prefects, expert engineers of bridges and roads. Set them all in motion, do not fall into the sleepy inactivity of routine office work."

Within a few months everything was ready. On 5 July 1808 the law to suppress begging was enacted. By what means? By means of the *dépôts,* which were so speedily transformed into penal institutions that in a short time the poor man could gain access to one only via a *police court.* Nevertheless, M. Noailles du Gard, a member of the legislative body, was able to declare, "Eternal gratitude to the hero who has found a refuge for the needy and the means of life for the poor. Childhood will no longer be abandoned, poor families will no longer lack resources, nor will workers go without encouragement and employment. *Nos pas ne seront plus arrêtés par l'image dégoûtante des infirmités et de la honteuse misère*" ("Our footsteps will no longer be halted by the disgusting image of infirmities and of shameful misery").

This last cynical statement is the only truth contained in this eulogy.

If Napoleon can turn to his advocates, prefects and engineers for counsel, why should not the King of Prussia turn to his authorities?

Why did not Napoleon simply decree the abolition of beggary *at a stroke?* This question is just as valid as that of our "Prussian" who asks: "Why does the King not decree the education of all deprived children at a stroke?" Does the "Prussian" understand what the King would have to decree? Nothing other than the *abolition of the proletariat*. To educate children it is necessary to *feed* them and free them from the *need to earn a livelihood*. The feeding and educating of destitute children, i.e. the feeding and educating of the *entire future* proletariat, would mean the abolition of the proletariat and of pauperism.

For a moment the *Convention* had the courage to *decree* the abolition of pauperism, not indeed "*at a stroke,*" as the "Prussian" requires of his King, but only after instructing the Committee of Public Safety to draw up the necessary plans and proposals and after the latter had made use of the extensive investigation by the Constituent Assembly into the state of poverty in France and, through Barère, had proposed the establishment of the "Livre de la bienfaisance nationale." etc. What was achieved by the decree of the Convention? Simply that there was now one decree more in the world and that *one* year later starving women besieged the Convention.

The Convention, however, represented the *maximum of political energy, political power* and *political understanding*.

No government in the whole world has issued *decrees* about pauperism *at a stroke* and without consulting the authorities. The English Parliament even sent emissaries to all the countries in Europe in order to discover the different administrative remedies in use. But in their attempts to come to grips with pauperism every government has stuck fast at *charitable* and *administrative measures* or even regressed to a more primitive stage than that.

Can the state do otherwise?

The *state* will never discover the source of *social* evils *in the "state and the organization of society,"* as the Prussian expects of his King.

Wherever there are political parties each party will attribute *every* defect of society to the fact that its rival is at the helm of the state instead of itself. Even the radical and revolutionary politicians look for the causes of evil not in the *nature* of the state but in a specific *form of the state* which they would like to replace with *another* form of the state.

From a *political* point of view the *state* and the *organization of society* are not *two* different things. The state is the organization of society. In so far as the state acknowledges the existence of *social* grievances it locates their origins either in the *laws of nature* over which no human agency has control, or in *private life,* which is independent of the state, or else in *malfunctions of the administration* which is dependent on it. Thus England finds poverty to be based on the *law of nature* according to which the population must always outgrow the available means of subsistence. From another point of view it explains *pauperism* as the consequence of the *bad will of the poor,* just as the King of Prussia explains it in terms of the *unchristian feelings of the rich* and the Convention explains it in terms of the *counter-revolutionary and suspect attitudes* of the *proprietors.* Hence England punishes the poor, the King of Prussia exhorts the rich and the Convention beheads the proprietors.

Lastly, *all* states seek the cause in *fortuitous* or *intentional defects in the administration* and hence the cure is sought in administrative measures. Why? Because the *administration* is the *organizing* agency of the state.

The contradiction between the vocation and the good intentions of the administration on the one hand and the means and powers at its disposal on the other cannot be eliminated by the state, except by abolishing itself; for the state is based on this contradiction. It is based on the contradiction between *public* and *private life,* between *universal* and *particular interests.* For this reason, the state must confine itself to *formal, negative* activities, since the scope of its own power comes to an end at the very point where civil life and work begin. Indeed, when we consider the consequences arising from the social nature of civil life, of private property, of trade, of industry, of the mutual plundering that goes on between the various groups in civil life, it becomes clear that the *law of nature* governing the administration is *impotence.* For, the fragmentation, the depravity and the *slavery of civil society* is the natural foundation of the *modern* state, just as the civil society of slavery was the natural foundation of the state in *antiquity.* The existence of the state is inseparable from the existence of slavery. The state and slavery in antiquity—frank and open *classical* antitheses—were not more closely *welded* together than the modern state and the cut-throat world of modern business—sanctimonious *Christian* antitheses. If the modern state desired to abolish the *impotence* of its administration it would have to abolish contemporary *private life*. And to abolish private life it would have to abolish itself, since it exists *only* as the antithesis of private life. However, no *living* person believes the defects of his existence to be based on the *principle,* the essential nature of his own life; they must instead be grounded in circumstances *outside* his own life. *Suicide* is contrary to nature. Hence the state cannot believe in the *intrinsic* impotence of its administration, i.e. of itself. It can *only* perceive formal, contingent defects in it and try to remedy them. If these modifications are inadequate, well, that just shows that social ills are natural imperfections, independent of man, they are a *law of God,* or else, the will of private individuals is too degenerate to meet the good intentions of the administration halfway. And how perverse private individuals are! They grumble about the government when it places limits on freedom and yet demand that the government should prevent the inevitable consequences of that freedom!

The more powerful a state and hence the *more political* a nation, the less inclined it is to explain the general principle governing *social* ills and to seek out their causes by looking at the *principle of the state,* i.e. at the *actual organization of society* of which the state is the active, self-conscious and official expression. *Political* understanding is just *political* understanding because its thought does not transcend the limits of politics. The sharper and livelier it is, the more incapable is it of comprehending social problems. The *classical* period of political understanding is the *French Revolution.* Far from identifying the principle of the state as the source of social ills, the heroes of the French Revolution held social ills to be the source of political problems. Thus Robespierre regarded great wealth and great poverty as an obstacle to *pure democracy.* He therefore wished to establish a universal system of *Spartan* frugality. The principle of politics is the *will.* The more one-sided, i.e. the more perfect, *political* understanding is, the more completely it puts its faith in the *omnipotence* of the will; the blinder it is towards the *natural* and spiritual *limitations* of the will, the more incapable it becomes of discovering the real source of the evils of society. No further arguments are needed to prove that when the "Prussian" claims that "the political understanding" is destined "to uncover the roots of social want in Germany" he is indulging in vain illusions.

It was foolish to expect the King of Prussia to exhibit a power not possessed by the Convention and Napoleon combined; it was foolish to expect him to possess a vision which could cross *all* political frontiers, a vision with which our clever "Prussian" is no better endowed than is his King. . . .

The "Prussian" predicts the suppression of the insurrections which are sparked off by the *"disastrous isolation of man from the community* and *of their thoughts from social principles."*

We have shown that in the Silesian uprising there was no separation of thoughts from social principles. That leaves *"the disastrous isolation of men from the community."* By community is meant here the *political community, the state.* It is the old song about *unpolitical Germany.*

But do not *all* rebellions without exception have their roots in *the disastrous isolation of man from the community?* Does not every rebellion necessarily presuppose isolation? Would the revolution of 1789 have taken place if French citizens had not felt disastrously isolated from the community? The abolition of this isolation was its very purpose.

But the community from which the worker is *isolated* is a community of quite different reality and scope than the *political* community. The community from which *his own labour* separates him is *life* itself, physical and spiritual life, human morality, human activity, human enjoyment, *human nature. Human nature is the true community of men.* Just as the disastrous isolation from this nature is disproportionately more far-reaching, unbearable, terrible and contradictory than the isolation from the political community, so too the transcending of this isolation and even a partial reaction, a *rebellion* against it, is so much greater, just as the *man* is greater than the *citizen* and *human life* than *political life.* Hence, however limited an industrial revolt may be, it contains within itself a *universal* soul: and however universal a political revolt may be, its *colossal* form conceals a *narrow* spirit.

The "Prussian" brings his essay to a close worthy of it with the following sentence:

> *A social revolution without a political soul* (i.e. without a central insight organizing it from the point of view of the totality) is impossible.

We have seen: a social revolution possesses a *total* point of view because—even if it is confined to only one factory district—it represents a protest by man against a dehumanized life, because it proceeds from the point of view of the *particular, real individual,* because the *community* against whose separation from himself the individual is reacting is the *true* community of man, *human* nature. In Contrast, the *political soul* of revolution consists in the tendency of the classes with no political power to put an end to their *isolation from the state* and from *power*. Its point of view is that of the state, of an abstract *totality* which exists *only* through its separation from real life and which is *unthinkable* in the absence of an organized antithesis between the universal idea and the individual existence of man. In accordance with the *limited* and *contradictory* nature of the political soul a revolution inspired by it organizes a dominant group within society at the cost of society. . . .

7

The Holy Family, or Critique of Critical Criticism: Contra Bruno Bauer and Company

This piece was written by Marx and, in very small part (a dozen pages), by Engels from September to November 1844. It was published in February 1845 in Frankfurt am Main. It consists of a long and detailed polemic against the young Hegelian Bruno Bauer and his friends of the *Allgemeine Literatur-Zeitung* in Berlin. Marx had been very close to Bruno Bauer, to his brother Edgar, and to the intellectual Hegelians of the Doctor's Club since he studied philosophy in Berlin in 1837; it was Bruno Bauer who had encouraged him to finish his doctoral thesis. In 1841, he found Bruno Bauer anew in Bonn, where the latter was teaching at the university prior to being called back by the Prussian government in October of the same year because of his openly held liberal opinions. At the *Rheinische Zeitung,* in 1842, Marx quickly became opposed to the intentionally provocative extremism and confused verbalism of "die Freien"— young Hegelians influenced by Bruno Bauer, Stirner, and the Berlin correspondents of the journal.

In the *Allgemeine Literatur-Zeitung,* Bruno Bauer and his friends, in the name of the superior rights of the spirit, of theory, and of the "critique," had since the end of 1843 been developing the idea of the intellectual "passivity" of the bourgeois and working-class "mass"; activity was, in their eyes, the privilege of exceptional historical personalities and of the "critical" intellectuals; fleeing before Prusso-German political "misery," Hegelian idealism found itself pushed to the extreme and falsified. At base, the position of "die Freien" of Berlin was not very different from Marx's in the his late 1843 text on Hegel's philosophy of right (see selection 5). But what they forgot, or wished not to see, was that the dialectic of theory and practice assumed at least the existence of the popular

MEW 2:125–31. Karl Marx and Friedrich Engels, *Collected Works* (New York: International Publishers, 1983), 4:118–14.

"masses" even though they were "passive"; the disdain "die Freien" exhibited for the masses would in turn falsify their practical existence.

Marx had evolved in the opposite direction: he was necessarily offended by the attitude of Bruno Bauer and his friends at a time when, in a letter to Feuerbach of 11 August 1844 (see MEW 27:426) and in a text known under the name of the *1844 Manuscripts* (MEW, EB, 1:533–54), he was praising the intellectual and practical activity as well as the organizational capacity and humanity of the Parisian workers.

Bruno Bauer presented the 1789 revolution as a battle of ideas for liberty and egality, and also as a failure for the bourgeoisie, whose "ideas" had foundered when confronted with the lack of interest on the part of the "masses" and with national and individual egoism. For Marx, on the other hand, the French Revolution was a practical battle between the bourgeois class and the privileged classes of the ancien régime; the masses' lack of interest in the bourgeoisie's battle was explained by the divergence of their respective material "interests."

To write *The Holy Family,* Marx used the notes he took at Kreuznach during the summer of 1843 (see selection 3) as well as those taken in Paris in late 1843 and early 1844, in particular on the history of the French Revolution and the Convention (see the Mémoires de Lavasseur de la Sarthe in K. Marx and F. Engels, *Gesamtausgabe,* (East Berlin: Dietz, 1975), sec. 4, 2:283–98 and 725).

• • •

Critical Battle Against the French Revolution

The *narrow-mindedness of the Mass* forced *the* "Spirit," *Criticism,* Herr Bauer, to consider the *French Revolution* not as the time of the revolutionary efforts of the French in the *"prosaic* sense" but "*only*" as the "*symbol* and *fantastic expression*" of the Criticial figments of his own brain. *Criticism* does *penance* of its "*oversight*" by submitting the *Revolution* to a *fresh examination.* At the same time it punishes the seducer of its innocence—"the Mass"—by communicating to it the results of this "fresh examination."

> The *French Revolution* was an experiment which still belonged entirely to the eighteenth century.

The chronological truth that an experiment of the eighteenth century like the French Revolution is still entirely an experiment of the eighteenth century, and not, for example, an experiment of the nineteenth, seems "still entirely" to be one of those truths which "are self-evident from the start." But in the terminology of *Criticism,* which is very prejudiced against "crystal-clear" truths, a truth like that is called an *"examination"* and therefore naturally has its place in a "fresh examination of the Revolution."

> The ideas to which the French Revolution gave rise did not, however, lead beyond the *order of things* that it wanted to abolish by force.

Ideas can never lead beyond an old world order but only beyond the ideas of the old world order. Ideas *cannot carry out anything* at all. In order to carry out ideas men are needed who can exert practical force. In its literal *sense* the Critical sentence is therefore another truth that is self-evident, and therefore another *"examination."*

Undeterred by this examination, the French Revolution gave rise to ideas which led beyond the *ideas* of the entire old world order. The revolutionary movement which began in 1789 in the *Cercle social,* which in the middle of its course had as its chief representatives *Leclerc* and *Roux,* and which finally with *Babeuf's* conspiracy was temporarily defeated, gave rise to the *communist* idea which *Babeuf's* friend *Buonarroti* re-introduced in France after the Revolution of 1830. This idea, consistently developed, is the *idea* of the *new world order.*

> After the Revolution had therefore" (!) "abolished the feudal barriers in the life of the people, it was compelled to sat-isfy and even to inflame the pure egoism of the nation and, on the other hand, to curb it by its necessary complement, the rec-ognition of a supreme being, by this higher confirmation of the general state system, which has to hold together the individual self-seeking atoms.

The egoism of the nation is the natural egoism of the general state system, as opposed to the egoism of the feudal classes. The su-preme being is the higher confirmation of the general state system, and hence also of the nation. Nevertheless, the supreme being is sup-posed to *curb* the egoism of the nation, that is, of the general state system! A really Critical task, to curb egoism by means of its confir-mation and even of its *religious* confirmation, i.e., by recognising that it is of a superhuman nature and therefore free of human restraint! The creators of the supreme being were not aware of this, their Critical intention.

Monsieur *Buchez,* who bases national fanaticism on religious fanaticism, understands his hero *Robespierre* better.[1]

Nationalism [*Nationalität*] led to the downfall of Rome and Greece. *Criticism* therefore says nothing specific about the French Revolution when it maintains that nationalism caused its downfall, and it says just as little about the nation when it defines its egoism as *pure.* This pure egoism appears rather to be a very dark, spontaneous egoism, combined with flesh and blood, when compared, for example, with the pure egoism of *Fichte's* "*ego.*" But if, in contrast to the egoism of the feudal classes, its purity is only relative, no "fresh examination of the revolution" was needed to see that the egoism which has a nation as its content is more general or purer than that which has as its content a particular social class or a particular corporation.

Criticism's explanations about the general state system are no less instructive. They are confined to saying that the general state system must hold together the individual self-seeking atoms.

Speaking exactly and in the prosaic sense, the members of civil society are not *atoms.* The *specific property* of the atom is that it has *no* properties and is therefore not connected with beings outside it by any relationship determined by its own *natural necessity.* The atom *has no needs,* it is *self-sufficient;* the world outside it is an absolute *vacuum,* i.e., is contentless, senseless, meaningless, just because the atom has *all fullness* in itself. The egoistic individual in civil society may in his non-sensuous imagination and lifeless abstraction inflate himself into an *atom,* i.e., into an unrelated, self-sufficient, wantless, *absolutely full,* blessed being. Unblessed *sensuous reality* does not bother about his imagination, each of his senses compels him to believe in the existence of the world and of individuals outside him, and even his *profane* stomach reminds him every day that the world outside *him is not empty,* but is what really *fills.* Every activity and property of his being, every one of his vital urges, becomes a *need,* a *necessity,* which his *self-seeking* transforms into seeking for other things and human beings outside him. But since the need of one individual has no self-evident meaning for another egoistic individual capable of satisfying that need, and therefore no direct connection with its satisfaction, each individual has to create this connection; it thus becomes the intermediary between the need of another and the objects of this need.

Therefore, it is *natural necessity,* the *essential human properties* however estranged they may seem to be, and *interest* that hold the members of civil society together; *civil,* not *political* life is their *real* tie. It is therefore not the *state* that holds the *atoms* of civil society together, but the fact that they are *atoms* only in *imagination,* in the *heaven* of their fancy, but in *reality* beings tremendously different from atoms, in other words, not *divine egoists,* but *egoistic human beings.* Only *political superstition* still imagines today that civil life must be held together by the state, whereas in reality, on the contrary, the state is held together by civil life.

> Robespierre's and *Saint-Just's* tremendous idea of making a *'free people'* which would live only according to the rules of *justice* and *virtue*—see, for example, Saint-Just's report on Danton's crimes and his other report on the general police—could be maintained for a certain time only by terror and was a *contradiction against which* the vulgar, self-seeking elements of *the popular community* reacted in the cowardly and insidious way that was only to be expected from them.

This phrase of *Absolute Criticism,* which describes a "free people" as a *"contradiction" against* which the elements of the *"popular community"* are bound to react, is absolutely hollow, for according to Robespierre and Saint-Just *liberty, justice* and *virtue* could, on the contrary, be only manifestations of the life of the *"people"* and only properties of the "popular community." Robespierre and Saint-Just spoke explicitly of "liberty, justice and virtue" of *ancient times,* belonging only to the *"popular community." Spartans, Athenians* and *Romans* at the time of their greatness were "free, just and virtuous peoples." "What," asks Robespierre in his speech on the principles of public morals (sitting of the Convention on February 5, 1794).

> is the *fundamental principle* of democratic or popular government? It is *virtue,* I mean *public* virtue, which worked such miracles in *Greece* and *Rome* and which will work still greater ones in republican France; virtue which is nothing but love of one's country and its laws."

Robespierre then explicitly calls the *Athenians* and *Spartans* *"peuples libres."* He continually recalls the ancient *popular community* and quotes its heroes as well as its corrupters—Lycurgus, Demosthenes, Miltiades, Aristides, Brutus and Catilina, Caesar, Clodius and Piso.

In his report on Danton's arrest (referred to by Criticism) *Saint-Just* says explicitly:

> The world has been empty since the *Romans,* and only their memory fills it and still prophesies *liberty.*

His accusation is composed in the ancient style and directed against *Danton* as against *Catilina.*

In *Saint-Just's* other report, the one on the *general police,* the *republican* is described exactly in the *ancient* sense, as *inflexible, modest, simple* and so on. The *police* should be an institution of the same nature as the Roman *censorship.*—He does not fail to mention Codrus, Lycurgus, Caesar, Cato, Catilina, Brutus, Antonius, and Cassius. Finally, *Saint-Just* describes the *"liberty,* justice and virtue" that he demands in a *single word* when he says:

> Que les hommes révolutionnaires soient des *Romains.*

Robespierre, Saint-Just and their party fell because they confused the ancient, *realistic-democratic commonweal* based on *real slavery* with the *modern spiritualistic-democratic representative state,* which is based on *emancipated slavery, bourgeois society.* What a terrible illusion it is to have to recognise and sanction in the *rights of man* modern bourgeois society, the society of industry, of universal competition, of private interest freely pursuing its aims, of anarchy, of self-estranged natural and spiritual individuality, and at the same time to want afterwards to annul the *manifestations of the life* of this society in particular individuals and simultaneously to want to model the *political head* of that society in the manner of *antiquity!*

The illusion appears tragic when Saint-Just, on the day of his execution, pointed to the large table of the *Rights of Man* hanging in the hall of the *Conciergerie* and said with proud dignity: "*C'est pourtant moi qui ai fait cela.*" It was just this table that proclaimed the *right* of a man who cannot be the man of the ancient commonweal any more than his *economic* and *industrial* conditions are those of *ancient* times.

This is not the place to vindicate the illusion of the *Terrorists* historically.

THE HOLY FAMILY, OR CRITIQUE OF CRITICAL CRITICISM

> After the fall of Robespierre the *political enlightenment* and *movement* hastened to the point where they became the prey of *Napoleon* who, shortly after 18 Brumaire, could say: "With my prefects, gendarmes and priests I can do what I like with France."

Profane history, on the other hand, reports: After the fall of Robespierre, the *political* enlightenment, which formerly had been *overreaching* itself and had been *extravagant,* began for the first time to develop *prosaically.* Under the government of the *Directory, bourgeois society,* freed by the Revolution itself from the trammels of feudalism and officially recognised in spite of the *Terror's* wish to sacrifice it to an ancient form of political life, broke out in powerful streams of life. A storm and stress of commercial enterprise, a passion for enrichment, the exuberance of the new bourgeois life, whose first self-enjoyment is pert, light-hearted, frivolous and intoxicating; a *real* enlightenment of the *land* of France, the feudal structure of which had been smashed by the hammer of the Revolution which, by the first feverish efforts of the numerous new owners, had become the object of all-round cultivation; the first moves of industry that had now become free—these were some of the signs of life of the newly emerged bourgeois society. *Bourgeois society* is *positively* represented by the *bourgeoisie.* The bourgeoisie, therefore, *begins* its rule. The *rights of man* cease to exist *merely* in *theory.*

It was not the revolutionary movement as a whole that became the prey of Napoleon on 18 Brumaire, as *Criticism* in its faith in a Herr von Rotteck or Welcker believes;[2] it was the *liberal bourgeoisie.* One only needs to read the speeches of the legislators of the time to be convinced of this. One has the impression of coming from the National Convention into a modern Chamber of Deputies.

Napoleon represented the last battle of *revolutionary terror* against the *bourgeois society* which had been proclaimed by this same Revolution, and against its policy. Napoleon, of course, already discerned the essence of the *modern state;* he understood that it is based on the unhampered development of bourgeois society, on the free movement of private interest, etc. He decided to recognise and protect this basis. He was no terrorist with his head in the clouds. Yet at the same time he still regarded the *state* as an *end in itself* and civil life only as a treasurer and his *subordinate* which must have no *will of its own.* He *perfected* the *Terror* by *substituting permanent war* for *permanent revolution.* He fed the egoism of the French nation to complete satiety but demanded also the sacrifice of bourgeois business, enjoyments, wealth, etc., whenever this was required by the political aim of conquest. If he despotically suppressed the liberalism of bourgeois society—the political idealism of its daily practice—he showed no more consideration for its essential *material* interests, trade and industry, whenever they conflicted with his political interests. His scorn of industrial *hommes d'affaires* was the complement to his scorn of *ideologists*. In his home policy, too, he combated bourgeois society as the opponent of the state which in his own person he still held to be an absolute aim in itself. Thus he declared in the State Council that he would not suffer the owner of extensive estates to cultivate them or not as he pleased. Thus, too, he conceived the plan of subordinating trade to the state by appropriation of *roulage*. French businessmen took steps to anticipate the event that first shook Napoleon's power. Paris exchange brokers forced him by means of an artificially created famine to delay the opening of the Russian campaign by nearly two months and thus to launch it too late in the year.

Just as the liberal bourgeoisie was opposed once more by revolutionary terror in the person of Napoleon, so it was opposed once more by counter-revolution in the Restoration in the person of the Bourbons. Finally, in 1830 the bourgeoisie put into effect its wishes of the year 1789, with the only difference that its *political enlightenment* was not *completed,* that as a means for achieving the ideal of the state, the welfare of the world and universal human aims but, on the contrary, had acknowledged it as the *official* expression of its own *exclusive* power and the *political* recognition of its own *special* interests.

The history of the French Revolution, which dates from 1789, did not come to an end in 1830 with the victory of one of its components enriched by the consciousness of its own *social* importance.

NOTES

1. This is a reference to Buchez and Roux, *Histoire Parlementaire de la Révolution française ou Journal des Assemblées nationales, depuis 1789 jusqu'en 1815,* 49 vols. (Paris, 1834–38).

2. Karl von Rotteck and Karl Theodor Welcker, both jurists and professors at the University of Freiburg (Breisgau), were liberal representatives in the Diet of Bade in 1830–31. Because of their liberal opinions and activities, they were stripped of their professorships in October 1832. From 1833–34 on, they undertook together the editing of a big critical dictionary of politics (*Das Staatslexikon*), which would become a required reference

work of the liberal German bourgeoisie until 1848. It is also worth noting that Bruno Bauer was to publish a history of constitutional and revolutionary movements in Southern Germany (*Geschichte der constitutionellen und revolutionären Bewegungen im südlichen Deutschland, 1831–1834,* 3 vols. (Berlin-Charlottenberg, 1845), in which Rotteck and Welcker are often the subject of discussion.

8

From Marx's Notes of 1845

This text, first published in 1932, was found in Marx's notebooks with his celebrated *Theses on Feuerbach,* a text drafted in spring 1845 and published for the first time by Engels in 1888.

• • •

[Civil Society and the Communist Revolution].

1. The *history of the genesis of the modern state,* or the *French Revolution.*

The arrogance of the political being—confusion with the state of antiquity. Relationships of revolutionaries to civil society. Doubling of all elements into civil beings and political beings.

2. The *proclamation of the rights of man* and the *state constitution.* Individual freedom and public power.

Freedom, equality and *unity.* Sovereignty of the people.

3. The state and civil society.

4. The *representative state* and the *Charters.*

The constitutional representative state, the democratic representative state.

5. The *division of powers.* Legislative and executive power.

6. *Legislative power* and legislative bodies. Political clubs.

7. *Executive power.* Centralization and hierarchy. Centralization and political civilization. The federal system and industrialism. The *state administration* and *local administration.*

8'. *Judicial power* and the *law.*

8''. *Nationality* and the *people.*

9'. *Political parties.*

9''. *Franchise,* the struggle for the *abolition* of the state and civil society.

MEW 3:537–38.

9

The German Ideology: Critique of the Most Recent German Philosophy as Represented by Feuerbach, B. Bauer, and Stirner, and of German Socialism as Represented by Its Various Prophets

This text was drafted by Marx and Engels at the end of 1845 and in 1846—it is impossible to determine exactly which part was written by whom—and was not published until 1932. In February 1845, Marx had been expelled from Paris along with the principal collaborators of *Vorwärts!* with the notable exception of Heine. In taking this measure, the French minister of the interior, Guizot, acceded to a pressing demand of the Prussian government in December 1845. Marx had, moreover, to renounce his Prussian citizenship in that month; he lived in Brussels from February 1845 to March 1848.

The German Ideology lengthened and deepened the critique of the extreme idealism of the young Hegelians already formulated in *The Holy Family*. The attacks centered principally on Bruno Bauer (referred to as "Saint Max," "Saint Sancho," or "Sancho") and on his book *Der Einzige und sein Eigentum,* which appeared in October 1844. But the critique of neo-Hegelian idealism was then extended to different representatives of "true socialism": Karl Grün, Georg Kuhlmann, and, to a certain extent, Moses Hess. The "true socialism"—thus called by its own partisans, in contradistinction to a primitive or elementary socialism stripped of any intellectual armor—represented an attempt to apply neo-Hegelian dialectical schemata to the world of the workers. Its representatives, intellectuals or autodidacts, were active principally through newspapers or periodicals, which were often ephemeral, such as Hermann Püttmann's *Rheinische Jahrbücher zur gesellschaftlichen Reform,* in the Prussian Rhineland, particularly in the industrial region of the Ruhr. The case of Moses Hess was somewhat exceptional: criticized by Marx and Engels in *The German Ideology,* Hess had himself criticized Stirner's book and had partially collaborated in the drafting of *The German Ideology.*

MEW 3:46–48, 159–63, 176–82, 362–64, 396–98. *Collected Works* (see source note to selection 7), 9:59–61, 175–79, 193–201, 379–81, 411–13.

The first part of the text, entitled "Feuerbach," in fact deals little with that particular philosopher but rather presents a philosophical conception of the world and of history that is at once the culmination of Marx's earlier evolution and the manifestation of a break with any neo-Hegelian or Feuerbachian idealism that remained in his thought. Now material interests (and no longer the "lightning flashes of thought"), that is, the interrelations of social classes, were presented as the decisive foundation not only of specific political changes and revolutions but also of ideological shifts, something even more abstract.

This shift in 1845–46 from what was still an idealist conception of the world and of history to a materialist conception was noted by commentators and by various interpreters. How the change was interpreted varied, to be sure, but there is no doubt when it occurred (at the turn of 1845–46) and what its principal content was (what is generally called "historical materialism").

Certain elements certainly played an important role in Marx's moving from what was still an idealist conception of the history of the revolution to a materialistic conception: the revolt of the Silesian weavers in 1844, his friend Engels's empirical studies of the English proletarian and industrial world, and his massive readings in economics in Paris from spring 1844 onward.

The following passage, drawn from the first part of *The German Ideology* ("Feuerbach"), applies implicitly and, toward the end, explicitly to the situation in France before 1789 and during the time of the Revolution.

• • •

For instance, in an age and in a country where royal power, aristocracy and bourgeoisie are contending for domination and where, therefore, domination is shared, the doctrine of the separation of powers proves to be the dominant idea and is expressed as an "eternal law."

The division of labour, which we already saw above as one of the chief forces of history up till now, manifests itself also in the ruling class as the division of mental and material labour, so that inside this class one part appears as the thinkers of the class (its active, conceptive ideologists, who make the formation of the illusions of the class about itself their chief source of livelihood), while the others' attitude to these ideas and illusions is more passive and receptive, because they are in reality the active members of this class and have less time to make up illusions and ideas about themselves. Within this class this cleavage can even develop into a certain opposition and hostility between the two parts, but whenever a practical collision occurs in which the class itself is endangered they automatically vanish, in which case there also vanishes the appearance of the ruling ideas being not the ideas of the ruling class and having a power distinct from the power of this class. The existence of revolutionary ideas in a particular period presupposes the existence of a revolutionary class; about the premises of the latter sufficient has already been said above.

If now in considering the course of history we detach the ideas of the ruling class from the ruling class itself and attribute to them an independent existence, if we confine ourselves to saying that these or those ideas were dominant at a given time, without bothering ourselves about the conditions of production and the producers of these ideas, if we thus ignore the individuals and world conditions which are the source of the ideas, then we can say, for instance, that during the time the aristocracy was dominant, the concepts honour, loyalty, etc., were dominant, during the dominance of the bourgeoisie the concepts freedom, equality, etc. The ruling class itself on the whole imagines this to be so. This conception of history, which is common to all historians, particularly since the eighteenth century, will necessarily come up against the phenomenon that ever more abstract ideas hold sway, i.e., ideas which increasingly take on the form of universality. For each new class which puts itself in the place of one ruling before it is compelled, merely in order to carry through its aim, to present its interest as the common interest of all the members of society, that is, expressed in ideal form: it has to give its ideas the form of universality, and present them as the only rational, universally valid ones. The class making a revolution comes forward from the very start, if only because it is opposed to a *class,* not as a class but as the representative of the whole of society, as the whole mass of society confronting the one ruling class.* It can do this because initially its interest really is as yet mostly connected with the common interest of all other non–ruling classes, because under the pressure of hitherto existing conditions its interest has not yet been able to develop as the particular interest of a particular class. Its victory, therefore, benefits also many individuals of other classes which are not winning a dominant position, but only insofar as it now enables these individuals to

* [Marginal note by Marx:] (Universality corresponds to 1) the class versus the estate, 2) the competition, world intercourse, etc., 3) the great numerical strength of the ruling class, 4) the illusion of the *common* interests, in the beginning this illusion is true, 5) the delusion of the ideologists and the division of labour.)

raise themselves into the ruling class. When the French bourgeoisie overthrew the rule of the aristocracy, it thereby made it possible for many proletarians to raise themselves above the proletariat, but only insofar as they became bourgeois. Every new class, therefore, achieves domination only on a broader basis than that of the class ruling previously; on the other hand the opposition of the non-ruling class to the new ruling class then develops all the more sharply and profoundly. Both these things determine the fact that the struggle to be waged against this new ruling class, in its turn, has as its aim a more decisive and more radical negation of the previous conditions of society than all previous classes which sought to rule could have.

• • •

In the section of *The German Ideology* devoted to Max Stirner ("Saint Max"), Marx and Engels show how Stirner pushed Hegelian idealism to the extreme and caricatured it, particularly when addressing the subject of the preeminence of the Spirit in history. They show, by manipulating citations, that Stirner was often content to recopy Hegel, merely modifying a few terms. They recognized in Hegel a profound understanding of "empirical history" and a respect for it, qualities that had disappeared among his lesser disciples. The latter had lost sight of, or did not wish to acknowledge, the realities of economics and social history, because of the difficulties these realities created for their schema of thought. Marx and Engels make an example of Stirner's description of the French Revolution from 1789 to 1794.

• • •

. . . From the above-quoted passages it also follows that Hegel: 1) appraises the French Revolution as a new and more perfect phase of this domination of spirit; 2) regards philosophers as the rulers of the world of the nineteenth century; 3) maintains that now only abstract ideas have validity among people; 4) that he already regards marriage, the family, the state, earning one's livelihood, civic order, property, etc., as "divine and holy", as the "*religious principle*" and 5) that *morality* as worldly sanctity or as sanctified worldliness is represented as the highest and ultimate form of the domination of spirit over the world— all these things are repeated *word for word* in "Stirner.". . .

If, like Hegel, one designs such a system for the first time, a system embracing the whole of history and the present-day world in all its scope, one cannot possibly do so without comprehensive, positive knowledge, without great energy and keen insight and without dealing at least in some passages with empirical history. On the other hand, if one is satisfied with exploiting an already existing pattern, transforming it for one's "own" purposes and demonstrating this conception of one's own by means of isolated examples (e.g., Negroes and Mongols, Catholics and Protestants, the French Revolution, etc.)—and this is precisely what our warrior against the holy does—then absolutely no knowledge of history is necessary. The result of all this exploitation inevitably becomes comic. . . .

By carrying over the old domination of the clerics to modern times, Saint Max interprets modern times as "*clericalism*"; and then by regarding this domination of the clerics carried over to modern times as something distinct from the old medieval clerical domination, he depicts it as domination of the ideologists, as "*scholasticism*." Thus clericalism=hierarchy as the domination of the spirit, scholasticism=the domination of the spirit as hierarchy.

"Stirner" achieves this simple transition to clericalism—which is no transition at all—by means of three weighty transformations.

Firstly, he "has" the "concept of clericalism" in anyone "who lives for a great idea, for a good cause" (still the good cause!), "for a doctrine, etc."

Secondly, in his world of illusion Stirner "comes up against" the "age-old illusion of a world that has not yet learned to dispense with clericalism," namely —"to live and create for the sake of an *idea, etc.*"

Thirdly, "it is the domination of the idea, i.e., clericalism," that is: "Robespierre, for example" (for example!), "Saint-Just, and so on" (and so on!) "were out-and-out priests," etc. All three transformations in which clericalism is "discovered," "encountered" and "called upon" (all this on p. 100), therefore, express nothing more than what Saint Max has already repeatedly told us, namely, the domination of spirit, of the idea, of the holy, over "life" (ibid.).

After the "domination of the idea, i.e., clericalism" has thus been foisted upon history, Saint Max can, of course, without difficulty find this "clericalism" again in the whole of preceding history, and thus depict "Robespierre, for example, Saint-Just, and so on" as priests and identify them with Innocent III and Gregory VII, and so all uniqueness vanishes in the face of *the unique*. All of them, properly speaking, are merely different *names,* different disguises for *one* person, "clericalism," which made all history from the beginning of Christianity. As to how, with this sort of conception of history, "all cats become grey," since all historical differences are "abolished" and "resolved" in the "notion of clericalism"—as to this, Saint Max at once gives us a striking example in his "Robespierre, for example,

Saint-Just, and so on". Here we are first given Robespierre as an "example" of Saint-Just, and Saint-Just—as an "and-so-on" of Robespierre. It is then said:

> These representatives of holy interests are confronted by a
> world of innumerable "personal," earthly interests.

By whom were they confronted? By the Girondists and Thermidorians, who (see "for example" R. Levasseur's *Mémoires,* "and so on," "i.e.," Nougaret, *Histoire des prisons:* Barère; *"Deux amis de la liberté"* (*et du commerce*); Montgaillard, *Histoire de France;* Madame Roland, *Appel à la postérité;* J. B. Louvet's *Mémoires* and even the disgusting *Essais historiques* by Beaulieu,[1] etc., etc., as well as all the proceedings before the revolutionary tribunal, "and so on") constantly reproached them, the real representatives of revolutionary power, i.e., of the class which *alone* was truly revolutionary, the "innumerable" masses, for violating "sacred interests," the constitution, freedom, equality, the rights of man, republicanism, law, *sainte propriété,* "for example" the division of powers, humanity, morality, moderation, "and so on." They were opposed by all the *priests,* who accused them of violating all the main and secondary items of the religious and moral catechism (see "for example" *Histoire du clergé de France pendant la révolution,* by M. R.,[2] Paris, libraire catholique, 1828, "and so on"). The historical comment of the bourgeois that during the *règne de la terreur* "Robespierre, for example, Saint-Just, and so on" cut off the heads of *honnêtes gens* (see the numerous writings of the simpleton Monsieur *Peltier,* "for example," *La conspiration de Robespierre* by *Montjoie,*[3] "and so on") is expressed by Saint Max in the following transformation:

> Because the revolutionary priests and school-masters served
> *Man,* they cut the throats of men.

This, of course, saves Saint Max the trouble of wasting even one "unique" little word about the actual, empirical grounds for the cutting off of heads—grounds which were based on extremely worldly interests, though not, of course, fo the stockjobbers, but of the "innumerable" masses. . . .

Blessed Max, who has found sufficient grounds for everything ("I have now found the ground into which my anchor is eternally fastened,"[4] in the idea, "for example," in the "clericalism," "and so on" of "Robespierre, for example, Saint-Just, and so on," George Sand,

Proudhon, the chaste Berlin seamstress, etc.)—this blessed Max "does not blame the class of the bourgeoisie for having asked its egoism how far it should give way to the revolutionary *idea as such.*" For Saint Max "the revolutionary idea" which inspired the *habits bleus* and *honnêtes gens* of 1789 is the same "idea" as that of the sansculottes of 1793, *the same* idea concerning which people deliberate whether to "give way" to it —but no further "space can be given" to any "idea" about this point. . . .

• • •

Further on, in the long development of the critique of Stirner's positions, Marx and Engels situate Stirner, and with him all of "left-leaning" neo-Hegelianism, in the long line of German idealists since Kant, and thus in a situation of dependency upon German economic and social backwardness and upon the German political "misery" of the late eighteenth century up to the 1840s: Stirner's errors of judgment about the French Revolution could, according to Marx and Engels, be explained essentially by the fact that he was a German intellectual, living in Germany, and thus incapable of conceiving of the bourgeois (or the *citoyen*) other than in the form of the Berlin "philistine"—apolitical and beer-drinking.

• • •

The key to the criticism of liberalism advanced by Saint Max and his predecessors is the history of the German bourgeoisie. We shall call special attention to some aspects of this history since the French Revolution.

The state of affairs in Germany at the end of the last century is fully reflected in Kant's *Critik der praktischen Vernunft*. While the French bourgeoisie, by means of the most colossal revolution that history has ever known, was achieving domination and conquering the Continent of Europe, while the already politically emancipated English bourgeoisie was revolutionising industry and subjugating India politically, and all the rest of the world commercially, the impotent German burghers did not get any further than "good will." Kant was satisfied with "good will" alone, even if it remained entirely without result, and he transferred the *realisation* of this good will, the harmony between it and the needs and impulses of individuals, to *the world beyond*. Kant's good will fully corresponds to the impotence, depression and wretchedness of the German burghers, whose petty interests were never capable of developing into the common, national interests of a class and who were, therefore, constantly exploited by the bourgeois of all other nations. These petty, local interests had as their counterpart, on the one hand, the truly local and provincial narrow-mindedness of the German burghers and, on the other hand, their cosmopolitan swollen-headedness. In general, from the time of the Reformation German development has borne a completely petty-bourgeois character. The old feudal aristocracy was, for the most part, annihilated in the peasant wars; what remained of it were either imperial petty princes who gradually achieved a certain independence and aped the absolute monarchy on a minute, provincial scale, or lesser landowners who partly squandered their little bit of property at the tiny courts, and then gained their livelihood from petty positions in the small armies and government offices—or, finally, Junkers from the backwoods, who lived a life of which even the most modest English squire or French *gentilhomme de province* would have been ashamed. Agriculture was carried on by a method which was neither parcellation nor large-scale production, and which, despite the preservation of feudal dependence and corvées, never drove the peasants to seek emancipation, both because this method of farming did not allow the emergence of any active revolutionary class and because of the absence of the revolutionary bourgeoisie corresponding to such a peasant class.

As regards the middle class, we can only emphasise here a few significant factors. It is significant that linen manufacture, i.e., an industry based on the spinning wheel and the hand-loom, came to be of some importance in Germany at the very time when in England those cumbersome tools were already being ousted by machines. Most characteristic of all is the position of the German middle class in relation to *Holland*. Holland, the only part of the Hanseatic League that became commercially important, tore itself free, cut Germany off from world trade except for two ports (Hamburg and Bremen) and since then dominated the whole of German trade. The German middle class was too impotent to set limits to exploitation by the Dutch. The bourgeoisie of little Holland, with its well-developed class interests, was more powerful than the far more numerous German middle class with its indifference and its divided petty interests. The fragmentation of interests was matched by the fragmentation of political organisation, the division into small principalities and free imperial cities. How could *political* concentration arise in a country which lacked all the *economic* conditions for it? The impotence of each separate sphere of life (one can speak here neither of estates nor of classes, but at most of former estates and classes not yet born) did not allow any one of them to gain exclusive domination. The inevitable consequence was that during the epoch of absolute monarchy, which assumed here its most stunted, semi–patriarchal form, the special sphere which, owing to division of labour, was responsible for the administration of public interests acquired as abnormal independence, which became still greater in the bureaucracy of modern times. Thus, the state built itself up into an apparently independent force, and this position, which in other countries was only transitory—a transition stage—it has maintained in Germany until the present day. This position of the state explains both the conscientiousness of the civil servant, which is found nowhere else, and all the illusions about the state which are current in Germany, as well as the apparent independence of German theoreticians in relation to the middle class—the seeming contradiction between the form in which these theoreticians express the interests of the middle class and these interests themselves.

The characteristic form which French liberalism, based on real class interests, assumed in Germany we find again in Kant. Neither he, nor the German middle-class, whose whitewashing spokesman he was, noticed that these theoretical ideas of the bourgeoisie had as their basis material interests and a *will* that was conditioned and determined by the material relations of production. Kant, therefore, separated this theoretical expression from the interests which it expressed; he made the materially motivated determinations of the will of the French bourgeois into *pure* self-determinations of "*free will*," of the will in and for itself, of the human will, and so converted it into purely ideological conceptual determinations and moral postulates. Hence the German petty bourgeois recoiled in horror from the practice of this energetic bourgeois liberalism as soon as this practice showed itself, both in the Reign of Terror and in shameless bourgeois profit-making.

Under the rule of Napoleon, the German middle class pushed its petty trade and its great illusions still further. As regards the petty-trading spirit which predominated in Germany at that time, Saint Sancho can, *inter alia,* compare Jean Paul, to mention only works of fiction, since they are the only source open to him. The German citizens, who railed against Napoleon for compelling them to drink chicory and for disturbing their peace with military billeting and recruiting of conscripts, reserved all their moral indignation for Napoleon and all their admiration for England; yet Napoleon rendered them the greatest services by cleaning out Germany's Augean stables and establishing civilised means of communication, whereas the English only waited for the opportunity to exploit them *à tort et à travers.* In the same petty-bourgeois spirit the German princes imagined they were fighting for the principle of legitimism and against revolution, whereas they were only the paid mercenaries of the English bourgeoisie. In the atmosphere of these universal illusions it was quite in the order of things that the estates privileged to cherish illusions—ideologists, school-masters, students, members of the *Tugendbund*[5]—should talk big and give a suitable highflown expression to the universal mood of fantasy and indifference.

The political forms corresponding to a developed bourgeoisie were passed on to the Germans from outside by the July revolution—as we mention only a few main points we omit the intermediary period. Since German economic relations had by no means reached the stage of development to which these political forms corresponded, the middle class accepted them merely as abstract ideas, principles valid in and for themselves, pious wishes and phrases, Kantian self-determinations of the will of human beings as they ought to be. Consequently their attitude to these forms was far more moral and disinterested than that of other nations, i.e., they exhibited a highly peculiar narrow-mindedness and remained unsuccessful in all their endeavours.

Finally the ever more powerful foreign competition and world intercourse—from which it became less and less possible for Germany to stand aside—compelled the diverse local interests in Germany to adopt some sort of common attitude. Particularly since 1840, the German middle class began to think about safeguarding these common interests; its attitude became national and liberal and it demanded protective tariffs and constitutions. Thus it has now got almost as far as the French bourgeoisie in 1789.

If, like the Berlin ideologists, one judges liberalism and the state within the framework of local German impressions, or limits oneself merely to criticism of German-bourgeois illusions about liberalism, instead of seeing the correlation of liberalism with the the real interests from which it originated and without which it cannot really exist—then, of course, one arrives at the most banal conclusions. This German liberalism, in the form in which it expressed itself up to the most recent period, is, as we have seen, even in its popular form, empty enthusiasm, ideological reflections about *real* liberalism. How easy it is, therefore, to transform its content wholly into philosophy, into pure conceptual determinations, into "rational cognition"! Hence if one is so unfortunate as to know even this bourgeoisified liberalism only in the sublimated form given it by Hegel and the school-masters who depend on him, then one will arrive at conclusions belonging exclusive to the sphere of the holy. . . .

We wish to give here a few examples of how Saint Max embellishes this property of his with historical arabesques. For this purpose he uses the French Revolution, concerning which a small contract to supply him with a few data has been negotiated by his history-broker, Saint Bruno.

On the basis of a few words from Bailly, obtained moreover through the intermediary of Saint Bruno's *Denkwürdigkeiten,* the statement is made that through the convening of the States General "those who hitherto were subjects arrive at the consciousness that they are proprietors" (p. 132). On the contrary, *mon brave!* By the convening of the States General, those who hitherto were proprietors show their consciousness of being no longer subjects—a consciousness which was long ago arrived at, for example in the Physiocrats, and—in polemical form against the bourgeoisie—in Linguet (*Théorie des lois civiles,* 1767), Mercier, Mably, and, in general, in the writings against the Physiocrats. This meaning was also immediately understood at the beginning of the revolution—for example by Brissot, Fauchet, Marat, in the *Cercle social* and by all the democratic opponents in Lafayette. If Saint Max had understood the matter as it took place independently of his history-broker, he would not have been surprised that "Bailly's words certainly *sound* [as if each man were now a proprietor . . .]."

. . . By carrying the motion,[6] the Assembly discarded the characteristic features of the old, feudal *Etats généraux.* Moreover, it was at that time by no means a question of the correct theory of popular representation, but of highly practical, essential problems. Broglie's army held Paris at bay and drew nearer every day; the capital was in a state of utmost agitation; hardly a fortnight had passed since the *jeu de paume* and the *lit de justice,* the court was plotting with the bulk of the aristocracy and the clergy against the National Assembly; lastly, owing to the still existing feudal provincial tariff barriers, and as a result of the feudal agrarian system as a whole, most of the provinces were in the grip of famine and there was a great scarcity of money. . . .

. . . At that moment it was a question of an *assemblée essentiellement active,* as Talleyrand himself put it, while the *Cahiers* of [the] aristocratic and other reactionary groups provided the court with an opportunity to declare [the] decision of the Assembly [void by referring] to the wishes of the constituents. The Assembly proclaimed its independence by carrying Talleyrand's motion and seized the power it required, which in the political sphere could, of course, only be done within the framework of political form and by making use of the existing theories of Rousseau, etc. (Cf. *Le point du jour,* par Barère de

Vieuzac, 1789, Nos. 15 and 17.) The National Assembly had to take this step because it was being urged forward by the immense mass of the people that stood behind it. By so doing, therefore, it did not at all transform itself into an "utterly egoistical chamber, completely cut off from the umbilical cord and ruthless" [p. 147]; on the contrary it actually transformed itself thereby into the *true organ* of the vast majority of Frenchmen, who would otherwise have crushed it, as they later crushed "utterly egoistical" deputies who "completely cut themselves off from the umbilical cord." But Saint Max, with the help of his history-broker, sees here merely the solution of a theoretical question; he takes the Constituent Assembly, six days before the storming of the Bastille, for a council of *church fathers* debating a point of dogma! The question regarding the "importance of each man, the individual," can, moreover, only arise in a democratically elected representative body, and during the revolution it only came up for discussion in the Convention, and for as empirical reasons as earlier the question of the *Cahiers*. A problem which the Constituent Assembly decided *also* theoretically was the distinction between the representative body of a ruling *class* and that of the ruling *estates;* and this political rule of the bourgeois *class* was determined by each individual's position, since it was determined by the relations of production prevailing at the time. The representative system is a very specific product of modern bourgeois society which is as inseparable from the latter as is the isolated individual of modern times. . . .

. . . "Stirner" thinks that as far as "the good burghers" are concerned, it makes no difference who defends them and their principles, whether an absolute or a constitutional king, a republic, etc.—For the "good burghers" who quietly drink beer in a Berlin beer-cellar this undoubtedly "makes no difference"; but for the historical bourgeois it is by no means a matter of indifference. The "good burgher" "Stirner" here again imagines—as he does throughout this section— that the French, American and English bourgeois are good Berlin beer-drinking philistines. If one translates the sentence above from the language of political illusion into plain language, it means: "it makes no difference" to the bourgeoisie whether it rules unrestrictedly or whether its political and economic power is counterbalanced by other classes. Saint Max believes that an absolute king, or someone else, *could* defend the bourgeoisie just as successfully as it defends itself. And even "its principles," which consist in subordinating state power to *"chacun pour soi, chacun chez soi"* and exploiting it for that purpose—an "absolute monarch" is supposed to be able to do that! Let Saint Max name any country with developed trade and industry and strong competition where the bourgeoisie entrusts its defence to an "absolute monarch."

After this transformation of the historical bourgeois into German philistines devoid of history, "Stirner," of course, does not need to know any other bourgeois than "comfortable burghers and loyal officials"(!!)—two spectres who only dare to show themselves on "holy" German soil—and can lump together the whole class as "obedient servants." Let him just take a look at these obedient servants on the stock exchanges of London, Manchester, New York and Paris.

• • •

Further along in this same section on Stirner, Marx and Engels comment at length on the notion of revolt (*"Empörung"*) in the work of "Saint Max." They denounce again the absolute idealism of Stirner's historical conceptions, in particular apropos of the relationship between socioeconomic and political factors at the time of the French Revolution: "Saint Max's" version of the Revolution as the triumph of the idea or the concept.

• • •

We already know what meaning "going beyond the framework of what exists" has. It is the old fancy that the state collapses of itself as soon as all its members leave and that money loses its validity if all the workers refuse to accept it. Even in a hypothetical form, this proposition reveals all the fantasy and impotence of pious desire. It is the old illusion that changing existing relations depends only on the good will of people, and that existing relations are ideas. The alteration of consciousness divorced from actual relations—a pursuit followed by philosophers as a profession, i.e., as a *business*—is itself a product of existing relations and inseparable from them. This imaginary rising above the world is the ideological expression of the impotence of philosophers in face of the world. Practical life every day gives the lie to their ideological bragging.

In any event, Sancho did not "rebel" against his own state of confusion when he wrote those lines. For him there is the "transformation of existing conditions" on one side, and "people" on the other side, and the two sides are entirely separate from each other. Sancho does not give the slightest thought to the fact that the "conditions" have always been the conditions of these people and it would never have been possible to transform them unless the people transformed themselves and, if it has to be expressed in this way, unless they became "dissatisfied with themselves" in the old conditions. He thinks he is dealing a mortal blow at revolution when he asserts that it aims at new arrangements, whereas rebellion leads to a position where we no longer allow others to arrange things for us, but arrange things for ourselves. But the very fact that "we" arrange things for "ourselves," that it is "we" who rebel, denotes that the individual, despite all Sancho's "repugnance," has to "allow" that "we" "arrange things" for him, and that therefore the only difference between revolution and rebellion is that in the former this is known, whereas in the latter people harbour illusions about it. Next Sancho leaves it open whether the rebellion "*prospers*" or not. One cannot understand why it should *not* "prosper," and even less why it should prosper, since each rebel goes his own way. Worldly conditions would have to intervene to show the rebels the necessity of a *joint* act, one which would be "political or social," irrespective of whether it arises from egoistical motives or not. A further "trashy distinction," based again on confusion, is that drawn by Sancho between the "overthrow" of what exists and "rising" above it, as though in overthrowing what exists he does not rise above it, and in rising above it, he does not overthrow it, if only insofar as it exists in him himself. Incidentally, neither "overthrow" by itself nor "rising" by itself tells us anything; that "rising" also takes place in revolution Sancho could have seen from the fact that "*Levons-nous!*"[7] was a well-known slogan in the French Revolution.

> Revolution bids [!] us to create *institutions*, rebellion urges us to *rise or rise up*. Revolutionary minds were occupied with the choice of a *constitution*, and the entire political period teems with constitutional struggles and constitutional questions, just as socially-gifted persons revealed extraordinary inventiveness as regards social institutions (phalansteries and such-like). To *be without a constitution* is the endeavour of the rebel.

That the French Revolution brought institutions in its train is a fact; that *Empörung* is derived from the word *empor* is also a fact; that during the revolution and after it people fought for constitutions is another fact, and equally so that various social systems were outlined; and it is no less a fact that Proudhon spoke about anarchy. From these five facts Sancho has concocted the above-quoted passage.

From the fact that the French Revolution led to "institutions," Sancho concludes that this is a "bidding" of revolution in general. From the fact that the political revolution was a political one in which the social transformation had also an official expression in the form of constitutional struggles, Sancho—faithfully following his history-broker—deduces that in it people fought over the best constitution. To this discovery he links, by means of the words "just as," a mention of social systems. In the epoch of the bourgeoisie, people occupied themselves with constitutional questions, "just as" in recent times various social systems have been devised. This is the train of thought in the above-quoted passage.

It follows from what was said above against Feuerbach that previous revolutions within the framework of division of labour were bound to lead to new political institutions; it likewise follows that the communist revolution, which removes the division of labour, ultimately abolishes political institutions, and, finally, it follows also that the communist revolution will be guided not by the "social institutions of inventive socially-gifted persons," but by the productive forces.

But "to be without a constitution is the endeavour of the rebel"! He who is "born free," who is from the outset rid of everything, endeavours at the end of time to get rid of the constitution.

It should be mentioned also that all sorts of earlier illusions of our bonhomme contributed to Sancho's concept of "rebellion." They include, among others, his belief that the individuals who make a revolution are linked by some ideal bond and that their "raising the standard of revolt" is limited to inscribing on it a new concept, fixed idea, spectre, or apparition—the holy.

• • •

Marx and Engels, still referring to Stirner, elaborated at length the "theory of utility and exploitation" ("*Nützichlichkeits- und Exploitationstheorie*") in England and in France, in relation to the real development of the bourgeois class before and after the French Revolution. Stirner was, to be sure, incapable of understanding the development of this bourgeois reality and theory, lost, as he was, in his German "philistine's" illusions.

• • •

The advances made by the theory of utility and exploitations, its various phases are closely connected with the various periods of development of the bourgeoisie. In the case of Helvétius and Holbach, the actual content of the theory never went much beyond paraphrasing the mode of expression of writings belonging to the period of the absolute monarchy. It was a different method of expression which reflected the desire to reduce all relations to the relation of exploitation and to explain the intercourse of people from their material needs and the ways of satisfying them, rather than the actual realisation of this desire. The problem was set. Hobbes and Locke had before their eyes not only the earlier development of the Dutch bourgeoisie (both of them had lived for some time in Holland) but also the first political actions by which the English bourgeoisie emerged from local and provincial limitations, as well as a comparatively highly developed stage of manufacture, overseas trade and colonisation. This particularly applies to Locke, who wrote during the first period of the English economy, at the time of the rise of joint-stock companies, the Bank of England and England's mastery of the seas. In their case, and particularly in that of Locke, the theory of exploitation was still directly connected with the economic content.

Helvetius and Holbach had before them, besides English theory and the preceding development of the Dutch and English bourgeoisie, also the French bourgeoisie which was still struggling for its free development. The commercial spirit, universal in the eighteenth century, had especially in France taken possession of all classes in the form of speculation. The financial difficulties of the government and the resulting disputes over taxation occupied the attention of all France even at that time. In addition, Paris in the eighteenth century was the only world city, the only city where there was personal intercourse among individuals of all nations. These premises, combined with the more universal character typical of the French in general, gave the theory of Helvétius and Holbach its peculiar universal colouring, but at the same time deprived it of the positive economic content that was still to be found among the English. The theory which for the English was still simply the registration of facts becomes for the French a philosophical system. This generality devoid of positive content, such as we find it in Helvétius and Holbach, is essentially different from the substantial comprehensive view which is first found in Bentham and Mill. The former corresponds to the struggling, still undeveloped bourgeoisie, the latter to the ruling, developed bourgeoisie.

The content of the theory of exploitation that was neglected by Helvétius and Holbach was developed and systematised by the Physiocrats—who worked at the same time as Holbach—but because their basis was the undeveloped economic relations of France where feudalism, under which landownership plays the chief role, was still unshaken, they remained in thrall to the feudal outlook insofar as they declared landownership and land cultivation to be that [productive force] which determines the whole structure of society.

The theory of exploitation owes its further development in England to Godwin, and especially to Bentham. As the bourgeoisie succeeded in asserting itself more and more both in England and in France, the economic content, which the French had neglected, was gradually re-introduced by Bentham. Godwin's *Political Justice* was written during the terror, and Bentham's chief works during and after the French Revolution and the development of large-scale industry in England. The complete union of the theory of utility with political economy is to be found, finally, in Mill.

At an earlier period political economy had been the subject of inquiry either by financiers, bankers and merchants, i.e., in general by persons directly concerned with economic relations, or by persons with an all-round education like Hobbes, Locke and Hume, for whom it was of importance as a branch of encyclopaedic knowledge. Thanks to the Physiocrats, political economy for the first time was raised to the rank of a special science and has been treated as such ever since. As a special branch of science it absorbed the other relations—political, juridical, etc.—to such an extent that it reduced them to economic relations. But it regarded this subordination of all relations to itself as only one aspect of these relations, and thereby allowed them for the rest an independent significance outside political economy. The complete subordination of all existing relations to the relation of utility, and its unconditional elevation to the sole content of all other relations, occurs for the first time in Bentham's works, where, after the French Revolution and the development of large-scale industry, the bourgeoisie is no longer presented as a special class, but as the class whose conditions of existence are those of the whole society. . . .

NOTES

1. René Levasseur de la Sarthe, *Mémoires,* vols. 1–4 (Paris, 1829–31). Pierre-Jean Baptiste Nougaret, *Histoire des prisons de Paris et des départements,* contenant des mémoires rares et précieux. Le tout pour servir à l'histoire de la Révolution française, notamment à la tyrannie de Robespierre et de ses agents et complices. Ouvrage dédié à tous ceux qui ont été détenus comme suspects (Paris, 1797). Bertrand Barère de Vieuzac (1755–1841) was one of the men who played a crucial role in the fall of Robespierre. Also under the pseudonym "Deux amis de la liberté," a multivolume *Histoire de la Révolution de France* was published in 1792, which was credited to the pen of F.-Marie Kerverseau and G. Clavelin. Marx added "et du commerce," a nickname he often gave to the bourgeois of the time. Guillaume-Honoré

Montagaillard's *Revue chronologique de l'histoire de Francd* covered the first Convention of the notables up until the departure of the foreign troops in 1787–1818. It was published in Paris in 1820. Jeanne-Manon Roland's *Appel à l'impartiale postérité* was subtitled "par la citoyenne Roland . . . ou recueil des écrits qu'elle a rédigés pendant sa détention aux prisons de l'Abbaye et de Sainte-Pélagie" (Paris, 1795). Jean-Baptiste Louvet de Couvray's *Mémoires* appeared in Paris in 1823, and the full title of Claude-François Beaulieu's book is *Essais historiques sur les causes et les effets de la Révolution de France* (Paris, 1801–3).

2. M. R. was Hippolyte Régnier d'Estourbet.

3. Jean-Gabriel Peltier (1765–1825) was a French royalist journalist. Félix-Christophe-Louis Montjoie, Ventre de Touloubre, *Histoire de la conjuration de Maximilien Robespierre* (Paris, 1795).

4. A line from a Protestant song.

5. The *Tugendbund* (literally "league of virtue") was a secret society, founded in Prussia in 1808. Its objective was to develop patriotic sentiments and to fight for the liberation of the territories occupied by France. At Napoleon's behest, the king of Prussia ordered the dissolution of the *Tugendbund* in 1809.

6. A motion raised on 4 July 1789 by Talleyrand.

7. The motto of the weekly *Les Révolutions de Paris*. Its complete text was: "Les Grands ne nous paraissent si grands que parce que nous sommes à genoux. Levons-nous!" (The Great look so great to us only because we are on our knees. Rise up!) This periodical appeared from July 1789 to February 1794 in Paris.

8. *Empor* means "upward"; *Empörung* means "uprising," "revolt."

10

Karl Grun's *Die soziale Bewegung in Frankreich und Belgien* (Darmstadt, 1845), or The Historiography of True Socialism

This piece was part of the section of *The German Ideology* (see selection 9) devoted to a critique of the representatives of "true" socialism. Drafted by Marx in the spring of 1846, it was published in August and September of 1847 in a review (of "true" socialism) that appeared in Bielefeld and Paderborn: *Das Westphälische Dampfboot.*

Marx wished to demonstrate that Karl Grün, despite his friendly relationship with Proudhon, was poorly versed in French socialism, knowing it only second hand, for example through Lorenz von Stein's *Der Socialismus und Communismus des heutigen Frankreichs: Ein Beitrag zur Zeitgeschichte* (Leipzig, 1842) or Louis Reybaud's two-volume *Etudes sur les réformateurs ou socialistes modernes* (Paris, 1842–43). He also showed that Grün completely missed the most important elements of Saint-Simonianism, of Fourierism, or of Etienne Cabet's *Voyage en Icarie* (1842). The reason for this weakness, in particular in the area of economic analysis, could, according to Marx, be found in the intellectual conceit and idealism of Grün, who, like other representatives of "true" socialism, was convinced of the superiority of German science and philosophy over the political and social practices of the French.

The critique of "true" socialism did not end with *The German Ideology;* indeed, Marx would publish a declaration against Grün in the *Deutsche Brüsseler Zeitung* of 8 April 1847 (see MEW 4:37–39), and Engels, in the September-December 1847 issue of the same journal, would publish an article on "German socialism in verse and prose" that was a critique of "true" socialist literature (see MEW 4:207–47). From January to April 1847, Engels resumed the critique of "true" socialism included in *The German Ideology,* but this work remained unfinished and unpublished until 1932 (see MEW 4:248–

MEW 3:502, 514–15. *Collected Works* (see source note to selection 7), 5:514–16, 525–26. Translated by Clemens Dutt.

90). The *Manifesto of the Communist Party* contains a section devoted
to the critique of "German" or "true" socialism; Marx and Engels
attacked once more the taste for abstraction and the denial of social
and economic realities characteristic—according to them—of German
intellectuals.

• • •

. . . While reproaching Fourier for his interpretation of the French
Revolution, Herr Grün gives us a glimpse of his own insight into the
revolutionary age:

> If association had only been known of forty years earlier
> [so he makes Fourier say], the Revolution could have been
> avoided. But how [asks Herr Grün] did it come about that Tur-
> got, the Minister, recognised the right to work and that, in
> spite of this, Louis XVI lost his head? After all, it would have
> been easier to discharge the national debt by means of the right
> to work than by means of hen's eggs (p. 211).

Herr Grün overlooks the trifling fact that the right to work,
which Turgot speaks of, is none other than free competition and that
this very free competition needed the Revolution in order to establish
itself. . . .

Cabet calls Turgot a Baron and a Minister, Herr Grün copies
this much from him, but by way of improving on Cabet, he changes
the youngest son of the prévôt of the Paris merchants into "one of the
oldest of the feudal lords." Cabet is wrong in attributing the famine
and the uprising of 1775 to the machinations of the aristocracy. Up to
the present, no one has discovered who was behind the outcry about
the famine and the movement connected with it. But in any case the
parliaments and popular prejudice had far more to do with it than the
aristocracy. It is quite in order for Herr Grün to copy this error of
"poor limited Papa" Cabet. He believes in him as in a gospel. On
Cabet's authority Herr Grün numbers Turgot among the communists, Turgot, one of the leaders of the physiocratic school, the most
resolute champion of free competition, the defender of usury, the
mentor of Adam Smith. Turgot was a great man, since his actions
were in accordance with the time in which he lived and not with the
illusions of Herr Grün, the origin of which we have shown already.

Let us now pass to the men of the French Revolution. Cabet
greatly embarrasses his bourgeois opponent by numbering Sieyès
among the forerunners of communism, by reason of the fact that he

recognised equality of rights, and considered that only the state sanctions property (Cabet, pp. 499–502). Herr Grün, who "is fated to find the French mind inadequate and superficial every time that he comes into close contact with it," cheerfully copies this, and imagines that an old party leader like Cabet is destined to preserve the "humanism" of Herr Grün from "the dust of erudition." Cabet continues: *"Ecoutez le fameux Mirabeau!"* (p. 504). Herr Grün says: "Listen to Mirabeau!" (p. 292) and quotes some of the passages stressed by Cabet, in which Mirabeau advocates the equal division of bequeathed property among brothers and sisters. Herr Grün exclaims: "Communism for the family!" (p. 292). On this principle, Herr Grün could go through the whole range of bourgeois institutions, finding in all of them traces of communism, so that taken as a whole they could be said to represent perfect communism. He could christen the *Code Napoléon* a *Code de la communauté!* And he could discover communist colonies in the brothels, barracks and prisons. . .

11

The Poverty of Philosophy: A Reply to Proudhon's
Philosophy of Poverty

The following passage constitutes the conclusion to *The Poverty of Philosophy;* it does not deal explicitly with the question of the French Revolution, but rather with the parallel between the social (or proletarian) revolution of the future and the political (or bourgeois) revolution of 1789. The relationship between these two types of revolution is at the core of Marx's reflections of 1847–48 (see, for example, *The Manifesto of the Communist Party*).

Marx wrote *The Poverty of Philosophy* between the end of December 1846 and April 1847, after reading Proudhon's *Système des contradictions économiques ou Philosophie de la misère,* published in 1846. Marx's book first appeared in French, in Paris and Brussels, in July 1847. It was translated into German in 1885 by Kautsky and Bernstein, with a preface by Engels.

In a sense, Marx rediscovered in Proudhon the autodidact the defects he had found so intolerable in the young Hegelians and the partisans of "true" socialism: an idealist conception of history, a schematic and systematic manner of thinking without concrete analysis, and intellectual conceit.

• • •

The first attempts of workers to *associate* among themselves always take place in the form of combinations.

Large-scale industry concentrates in one place a crowd of people unknown to one another. Competition divides their interests. But the maintenance of wages, this common interest which they have against their boss, unites them in a common thought of resistance—*combination*. Thus combination always has a double aim, that of stopping

MEW 4:180–82. *Collected Works* (see source note to selection 7), 6:210–12. Translated by Frida Knight.

competition among the workers, so that they can carry on general competition with the capitalist. If the first aim of resistance was merely the maintenance of wages, combinations, at first isolated, constitute themselves into groups as the capitalists in their turn unite for the purpose of repression, and in face of always united capital, the maintenance of the association becomes more necessary to them than that of wages. This is so true that English economists are amazed to see the workers sacrifice a good part of their wages in favour of associations, which, in the eyes of these economists, are established solely in favour of wages. In this struggle—a veritable civil war—all the elements necessary for a coming battle unite and develop. Once it has reached this point, association takes on a political character.

Economic conditions had first transformed the mass of the people of the country into workers. The domination of capital has created for this mass a common situation, common interests. This mass is thus already a class as against capital, but not yet for itself. In the struggle, of which we have pointed out only a few phases, this mass becomes united, and constitutes itself as a class for itself. The interests it defends become class interests. But the struggle of class against class is a political struggle.

In the bourgeoisie we have two phases to distinguish: that in which it constituted itself as a class under the regime of feudalism and absolute monarchy, and that in which, already constituted as a class, it overthrew feudalism and monarchy to make society into a bourgeois society. The first of these phases was the longer and necessitated the greater efforts. This too began by partial combinations against the feudal lords.

Much research has been carried out to trace the different historical phases that the bourgeoisie has passed through, from the commune up to its constitution as a class.

But when it is a question of making a precise study of strikes, combinations and other forms in which the proletarians carry out before our eyes their organisation as a class, some are seized with real fear and others display a *transcendental* disdain.

An oppressed class is the vital condition for every society founded on the antagonism of classes. The emancipation of the oppressed class thus implies necessarily the creation of a new society. For the oppressed class to be able to emancipate itself it is necessary that the productive powers already acquired and the existing social relations should no longer be capable of existing side by side. Of all the instruments of production, the greatest productive power is the revolutionary class itself. The organisation of revolutionary elements as a class supposes the existence of all the productive forces which could be engendered in the bosom of the old society.

Does this mean that after the fall of the old society there will be a new class domination culminating in a new political power? No.

The condition for the emancipation of the working class is the abolition of all classes, just as the condition for the emancipation of the third estate, of the bourgeois order, was the abolition of all estates and all orders.

The working class, in the course of its development, will substitute for the old civil society an association which will exclude classes and their antagonism, and there will be no more political power properly so-called, since political power is precisely the official expression of antagonism in civil society.

Meanwhile the antagonism between the proletariat and the bourgeoisie is a struggle of class against class, a struggle which carried to its highest expression is a total revolution. Indeed, is it at all surprising that a society founded on the *opposition* of classes should culminate in brutal *contradiction,* the shock of body against body, as its final denouement?

Do not say that social movement excludes political movement. There is never a political movement which is not at the same time social.

It is only in an order of things in which there are no more classes and class antagonisms and *social evolutions* will cease to be *political revolutions*. Till then, on the eve of every general reshuffling of society, the last word of social science will always be:

> Le combat ou la mort; la lutte sanguinaire ou le néant.
> C'est ainsi que la question est invinciblement posée."
> —George Sand

12

The Communism of the *Rheinische Beobachter*

This article was published by Marx in the *Deutsche Brüsseler Zeitung* of 12 September 1847. It constitutes a response to an article that appeared slightly earlier in a conservative, progovernment journal of Cologne, the *Rheinische Beobachter*. The *Reinische Beobachter* article was the work of a "Consistorial Counsellor" of the Prussian minister of Religious Worship, Education, and Medicine, Eichhorn; the "Consistorial Counsellor" in question may have been Hermann Wagener, who would play an important role in the "socially" oriented conservatism during Bismarck's era, from 1871 on.

The argument of the *Rheinische Beobachter* was as follows: it was in the Prussian government's interest to concern itself with the "social question" because the interests of the monarchy and of the "people" coincide and are both opposed to the interests of the liberal bourgeoisie. This last, in return, used the "people" in order to advance its political and economic demands but had only its own egotistical interests in view. The "Consistorial Counsellor" added that the social politics of the government had to rely on the principles of Christianity, which, put into practice, would make "communist" propaganda superfluous.

Marx's reply pointed up the progressive historical role of the liberal bourgeoisie, which, indeed, demanded and created the juridical and political forms that facilitated the development of the workers' movement and its political struggle, including its struggle against the liberal bourgeoisie itself. Marx offered England and France as examples, in contrast to Germany. According to Marx, the proletariat, without fostering any illusions about the liberal bourgeoisie, had to use this bourgeoisie's political struggle against the Prussian absolute monarchy and bureaucracy to further its own de-

MEW 4:200–203. *Collected Works* (see source note to selection 7), 6:231–34. Translated by Frida Knight.

mands and its own interests, and had to refuse any collusion with the monarchy and the Prussian government.

On 23 February 1865, Marx and Engels explicitly referred to Marx's article of 12 September 1847 to reject the policy of an alliance between the proletarian forces and Bismarck's government against the liberal bourgeoisie, a policy advocated and put into action in the early 1860s by Lassalle and his partisans (see MEW 16:79).

In the 1880s, Bismarck's political policy of social protection, the "socialism of the flesh" and the "social protestantism" of Pastor Stöcker, and other "social Christian" currents would represent a more elaborate version of the politics advocated since 1847 by the "Consistorial Counsellor" criticized by Marx.

• • •

. . . The social principles of Christianity have now had eighteen hundred years to be developed, and need no further developments by Prussian Consistorial Counsellors.

The social principles of Christianity justified the slavery of antiquity, glorified the serfdom of the Middle Ages and are capable, in case of need, of defending the oppression of the proletariat, even if with somewhat doleful grimaces.

The social principles of Christianity preach the necessity of a ruling and an oppressed class, and for the latter all they have to offer is the pious wish that the former may be charitable.

The social principles of Christianity place the Consistorial Counsellor's compensation for all infamies in heaven, and thereby justify the continuation of these infamies on earth.

The social principles of Christianity declare all the vile acts of the oppressors against the oppressed to be either a just punishment for original sin and other sins, or trials which the Lord, in his infinite wisdom, ordains for the redeemed.

The social principles of Christianity preach cowardice, self-contempt, abasement, submissiveness and humbleness, in short, all the qualities of the rabble, and the proletariat, which will not permit itself to be treated as rabble, needs its courage, its self-confidence, its pride and its sense of independence even more than its bread.

The social principles of Christianity are sneaking and hypocritical, and the proletariat is revolutionary.

So much for the social principles of Christianity.

Further:

> We have acknowledged social reform to be the most distin-
> guished vocation of the monarchy.

Have we? There has not been a single word of this hitherto.
However, let it stand. And what does the social reform of the monarchy consist in? In promulgating an Income Tax stolen from the liberal
press, which is to provide surpluses the Minister of Finance knows
nothing about, in the abortive Land Annuity Banks, in the Prussian
Eastern Railway, and in particular in the profits from a vast capital of
original sin and redemption!

"The interests of the monarchy itself makes this advisable"—
how low, then, the monarchy must have sunk!

"The distress in society demands this"—for the moment it demands protective tariffs far more than dogmas.

"The gospel recommends this"—this is recommended by everything in general, only not by the terrifyingly barren condition of the
Prussian State treasury, this abyss, which, within three years, will ir-
revocably have swallowed up the 15 Russian millions. The gospel recommends a great deal besides, among other things also castration as
the beginning of social reform with oneself (Matth[ew] 19:12).

> The monarchy [declares our Consistorial Counsellor] is
> one with the people.

This pronouncement is only another form of the old "*l'état c'est
moi*"; and precisely the same form, in fact, as was used by Louis XVI
against his rebellious estates on June 23, 1789: "If you do not obey,
then I shall send you back home"—"*et seul je ferai le bonheur de mon
peuple.*"

The monarchy must indeed be very hard-pressed if it decides to
make use of this formula, and our learned Consistorial Counsellor
certainly knows how the French people thanked Louis XVI for its use
on that occasion.

> The throne [the Herr Consistorial Counsellor assures us
> further] must rest on the broad foundation of the people, there
> it stands best.

So long, that is, as those broad shoulders do not, with one powerful heave, throw this burdensome superstructure into the gutter.

> The *aristocracy* [thus concludes the Herr Consistorial Counsellor] leaves the monarchy its dignity and gives it a poetical adornment, but removes real power from it. The *bourgeoisie* robs it of both its power and its dignity, and only gives it a civil list. The *people* preserves to the monarchy its power, its dignity and its poetry.

In this passage the Herr Consistorial Counsellor has unfortunately taken the boastful appeal *To His People,* made by Frederick William in his Speech from the Throne,[1] too seriously. Its last word is—overthrow of the aristocracy, overthrow of the bourgeoisie, creation of a monarchy drawing its support from the people.

If these demands were not pure fantasies they would contain in themselves a complete revolution.

We have not the slightest wish to argue in detail that the aristocracy cannot be overthrown in any other manner than by the bourgeoisie and the people together, that rule of the people in a country where the aristocracy and the bourgeoisie still exist side by side is a piece of sheer nonsense. One cannot reply to such yarn-spinnings from one of Eichhorn's Consistorial Counsellors with any serious developments of ideas.

We merely wish to make some well-intentioned comments to those gentlemen who would like to rescue the apprehensive Prussian monarchy by means of a somersault into the people.

Of all political elements the people is by far the most dangerous for a king. Not the people of which Frederick William speaks, which offers thanks with moist eyes for a kick and a silver penny; this people is completely harmless, for it only exists in the king's imagination. But the real people, the proletarians, the small peasants and the plebs—this is, as Hobbes says, *puer robustus, sed malitiosus,* a robust, but ill-natured youth, which permits no kings, be they lean or fat, to get the better of him.

This people would above all else extort from His Majesty a constitution, together with a universal franchise, freedom of association, freedom of the press and other unpleasant things.

And if it had all this, it would use it to pronounce as rapidly as possible on the *power,* the *dignity* and the *poetry* of the monarchy.

The current worthy occupant of this monarchy could count himself fortunate if the people employed him as a public barker of the Berlin Artisans' Association with a civil list of 250 talers and a cool pale ale daily.

If the Consistorial gentlemen now directing the destiny of the Prussian monarchy and the *Rhein[ische] Beobachter* should doubt this, then let them merely cast a glance at history. History provides quite different horoscopes for kings who appealed to their people.

Charles I of England also appealed *to His People* against his estates. He called his people to arms against parliament. The people, however, declared itself to be against the king, threw all the members who did not represent the people out of parliament and finally caused parliament, which had thus become the real representative of the people, to behead the king. Thus ended the appeal of Charles I to his people. This occurred on January 30, 1649, and has its bicentenary in the year 1849.

Louis XVI of France likewise appealed *to His People*. Three years long he appealed from one section of the people to another, he sought *His* people, the true people, the people filled with enthusiasm for him, and found it nowhere. Finally he found it in the encampment of Koblenz, behind the ranks of the Prussian and Austrian army. This, however, was too much of a good thing for his people in France. On August 10, 1792, it locked up the appellant in the Temple and summoned the National Convention, which represented it in every respect.

This Convention declared itself competent to judge the *appeal* of the ex-king, and after some consultation the appellant was taken to the Place de la Révolution, where he was guillotined on January 21, 1793.

That is what happens when kings *appeal to Their People*. Just what happens, however, when Consistorial Counsellors wish to found a democratic monarchy, we shall have to wait and see.

NOTE

1. Frederick William IV, the King of Prussia, had declared on 11 April 1847, at the opening of the United Diet of Prussia—a meeting of the eight provincial Diets of Prussia—that he would never allow the "natural" link between him and his people be transformed into a juridical and constitutional relation: an affirmation of the romantic theory of the organic unity between the king (or the king and queen) and the people considered as a living totality, independent from the individual and political rights codified in the French manner (see, for example, Novalis's *Glauben und Liebe, oder der König und die Königin* published in 1797 when Frederick William III and his wife, Queen Louise, ascended the throne.

13

Moralizing Criticism and Critical Morality: A Contribution to German Cultural History—contra Karl Heinzen

This long article of Marx's appeared in the *Deutsche Brüsseler Zeitung* 28–30 October, and 11, 18, and 25 November, 1847. It is an addition to the long critique of Heinzen developed by Engels in the same journal at the beginning of October 1847 ("Die Kommunisten und Karl Heinzen" MEW 5:309–24). Heinzen himself had also published articles on the communists, and on Engels in particular, in the same Brussels journal. This very active republican journalist, who was hostile to the Prussian state and its bureaucracy, favored the idea of a German republic of a federal type, like the numerous other German "Radicals" of the 1840s. Although he did indeed frequent the young Hegelians and the partisans of "true" socialism, he was hostile to these intellectual refinements of Hegelianism and considered the struggle of the "communists" to be an obstacle to the fundamental battle: the fight of the republicans and democrats against the aristocracy, the absolute monarchy, and the bureaucracy.

Heinzen's many articles and leaflets have been collected in several books, in particular, *Mehr als zwanzig Bogen* (Darmstadt, 1845—books of no more than twenty pages were not subject to censorship under the German Confederation); *Die Preussische Büreaukratie* (Darmstadt, 1845), and *Deutsche Revolution* (Bern, 1847).

Marx basically reproached Heinzen for the primitive, simplistic, and nondialectic character of his political positions; he took him particularly to task for having opposed simple common sense to Hegelian philosophy and the republican struggle to the analysis of social and political opposition between the liberal bourgeoisie and the proletariat. One might say that Marx reproached Heinzen for succumbing to the Jacobin illusion of a republican battle uniting the proletariat and the bourgeoisie beyond the confrontation between social classes.

MEW 4:38–42, 345–46. *Collected Works,* 6:319–23, 326. Translated by Christopher Upward.

   This selection complements the preceding one (12): the rejection of collusion with the Prussian monarchy should not lead to a
lack of awareness about the irreducible opposition between the bourgeoisie (even the liberal bourgeoisie) and the proletariat. But what
has happened to the "people," the "real people, the proletarians,
the small peasants and the plebs" about whom Marx spoke in his
12 September 1847 article "The Communism of the Rheinischer
Beobachter"? There indeed lay the problem of the failure of the German revolution of 1848 and, moreover, of any autonomous
proletarian strategy: this is the problem that the *Manifesto of the
Communist Party* would pose and attempt to solve.

· · ·

   . . . Incidentally, if the bourgeoisie is politically, that is, by its state
power, "maintaining injustice in property relations," it is not *creating*
it. The "injustice in property relations" which is determined by the
modern division of labour, the modern form of exchange, competition, concentration, etc., by no means arises from the political rule of
the bourgeois class, but vice versa, the political rule of the bourgeois
class arises from these modern relations of production which bourgeois economists proclaim to be necessary and eternal laws. If therefore the proletariat overthrows the political rule of the bourgeoisie, its
victory will only be temporary, only an element in the service of the
bourgeois revolution itself, as in the year 1794, as long as in the course of
history, in its "movement," the material conditions have not yet been
created which make necessary the abolition of the bourgeois mode of
production and therefore also the definitive overthrow of the political
rule of the bourgeoisie. The terror in France could thus by its mighty
hammer-blows only serve to spirit away, as it were, the ruins of feudalism from French soil. The timidly considerate bourgeoisie would
not have accomplished this task in decades. The bloody action of the
people thus only prepared the way for it. In the same way, the overthrow of the absolute monarchy would be merely temporary if the
economic conditions for the rule of the bourgeois class had not yet
become ripe. Men build a new world for themselves, not from the
"treasures of this earth," as grobian superstition imagines, but from
the historical achievements of their declining world. In the course of
their development they first have to *produce* the *material conditions* of a
new society itself, and no exertion of mind or will can free them from
this fate.
   It is characteristic of the whole *grobianism* of "sound common

sense," which feeds upon the "fulness of life" and does not stunt its *natural* faculties with any philosophical or other studies, that where it succeeds in seeing *differences,* it does not see *unity,* and that where it sees *unity,* it does not see *differences.* If it propounds *differentiated determinants,* they at once become fossilised in its hands, and it can see only the most reprehensible sophistry when these wooden concepts are knocked together so that they take fire.

When Herr Heinzen, for instance, says that *money* and *power, property* and *rule,* the *acquisition of money* and the *acquisition of power* are not *the same,* he is committing a *tautology* inherent in the mere words themselves, and this merely verbal differentiation he considers an heroic deed which with all the faculties of a *clairvoyant* he brings into play against the Communists, who are so "blind" as not to stop in their tracks at this childlike first perception.

How "acquisition of money" turns into "acquisition of power," how "property" turns into "political rule," in other words, how instead of the rigid difference to which Herr Heinzen gives the force of *dogma,* there are rather effective relations between the two forces up to the point where they merge, of this he may swiftly convince himself by observing how the serfs *bought* their freedom, how the communes *bought* the municipal rights, how the townspeople on the one hand, by trade and industry, attracted the money out of the pockets of the feudal lords and vaporised their landed property into bills of exchange, and on the other hand helped the absolute monarchy to its victory over the thus undermined feudal magnates, and *bought* privileges from it; how they later themselves exploited the financial crises of the absolute monarchy itself, etc., etc.; how the most absolute monarchies become dependent on the stock-exchange barons through the system of state debts—a product of modern industry and modern trade; how in international relations between peoples, industrial monopoly turns directly into political rule, as for instance, the Princes of the Holy Alliance in the "German war of liberation" were merely the hired mercenaries of England, etc., etc. . . .

The *political* relationships of men are of course also *social, societal* relationships, like all relations between men and men. All questions that concern the relations of men with each other are therefore also social questions.

With this view, which belongs in a catechism for eight-year-old children, this grobian naivety believes it has not only said something but has affected the balance in the conflicts of modern times.

It so happens that the "social questions" which have been "dealt with in *our own* day" increase in importance in proportion as we leave behind us the realm of absolute monarchy. Socialism and communism did not emanate from Germany but from England, France and North America.

The first manifestation of a truly active communist party is contained within the bourgeois revolution, at the moment when the constitutional monarchy is eliminated. The most consistent *republicans,* in England the *Levellers,* in France *Babeuf, Buonarroti,* etc., were the first to proclaim these "social questions." *The Babeuf Conspiracy,* by Babeuf's friend and party-comrade Buonarroti, shows how these republicans derived from the "movement" of history the realisation that the disposal of the social question of *rule by princes* and *republic* did not mean that even a single "social question" has been solved in the interests of the proletariat.

The *question of property* as it has been raised in "*our own* day" is quite unrecognisable even formulated as a question in the form Heinzen gives it: "whether it is *just* that one man should *possess* everything and another man nothing . . . , whether the individual *should be permitted* to possess anything at all" and similar simplistic questions of conscience and clichés about justice.

The question of property assumes different forms according to the different levels of development of industry in general and according to its particular level of development in the different countries.

For the *Galician* peasant, for instance, the question of property is reduced to the transformation of feudal landed property into small bourgeois landownership. For him it has the same meaning as it had for the *French* peasant before 1789; the *English* agricultural day labourer on the other hand has no relationship with the landowner at all. He merely has a relationship with the tenant farmer, in other words, with the industrial capitalist who is practising agriculture in factory fashion. This industrial capitalist in turn, who pays the landowner a rent, has on the other hand a direct relationship with the landowner. The abolition of landed property is thus the most important question of property as it exists for the English industrial bourgeoisie, and their struggle against the Corn Laws had no other significance. The abolition of capital on the other hand is the question of property as it affects the English agricultural day labourer just as much as the English factory worker.

In the English as well as the French revolution, the question of property presented itself in such a way that it was a matter of asserting free competition and of abolishing all feudal property relations, such

as landed estates, guilds, monopolies, etc., which had been transformed into fetters for the industry which had developed from the
16th to the 18th century.

In *"our own* day," finally, the significance of the question of
property consists in it being a matter of eliminating the conflicts
which have arisen from large-scale industry, the development of the
world market and free competition.

The question of property, depending on the different levels of
development of industry, has always been the vital question for a particular class. In the 17th and 18th centuries, when the point at issue
was the abolition of *feudal* property relations, the question of property was the vital question for the *bourgeois* class. In the 19th century,
when it is a matter of abolishing *bourgeois* property relations, the
question of property is a vital question for the *working class.*

The question of property, which in *"our own* day" is a question
of world-historical significance, has thus a meaning only in *modern
bourgeois society.* The more advanced this society is, in other words,
the further the bourgeoisie has developed economically in a country
and therefore the more state power has assumed a bourgeois character, the more glaringly does the *social* question obtrude itself, in
France more glaringly than in Germany, in England more glaringly
than in France, in a constitutional monarchy more glaringly than in
an absolute monarachy, in a republic more glaringly than in a constitutional monarchy. Thus, for example, the conflicts of the credit
system, speculation, etc., are nowhere more acute than in North
America. Nowhere, either, does *social* inequality obtrude itself more
harshly than in the eastern states of North America, because nowhere
is it less disguised by political inequality. If pauperism has not yet developed there as much as in England, this is explained by economic
circumstances which it is not our task to elucidate further here. . . .

Herr Heinzen sees the princes at the peak of the social structure
in Germany. He does not for a moment doubt that they have created
its social foundation and are re-*creating* it each day. What *simpler* explanation could there be for the connection between the monarchy
and social conditions, whose *official* political expression it is, than by
having the princes *create* this connection! What is the connection between the representative assemblies and modern bourgeois society
which they represent? They *created* it. The political deity with its ap-
paratus and gradations has thus *created* the secular world, whose most
sacred object it is. In the same way the *religious* deity will have created
earthly conditions, which are fantastically and in deified form reflected in it.

The grobianism which retails such homespun wisdom with appropriate sentiment cannot of course fail to be equally astonished and morally outraged at the opponent who toils to demonstrate to it that the apple did not create the apple-tree.

Modern histories have demonstrated that *absolute monarchy* appears in those transitional periods when the old feudal estates are in decline and the medieval estate of burghers is evolving into the modern bourgeois class, without one of the contending parties having as yet finally disposed of the other. The elements on which absolute monarchy is based are thus by no means its own product; they rather form its social prerequisite, whose historical origins are too well known to be repeated here. The fact that absolute monarchy took shape later in Germany and is persisting longer, is explained solely by the stunted pattern of development of the German bourgeois class. The answers to the puzzles presented by this pattern of development are to be found in the history of trade and industry. . . .

14

Manifesto of the Communist Party

The first Party Congress of the Communist League, successor to the League of the Just, took place in London in June 1847; in August, Marx had been elected president of the Brussels section of the league. At the end of November 1847, the league's Second Congress, in London, charged Marx and Engels with drafting the organization's "manifesto." Engels later insisted that Marx was the real author of the *Manifesto* (see the preface to the German 1883 edition of MEW 4:577); the literary form of the text is obviously due to Marx. The text was drafted essentially in January 1848 and appeared in London, in German, in late February.

One of the essential political questions debated by Marx since 1843–44 was the relationship between political revolution (bourgeois" or "bourgeois democratic") and social revolution ("proletarian"); this remained one of the principal questions of the *Manifesto*. The French Revolution appears relatively little, in an explicit fashion, in the text of the *Manifesto,* but when it does appear, it is always in connection with the relationship between political and social revolution.

In the passages that appear here, "socialist and communist literature" refers to the literature of "true" socialism. Marx and Engels were establishing a parallel between, on the one hand, relationship of the theoreticians of "true" socialism to French socialism and communism of the 1830s and 1840s and, on the other, the relationship of eighteenth-century German philosophers (Kant

MEW 4:474–75, 485–86, 489, 492–93. Karl Marx, *The Revolutions of 1848,* edited by David Fernbach (Pelican Marx Library, 1973; New York: Vintage Books, 1974). 80, 90–91, 94, 97–98. ©1973 by New Left Review. Reproduced by permission of Penguin Books, Ltd., and Random House, Inc. All further excerpts from this work are also reproduced by permission of these publishers. This translation was first published in 1888.

and perhaps Fichte also, to judge from the evidence) to the French Revolution. Was this a repetition of the "tragedy" as a "farce," at least insofar as German intellectuality was concerned? The question is reasonable, especially in light of the sarcasm Marx and Engels heaped earlier on the adherents of "true" socialism (see selections 9 and 10).

• • •

. . . The theoretical conclusions of the Communists are in no way based on ideas or principles that have been invented, or discovered, by this or that would-be universal reformer.

They merely express, in general terms, actual relations springing from an existing class struggle, from a historical movement going on under our very eyes. The abolition of existing property relations is not at all a distinctive feature of communism.

All property relations in the past have continually been subject to historical change consequent upon the change in historical conditions.

The French Revolution, for example, abolished feudal property in favour of bourgeois property.

The distinguishing feature of communism is not the abolition of property generally, but the abolition of bourgeois property. . . .

. . . The socialist and communist literature of France, a literature that originated under the pressure of a bourgeoisie in power, and that was the expression of the struggle against this power, was introduced into Germany at a time when the bourgeoisie, in that country, had just begun its contest with feudal absolutism.

German philosophers, would-be philosophers and *beaux esprits* eagerly seized on this literature, only forgetting that when these writings immigrated from France into Germany, French social conditions had not immigrated along with them. In contact with German social conditions, this French literature lost all its immediate practical significance, and assumed a purely literary aspect. It was bound to appear as idle speculation about the realization of the essence of man. Thus, to the German philosophers of the eighteenth century, the demands of the first French revolution were nothing more than the demands of "practical reason" in general, and the utterance of the will of the revolutionary French bourgeoisie signified in their eyes the laws of pure will, of will as it was bound to be, of true human will generally.

. . . We do not here refer to that literature which, in every great modern revolution, has always given voice to the demands of the proletariat, such as the writings of Babeuf and others.

The first direct attempts of the proletariat to attain its own ends, made in times of universal excitement, when feudal society was being overthrown, these attempts necessarily failed, owing to the then undeveloped state of the proletariat, as well as to the absence of the economic conditions for its emancipation, conditions that had yet to be produced, and could be produced by the impending bourgeois epoch alone. The revolutionary literature that accompanied these first movements of the proletariat had necessarily a reactionary character. It inculcated universal asceticism and social levelling in its crudest form. . . .

In Poland they support the part that insists on an agrarian revolution as the prime condition for national emancipation, that party which fomented the insurrection of Cracow in 1846.

In Germany they fight with the bourgeoisie whenever it acts in a revolutionary way, against the absolute monarchy, the feudal squirearchy, and the petty bourgeoisie.

But they never cease, for a single instant, to instil into the working class the clearest possible recognition of the hostile antagonism between bourgeoisie and proletariat, in order that the German workers may straightway use, as so many weapons against the bourgeoisie, the social and political conditions that the bourgeoisie must necessarily introduce along with its supremacy, and in order that, after the fall of the reactionary classes in Germany, the fight against the bourgeoisie itself may immediately begin.

The Communists turn their attention chiefly to Germany, because the country is on the eve of a bourgeois revolution that is bound to be carried out under more advanced conditions of European civilization, and with a much more developed proletariat, than that of England was in the seventeenth, and of France in the eighteenth century, and because the bourgeois revolution in Germany will be but the prelude to an immediately following proletarian revolution.

In short, the Communists everywhere support every revolutionary movement against the existing social and political order of things.

In all these movements they bring to the front, as the leading question in each, the property question, no matter what its degree of development at the time. . . .

15

Speech on the Second Anniversary of the Polish Revolution of 22 February 1846

The second anniversary of the 1846 Polish revolution was celebrated in Brussels with speeches by A. J. Senault, Marx, Lelewel, Engels, and Louis Lubliner (a lawyer). Marx's speech appears on pages 10–14 of the thirty-two-page brochure containing the speeches, which was published by C. G. Vogler (Brussels, 1848).

The 1815 Congress of Vienna, after the Napoleonic period, divided the Polish territories between Prussia, Austria, and Russia; the first received the western territories (essentially Posen), the second the southern territories (Galicia), and the third, the most extensive territories in the center and to the east, called the Kingdom of Poland or the Poland of the Vienna Congress. Thus the focus returned to the politics of division at the end of the eighteenth century (1772, 1793, and 1795) among the three powers.

The failure of the national uprising of 1830–31 in the Russian zone had as its consequence, in all three zones, a mounting of anti-nationalist repression and of Germanization (or Russification) of instruction and administration. The Polish nationalists of the three zones had a great deal of difficulty unifying their efforts; what is more, they were divided into opposing factions, the liberals and democrats, bourgeois and intellectuals, stressing the liberation of the peasants, which the aristocrats opposed. These divisions were, moreover, in part responsible for the failure of the movement of 1830–31.

Since 1815, the little republic of Cracow had been the only independent fragment of Poland. It was the principal seat of nationalist propaganda in the three zones, but especially in Galicia. On the night of 21–22 February 1846, a national government established in Cracow proclaimed a national insurrection and the abolition of peas-

Karl Marx and Friedrich Engels, *Gesamtausgabe* (complete works) (East Berlin: Dietz, 1956–), 1:5(1932):409–11. *The Revolutions of 1848* (see source note to selection 14), 102–5. Translated by Paul Jackson.

ant corvée. The Galician peasant masses remained at a distance from the movement; but the Ruthenian peasants of the region—different from the Polish peasants in their orthodox religion—attacked the châteaus of the Polish landowners and supported the Austrian troops who had come to crush the revolutionary movement.

In November 1846, with the authorization of Russia and Prussia, Austria annexed the Republic of Cracow. The Viennese government thanked the Galician peasants for their "patriotism" and then sent troops to compel them to submit once more to corvée.

• • •

Gentlemen,

There are some striking analogies in history. The Jacobin of 1793 has become the communist of our own day. In 1793, when Russia, Austria and Prussia divided Poland, the three powers justified themselves by citing the constitution of 1791, which was condemned by general agreement on the grounds of its reputedly Jacobin principles.

And what had the Polish constitution of 1791 proclaimed? No more and no less than constitutional monarchy: legislation to be placed in the hands of the country's representatives, freedom of the press, freedom of conscience, judicial hearings to be made public, serfdom to be abolished, etc. And all this was at that time simply called Jacobinism! So, gentlemen, you see how history has progressed. The Jacobinism of that time has today become, in the form of liberalism, all that is most moderate.

The three powers have moved with the times. In 1846, when they took away the last vestiges of Polish nationality by incorporating Cracow into Austria, they referred to what they used to call Jacobinism as communism.

But what was communist about the Cracow revolution? Was it communist to want to re-establish Polish nationality? One might equally say that the war of the European Coalition against Napoleon to save the various nationalities was a communist war, and that the Congress of Vienna was made up of communists with crowned heads. Or was the Cracow revolution communist for wanting to set up a democratic government? No one would accuse the millionaires of Berne or New York of communist tendencies.

Communism denies the need for classes to exist: it wants to get rid of all classes and all class distinctions. But the Cracow revolutionaries merely wanted to get rid of *political* distinctions between the classes; they wanted to give all classes equal rights.

Just what then was communist about that Cracow revolution?

Was it possibly that it was trying to break the chains of the feudal system, to liberate land subject to tribute and transform it into free, modern property?

If one were to say to French landowners: "Do you realize what the Polish democrats want? They want to bring into their country the form of ownership already existing in your country," then the French landowners would answer: "They are doing the right thing." But say, like M. Guizot, to the French landowners: "The Poles want to get rid of landownership as established by you in the 1789 revolution, and as it still exists in your country," 'Good God!' they would cry, "then they are revolutionaries, communists! These evil men must be crushed." The abolition of guild wardens and corporations, and the introduction of free competition, is now in Sweden called communism. The *Journal des Débats* goes further: abolishing the income which the two hundred thousand electors' right of corruption brings in—that means abolishing a source of revenue, destroying an existing property, communism. Certainly the Cracow revolution also wanted to abolish a form of property. But what kind of property? A kind which can no more be destroyed anywhere else in Europe, than can the Sonderbund[1] in Switzerland, because it simply does not exist any more.

No one will deny that in Poland the political question is linked with a social question. The one is always inseparable from the other.

You can ask the reactionaries about that! Under the Restoration, were they only struggling against political liberalism and its necessary corollary, Voltaireanism? One respected reactionary writer freely admitted that the highest metaphysic of a de Maistre and a de Bonald came down ultimately to a question of money, and is not every question of money a social question? The men of the Restoration did not hide the fact that to return to sound politics, they had to bring back sound property, feudal property, moral property. Everyone knows that faithful royalism cannot manage without tithes and *corvée*.

Let us go back further: in 1789 the political question of human rights concealed the social question of free competition.

And what is happening in England? In all matters from the Reform Bill to the repeal of the Corn Laws, have the political parties fought for anything but changes of property, questions of property—social questions?

Here, in Belgium itself, is the battle between liberalism and Catholicism anything other than a battle between industrial capital and the large landowners?

And all the political questions that have been debated for the past seventeen years—are they not all at bottom social questions?

So whatever point of view you may adopt, whether it be liberal, radical or even aristocratic, you can hardly still dare to blame the Cracow revolution for having attached a social question to a political one.

The men who led the revolutionary movement in Cracow were absolutely convinced that only a democratic Poland could be free, and that there could be no democratic Poland without the abolition of all feudal rights, and without an agrarian movement which would transform the peasants from landowners forced to pay tribute into free, modern landowners.

If the Russian autocrat were to be replaced by Polish aristocrats, then despotism would merely have taken out naturalization papers. Thus the Germans, in their battle against the foreigner, exchanged one Napoleon for thirty-six Metternichs. Though the Polish lord would no longer have a Russian lord over him, the Polish peasant would still have a lord over him—only a lord who was free rather than one who was a slave. This particular political change involves no social change at all.

The Cracow revolution has given all of Europe a magnificent example by identifying the cause of nationhood with the cause of democracy and the liberation of the oppressed class.

Though that revolution has for the time been stifled by the bloodstained hands of paid assassins, it is rising again in glory and triumph in Switzerland and Italy. It is finding its principles confirmed in Ireland, where the purely nationalist party has gone to the grave with O'Connell, and the new national party is above all reforming and democratic.

It is still Poland that has taken the initiative—not the feudal Poland of the past, but democratic Poland—and from now on its liberation has become a point of honour for all the democrats in Europe.

NOTE

1. The civil war of the *Sonderbund* (separatist league) in Switzerland, brought a minority of Catholic, conservative cantons into conflict with the radical, laicized cantons, which were in the majority. The former were very quickly defeated.

16

The Bill for the Abolition of Feudal Burdens

This article of Marx's appeared in the 30 July 1848 edition of the *Neue Rheinische Zeitung*.

At the beginning of March 1848, Marx, expelled from Belgium, was invited to return to France by the provisional government of the Republic. In a leaflet drafted at the end of March, distributed in Paris and then reproduced in various German newspapers and entitled *Forderungen der kommunistischen Partei in Deutschland* (*Demands of the Communist Party in Germany*), Marx and Engels pronounced themselves in favor of the creation of a "one and indivisible" German republic (see MEW 5:3). In April, Marx left Paris for Cologne with Engels and several other members of the Communist League. At Cologne, the capital of the Prussian Rhineland, Marx and Engels actively engaged in the creation and then the editing and distribution of a democratic and revolutionary daily, the *Neue Rheinische Zeitung,* which was subtitled "organ for democracy." The journal appeared from 1 June 1848 to 19 May 1849, under Marx's direction.

The German revolution of March 1848 represented for Marx the possibility that a proletarian revolution could follow a successful bourgeois revolution, a hypothesis he had envisaged in his texts of 1847 and in the *Manifesto*. The *Neue Rheinische Zeitung* furthermore addressed not only the proletarian forces influenced by the Communist League, but also the collection of popular and democratic forces and even the liberal bourgeoisie: the social revolution was, in effect, conditional upon the preliminary success of the political revolution. The divisions that appeared immediately (from summer of 1848) between the working class (or popular) forces and the bourgeois forces, and the dynastic and aristocratic counteroffensive—including a military one—in Vienna and Berlin, caused the revolution to fail. From summer 1848 on, Marx deplored the reconciliation between the bourgeoisie and the existent dynasties against the popular move-

MEW 5:278, 282–83. *The Revolutions of 1848* (see source note to selection 14), 137–38, 142–43. Translated by Paul Jackson.

ment: the political weakness of the German bourgeoisie—which he had diagnosed in the early 1840s—brought on, according to him, the resurgence of the revolutionary movement.

Marx devoted many articles to this "treason" by the German bourgeoisie, who allied themselves with the aristocracy and the dynasties and abandoned their "natural" allies—the working class and the peasant masses. This was the case in an article published in the 3 July issue, in which Marx emphasized the political split between the Rhineland, where a part of the revolutionary and Napoleonic inspiration remained in force after 1815 (in particular the abolition of the feudal burdens and the Civil Code), and the rest of Prussia, still subject to laws of a "feudal" type.

• • •

Cologne, 29 July

If any Rhinelander has forgotten what he owes to "foreign domination" and the "oppression of the Corsican tyrant," he should read the bill for the abolition of various burdens and dues without compensation which Herr Hansemann,[1] in the year of grace 1848, has allowed the *Vereinbarungsversammlung*[2] to see "for clarification." Fealty, enfranchisement-money, relief, heriot, protection-money, jurisdiction-tax, village court tax, wardship, sealing-money, cattle-tithe, bee-tithe, etc.—how strange, how barbaric, is the sound of these preposterous names to our ears which have been civilized by the Code Napoléon, by the French Revolution's destruction of feudal survivals! How incomprehensible to us is this whole jumble of semi-medieval services and dues, this natural history museum of the mouldiest plunder of antediluvian times!

But take off your shoes, German patriot, for you are standing on hallowed ground! These barbarisms are the remnants of the glory of Germanic Christendom, they are the final links of a chain which weaves its way through history and unites you with the majesty of your forefathers, right back to the Cheruskans in their woods. This stink of putrefaction, this feudal slime, found here in its classical purity, is the most genuine product of our fatherland, and he who is a true German must exclaim, with the poet:

> This is truly my native air!
> It touched my cheeks, and they glowed!
> And this is the muck of my fatherland:
> This mud of the country road![3]

THE BILL FOR THE ABOLITION OF FEUDAL BURDENS

. . . Of course the minister is attacking property—that is undeniable—but it is feudal, not modern bourgeois property he is attacking. Bourgeois property, which raises itself on the ruins of feudal property, is *strengthened* by this attack on feudal property. The only reason for Herr Gierke's[4] refusal to revise the redemption contracts is that those contracts have changed feudal property relations into *bourgeois* property relations, and that he cannot therefore revise them without at the same time formally injuring bourgeois property. And bourgeois property is naturally just as holy and untouchable as feudal property is assailable, and, depending on the level of the minister's need and courage, actually assailed.

What, then, is the short meaning of this long law?

It is the most conclusive proof that the German revolution of 1848 is only a parody of the French revolution of 1789.

The French people finished with the feudal burdens in *one day,* the fourth of August 1789, three weeks after the storming of the Bastille.

On 11 July 1848, four months after the March barricades, the feudal burdens finished with the German people, as testified by Gierke and Hansemann.

The French bourgeoisie of 1789 did not leave its allies the peasants in the lurch for one moment. It knew that the basis of its rule was the destruction of feudalism on the land and the establishment of a class of free peasant landowners.

The German bourgeoisie of 1848 does not hesitate to betray the peasants who are its *natural allies,* its own flesh and blood, and without the peasants this bourgeoisie is powerless against the nobility.

The continued existence of feudal rights, their sanctioning in the form of their (illusory) abolition, that then is the result of the German revolution of 1848. The mountain moved and lo!—a mouse emerged.

NOTES

1. David Justus Hansemann (1790–1864), industrialist, was one of the leaders of the liberal Rhineland's bourgeoisie. He was a representative in the Prussian National Assembly, and Prussian minister of finance from March to September 1848.

2. Marx is here referring to the theory of *Vereinbarung* (agreement), developed by the moderate liberal ministry that formed in Prussia around Camphausen and Hansemann at the end of 1848: a negation of the principle of popular sovereignty and thus of a Prussian Constituant Assembly, an

affirmation of the sovereignty of the monarch, it betokened an "agreement" between the liberal bourgeoisie and the King of Prussia against the revolutionary movement of 1848.

3. From Heinrich Heine, *Deutschland: Ein Wintermärchen,* chapter 8.

4. Gierke was a liberal representative at the Prussian National Assembly, and Prussian minister of agriculture from March to September 1848.

17

The Bourgeoisie and the Counterrevolution

This article of Marx's appeared in the *Neue Rheinische Zeitung* (see selection 16 for information concerning this newspaper) of 10–31 December 1848. Marx took stock of the sad political comportment of the German bourgeoisie, especially the Prussian bourgeoisie, since March 1848: they had abandoned their working-class allies and capitulated—once their interests were safe—to the dynasties and the aristocracy. This long article concludes with the following words: "The history of the Prussian bourgeoisie demonstrates, as indeed does that of the whole German bourgeoisie from March to December, that a purely *bourgeois revolution,* along with the establishment of *bourgeois hegemony* in the form of a *constitutional monarchy,* is impossible in Germany. What *is* possible is either feudal and absolutist counterrevolution or *social-republican revolution.*"

• • •

. . . The Prussian March revolution must not be confused either with the English revolution of 1648 or with the French revolution of 1789.

In 1648 the bourgeoisie was in alliance with the modern nobility against the monarchy, the feudal nobility and the established church.

In 1789 the bourgeoisie was in alliance with the people against the monarchy, the nobility and the established church.

The revolution of 1789 was (at least in Europe) only prefigured by the revolution of 1648, which in turn was only prefigured by the rising of the Netherlands against Spain. Both revolutions were approximately a century in advance of their predecessors, not only in time but also in content.

In both revolutions, the bourgeoisie was the class which was

MEW 6:107–9. *The Revolutions of 1848* (see source note to selection 14), 192–94. Translated by Paul Jackson.

genuinely to be found at the head of the movement. The proletariat, and the other sections of the town population which did not form a part of the bourgeoisie, either had as yet no interests separate from those of the bourgeoisie, or they did not yet form independently developed classes or groups within classes. Therefore, where they stood in opposition to the bourgeoisie, as for example in 1793 and 1794 in France, they were in fact fighting for the implementation of the interests of the bourgeoisie, although not *in the manner* of the bourgeoisie. The *whole of the French terror* was nothing other than a *plebeian manner* of dealing with the *enemies of the bourgeoisie,* with absolutism, feudalism and parochialism.

The revolutions of 1648 and 1789 were not *English* and *French* revolutions; they were revolutions of a *European* pattern. They were not the victory of a *particular* class of society over the *old political order;* they were the *proclamation of the political order for the new European society.* In these revolutions the bourgeoisie gained the victory; but the *victory of the bourgeoisie* was at that time the *victory of a new social order,* the victory of bourgeois property over feudal property, of nationality over provincialism, of competition over the guild, of the partition of estates over primogeniture, of the owner's mastery of the land over the land's mastery of its owner, of enlightenment over superstition, of the family over the family name, of industry over heroic laziness, of civil law over privileges of medieval origin. The revolution of 1648 was the victory of the seventeenth century over the sixteenth century, the revolution of 1789 was the victory of the eighteenth century over the seventeenth century. Still more than expressing the needs of the parts of the world in which they took place, England and France, these revolutions expressed the needs of the whole world, as it existed then.

Nothing of this is to be found in the *Prussian March revolution.*

The February revolution had *done away with* the constitutional monarchy in reality and the rule of the bourgeoisie in the mind. The purpose of the Prussian March revolution was to *establish* the constitutional monarchy in the mind and the rule of the bourgeoisie in reality. Far from being a *European revolution* it was merely the stunted echo, in a backward country, of a European revolution. Instead of being in advance of its own age it was behind it by more than half a century. It was *secondary* from the very beginning, but, as is well known, secondary diseases are more difficult to cure, and, at the same time, ravage the body more, than original ones. Here it was not a matter of setting up a new social order, but of the rebirth in Berlin of the society which had expired in Paris. The Prussian March revolution was not even *national* and *German;* it was from its inception *pro-*

vincial and *Prussian.* All kinds of provincial uprisings—e.g. those in Vienna, Kassel and Munich—swept along beside it and contested its position as the main German revolution.

Whereas 1648 and 1789 had the infinite self-confidence that springs from standing at the summit of creativity, it was Berlin's ambition in 1848 to form an anachronism. Its light was like the light of those stars which first reaches the earth when the bodies which radiated it have been extinct for a hundred thousand years. The Prussian March revolution was such a star for Europe—only on a small scale, just as it was everything on a small scale. Its light was light from the corpse of a society long since putrefied.

The German bourgeoisie had developed so sluggishly, so pusillanimously and so slowly, that it saw itself threateningly confronted by the proletariat, and all those sections of the urban population related to the proletariat in interests and ideas, at the very moment of its own threatening confrontation with feudalism and absolutism. And as well as having this class *behind* it, it saw *in front of* it the enmity of all Europe. The Prussian bourgeoisie was not, like the French bourgeoisie of 1789, the class which represented the *whole* of modern society in face of the representatives of the old society, the monarchy and the nobility. It had sunk to the level of a type of *estate,* as clearly marked off from the people as from the Crown, happy to oppose either, irresolute against each of its opponents, taken individually, because it always saw the other one in front of it or to the rear; inclined from the outset to treachery against the people and compromise with the crowned representative of the old society, because it itself already belonged to the old society; representing not the interests of a new society against an old but the renewal of its own interests within an obsolete society; at the steering-wheel of the revolution, not because the people stood behind it but because the people pushed it forward; at the head of the movement, not because it represented the initiative of a new social epoch, but only because it represented the malice of an old; a stratum of the old state which had not been able to break through to the earth's surface but had been thrown up by an earthquake; without faith in itself, without faith in the people, grumbling at those above, trembling before those below, egoistic in both directions and conscious of its egoism, revolutionary in relation to the conservatives and conservative in relation to the revolutionaries, mistrustful of its own slogans, which were phrases instead of ideas, intimidated by the storm of world revolution yet exploiting it; with no energy in any respect, plagiaristic in all respects; common because it lacked originality, original in its commonness; making a bargaining-counter of its own wishes, without initiative, without faith in itself, without faith in the people, without a world-historical function; an accursed old man, who found himself condemned to lead and mislead the first youthful impulses of a robust people in his own senile interests—sans teeth, sans eyes, sans taste, sans everything—this was the nature of the *Prussian bourgeoisie* which found itself at the helm of the Prussian state after the March revolution.

18

Review of François Guizot's *Pourquoi la révolution d'Angeleterre a-t-elle réussi? Discours sur l'histoire de la révolution d'Angleterre* (Paris, 1850)

In July and August 1849, Marx left Germany for Paris and, eventually, London. The failure of the German revolution had not discouraged him and he hypothesized a new revolutionary wave in Europe within a relatively short time. He and Engels, along with the members of the Communist League, the French Blanquists and the English Chartists, constituted an embryonic international proletarian revolutionary party: the Universal Society of Revolutionary Communists. In April 1850, Marx and Engels attended an international meeting commemorating Robespierre's birthday.

To succeed the *Neue Rheinische Zeitung* of 1848–49, Marx and Engels had created a new periodical, the *Neue Rheinische Zeitung: Politisch-ökonomische Revue,* the first issue of which appeared in Hamburg at the end of January 1850. Later issues included important writings by Engels and Marx—in particular, Engels's "The Constitutional Campaign in Germany" and "The Peasant War," and Marx's "The Class Struggles in France 1848–1850."

The review of Guizot's book appeared in the second issue, dated February 1850.

• • •

. . . M. Guizot ascribes the fact that the English revolution fared better than the French to two particular causes: the first is that the English revolution had a distinctly religious character and thus by no means broke with all the traditions of the past; the second is that from its inception it operated not as a destructive but as a conservative

MEW 7:208–11. Karl Marx, *Surveys from Exile,* edited by David Fernbach (Pelican Marx Library, 1974; New York: Vintage Books, 1974) 252–254. ©1973 by New Left Review. Reproduced by permission of Penguin Books, Ltd., and Random House, Inc. All further excerpts from this work are also reproduced by permission of these publishers. Translated by Paul Jackson.

force, in that Parliament was defending old existing laws against the encroachments of the Crown.

As far as the first point is concerned, M. Guizot forgets that free thought, which causes his flesh to creep so badly in connection with the French revolution, was exported to France from England, no less. Locke had been its father and in Shaftesbury and Bolingbroke it had already assumed that intellectually acute form which was later developed so brilliantly in France. We thus come to the strange conclusion that this same free thought which, according to M. Guizot, caused the French revolution to come to grief, was one of the most important products of the religious revolution in England.

As for the second point, M. Guizot completely forgets that the French revolution began just as conservatively, if not more so, than the English revolution. Absolutism, particularly as it finally manifested itself in France, was also an innovation there, and the *parlements* rose up against this innovation in defence of the old laws, the *us et coutumes* of the old monarchy based on the estates. And whereas the first step taken by the French revolution was to revive the Estates General, which had lain dormant since Henri IV and Louis XIII, the English revolution does not reveal any evidence of the same classical conservatism. . . .

The great puzzle of the conservative character of the English revolution, which M. Guizot can solve only by attributing it to the superior intelligence of the English, is in fact explained by the lasting alliance of the bourgeoisie with the great landowners, an alliance which fundamentally distinguishes the English from the French revolution, the latter having destroyed large landed property by dividing it up into smallholdings. This class of large landowners allied with the bourgeoisie, which, it may be added, had already arisen under Henry VIII, was not, as were the French feudal landowners of 1789, in conflict with the vital interests of the bourgeoisie, but rather in complete harmony with them. Their estates were indeed not feudal but bourgeois property. . . .

19

The Class Struggles in France, 1848–1850

This text was published by Marx in the form of a series of articles in the *Neue Rheinische Zeitung: Politisch-ökonomische Revue* from January to October 1850. Engels did not publish it as a pamphlet until 1895. Marx, preoccupied with the question of a new revolutionary wave in Europe after the failure of the movements of 1848, wished to show that the French-style "bourgeois republic" was only an illusion that masked the decisive confrontations between the bourgeoisie, the petite bourgeoisie, and the proletariat. His proof often rested upon a comparison between the movements of 1848–49 and those of the 1790s, the former sometimes appearing to have been a parody or caricature of the latter. This is the case, in the following passages, apropos of the actions of the provisional government of 1848, the bloody confrontations of June 1848, and Louis Napoleon Bonaparte's election to the presidency of the republic on 10 December 1848.

• • •

. . . It remains to the credit of the Luxembourg Commission, this creation of the Paris workers, that it disclosed the secret of the revolution of the nineteenth century from a European platform: *the emancipation of the proletariat*. The *Moniteur* could not help blushing when it had officially to propagate the "wild ravings" which hitherto had lain buried in the apocryphal writings of the socialist and had only reached the ears of the bourgeoisie from time to time as remote legends, half-terrifying, half-ludicrous. Europe started up in surprise from its bourgeois doze. Thus, in the ideas of the proletarians, who confused the financial aristocracy with the bourgeoisie in general, in

MEW 7:21–22, 31–33, 45–46. *Surveys from Exile* (see source note to selection 18), 47–48, 58–61, 73–74. Translated by Paul Jackson.

the imagination of republican worthies, who even denied the existence of classes or who at most admitted them to be the result of the constitutional monarchy, in the hypocritical phrases of those bourgeois fractions which had been excluded from power up to now, the *rule of the bourgeoisie* was abolished with the establishment of the republic. At that time all the royalists turned into republicans and all the millionaires of Paris turned into workers. The phrase which corresponded to this imaginary abolition of class relations was *fraternité,* general fraternization and brotherhood. This pleasant abstraction from class antagonisms, this sentimental reconciliation of contradictory class interests, this fantastic transcendence of the class struggle, this *fraternité* was the actual slogan of the February revolution. The classes had been divided by a mere *misunderstanding* and Lamartine christened the Provisional Government of 24 February *"un gouvernement qui suspend* ce malentendu terrible qui existe entre les différentes classes." The Paris proletariat revelled in this magnanimous intoxication of brotherhood.

Having been forced to proclaim the republic the Provisional Government, for its part, did everything to make it acceptable to the bourgeoisie and to the provinces. The bloody terror of the first French republic was disavowed with the abolition of the death penalty for political crimes; the press was opened to all opinions; the army, the courts and administration remained, with few exceptions, in the hands of the old dignitaries; none of the great culprits of the July monarchy was called to account. The bourgeois republicans of the *National* enjoyed themselves exchanging monarchist names and customs for those of the First Republic. As far as they were concerned the Republic was only a new evening dress for the old bourgeois society. The young republic sought its chief virtue not in frightening others but rather in constantly taking fright itself, and in disarming resistance and ensuring its further existence by its own soft compliance and lack of resistance. It was loudly announced to the privileged classes at home and the despotic powers abroad that the republic was of a peaceable nature. Its motto was: Live and let live. In addition, shortly after the February revolution the Germans, Poles, Austrians, Hungarians, Italians—all peoples revolted in a manner corresponding to their own situations. Russia and England—the former intimidated, the latter itself agitated—were unprepared. The republic, therefore, was not confronted by a *national* enemy. Consequently there were no great foreign complications to kindle energy, to accelerate the revolutionary process, to drive forward or throw overboard the Provisional Government.

The Paris proletariat, which saw in the republic its own creation, naturally acclaimed every act of the Provisional Government,
making it easier for the latter to establish itself in bourgeois society. It
willingly allowed itself to be used by Caussidière for police services,
to protect property in Paris, just as it allowed Louis Blanc to arbitrate
in wage disputes between workers and masters. It was a *point d'hon-
neur* to keep the bourgeois honour of the republic unsullied in the eyes
of Europe.

The republic encountered no resistance either at home or abroad.
As a result it was disarmed. Its task was no longer to transform the
world by revolution but only to adapt itself to the conditions of bourgeois society. . . .

The workers were left with no choice; they had either to starve
or to strike out. They answered on 22 June with the gigantic insurrection, in which the first great battle was fought between the two great
classes which divide modern society. It was a fight for the preservation or destruction of the *bourgeois* order. The veil which shrouded
the republic was torn asunder.

It is well known how the workers, with unheard-of bravery and
ingenuity, without leaders, without a common plan, without sup-
plies, and for the most part lacking weapons, held in check the army,
the Mobile Guard, the Paris National Guard and the National Guard
which streamed in from the provinces, for five days. It is well known
how the bourgeoisie sought compensation for the mortal terror it had
suffered in outrageous brutality, massacring over 3,000 prisoners.

The official representatives of French democracy were so immersed in republican ideology that the meaning of the June battle
only began to dawn on them after a few weeks. It was as though they
were stupefied by the powder and smoke in which their fantastic republic dissolved.

The immediate impression which the news of the June defeat
made on us, the reader will allow us to describe in the words of the
Neue Rheinische Zeitung.

> The last official remnant of the February revolution, the
> Executive Commission, has melted away like an apparition be-
> fore the seriousness of events. Lamartine's fireworks have
> turned into Cavaignac's incendiary rockets. "*Fraternité,*" the
> brotherhood of opposing classes, one of which exploits the
> other, this "*fraternité*" was proclaimed in February and written
> in capital letters on the brow of Paris, on every prison and every
> barracks. But its true, genuine, prosaic expression is *civil war* in

its most terrible form, the war between labour and capital. This fraternity flamed up in front of all the windows of Paris on the evening of 25 June. The Paris of the bourgeoisie was illuminated, while the Paris of the proletariat burned, bled and moaned in its death agony.

Fraternity lasted only as long as there were a fraternity of interests between bourgeoisie and proletariat. Pedants of the old revolutionary traditions of 1793; constructors of socialist systems, who went begging to the bourgeoisie on behalf of the people, and who were allowed to preach long sermons and to compromise themselves as long as the proletarian lion had to be lulled to sleep; republicans, who wanted to keep the whole of the old bourgeois order, but remove the crowned head; supporters of the dynastic opposition, upon whom chance had foisted the fall of a dynasty instead of a change of ministers; Legitimists, who wanted not to cast aside the livery but to change its cut: all these were the allies with whom the people made its February. . . .

The February revolution was the *beautiful* revolution, the revolution of universal sympathy, because the conflicts which erupted in the revolution against the monarchy slumbered harmoniously side by side, as yet *undeveloped,* because the social struggle which formed its background had only assumed an airy existence—it existed only as a phrase, only in words. The June revolution is the *ugly* revolution, the repulsive revolution, because realities have taken the place of words, because the republic has uncovered the head of the monster itself by striking aside the protective, concealing crown.

Order! was Guizot's battle-cry. *Order!* screamed Sébastiani, Guizot's follower, when Warsaw became Russian. *Order!* screamed Cavaignac, the brutal echo of the French National Assembly and the republican bourgeoisie. *Order!* thundered his grapeshot, as it lacerated the body of the proletariat.

None of the innumerable revolutions of the French bourgeoisie since 1789 was an attack on *order;* for they perpetuated class rule, the slavery of the workers, *bourgeois* order, no matter how frequent the changes in the political form of this rule and this slavery. June has violated this order. Woe unto June!

"Woe unto June!" the echo resounds from Europe.

The Paris proletariat was *forced* into the June insurrection by the bourgeoisie. This in itself sealed its fate. It was neither impelled by its immediate, avowed needs to fight for the overthrow of the bourgeoisie by force, nor was it equal to this task. It had to be officially informed by the *Moniteur* that the time was past when the republic found itself obliged to show deference to its illusions; only its defeat convinced it of the truth that the smallest improvement in its position remains a *utopia* within the bourgeois republic, a utopia which becomes a crime as soon as it aspires to become reality. In place of demands which were exuberant in form but petty and even bourgeois in content, which it had hoped to wring from the February republic, the bold, revolutionary battle-cry appeared: *Overthrow of the bourgeoisie! Dictatorship of the working class!*

By making its burial place the birthplace of the *bourgeois republic,* the proletariat forced this republic to appear in its pure form, as the state whose avowed purpose it is to perpetuate the rule of capital and the slavery of labour. . . .

The petty bourgeoisie and proletariat had voted *en bloc for* Napoleon in order to vote *against* Cavaignac and, by combining their votes, to rob the Constituent Assembly of the final decision. The most progressive sections of each class, however, put forward their own candidates. Napoleon was the *common name* for all the parties in coalition against the bourgeois republic; Ledru-Rollin and Raspail were the *proper names,* the former of the democratic petty bourgeoisie, the latter of the revolutionary proletariat. The votes for Raspail—as the proletarians and their socialist spokesmen declared aloud—were intended as a mere demonstration: each vote a protest against the presidency as such, that is, against the Constitution itself, each vote a vote against Ledru-Rollin; the first act by which the proletariat declared itself to be an independent political party distinct from the democratic party. This party, however—the democratic petty bourgeoisie and its parliamentary representative, the Montagne—treated the candidature of Ledru-Rollin with the seriousness which it habitually uses to solemnly dupe itself. This, it may be added, was its last attempt to set itself up against the proletariat as an independent party. The democratic petty bourgeoisie and its Montagne, as well as the republican bourgeois party, were beaten on 10 December.

Besides a Montagne France now possessed a Napoleon, a proof that both were only the lifeless caricatures of the great realities whose name they bore. Louis Napoleon, with the emperor's hat and the eagle, parodied the old Napoleon no more wretchedly than the Montagne, with its phrases borrowed from 1793 and its demagogic poses, parodied the old Montagne. The traditional superstitious belief in 1793 was thus shed with the traditional belief in Napoleon. The revolution could only come into its own when it had won its *own, original* name and it could only do this when the modern revolutionary class, the industrial proletariat, came to the fore as a dominant force. It may be said that 10 December took the Montagne by surprise and sowed confusion in its mind precisely because on this day the classical analogy with the old revolution was interrupted, with a laugh, by a derisive peasant joke. . . .

20

Address of the Central Committee to the Communist League (March 1850)

This address was drafted by Marx and Engels at the end of March 1850, and was distributed to the German and émigré members of the Communist League. Marx and Engels envisaged, with both hope and anxiety, a rapid return to a revolutionary situation and to revolutionary movements in Europe and Germany. It was within this perspective that they formulated their directives: autonomous organization and action of the proletariat against the liberal bourgeoisie, certainly, but even more against the republican and democratic petite bourgeoisie that, at that moment, constituted the major opposition to the powers that were in place in Germany; employment, in achieving the goals of the socialist revolution, of the rapid succession of revolutionary phases foreseen for the near future. On this last point, it is possible that Marx and Engels were influenced by the French revolutionary model of the 1790s.

In the *Manifesto,* drafted after the 1848 revolution, Marx and Engels proposed that the "proletarian part" supported at least on a provisional basis the liberal bourgeoisie in its battle against the old order. After the failure of the revolution and the treason of the German bourgeoisie, they needed to believe that the bourgeoisie was capable of revolutionary action, and their mistrust extended to the republican petite bourgeoisie, which was even more dangerous, according to them, to the proletariat than was the liberal bourgeoisie. Marx and Engels alluded to the French Revolution of 1789 on two precise points in order to explain the necessity of a clear distinction between the goals of the workers' party and those of the republican petite bourgeoisie (the "bourgeois democrats"): peasant ownership and the question of political and administrative centralization.

• • •

MEW 7:251–52. *The Revolutions of 1848* (see source note to selection 14), 327–29. Translated by Paul Jackson.

. . . The first point over which the bourgeois democrats will come into conflict with the workers will be the abolition of feudalism; as in the first French revolution, the petty bourgeoisie will want to give the feudal lands to the peasants as free property; that is, they will try to perpetuate the existence of the rural proletariat, and to form a petty-bourgeois peasant class which will be subject to the same cycle of impoverishment and debt which still afflicts the French peasant. The workers must oppose this plan both in the interest of the rural proletariat and in their own interest. They must demand that the confiscated feudal property remain state property and be used for workers' colonies, cultivated collectively by the rural proletariat with all the advantages of large-scale farming and where the principle of common property will immediately achieve a sound basis in the midst of the shaky system of bourgeois property relations. Just as the democrats ally themselves with the peasants, the workers must ally themselves with the rural proletariat.

The democrats will either work directly towards a federated republic, or at least, if they cannot avoid the one and indivisible republic they will attempt to paralyse the central government by granting the municipalities and provinces the greatest possible autonomy and independence. In opposition to this plan the workers must not only strive for the one and indivisible German republic, but also, within this republic, for the most decisive centralization of power in the hands of the state authority. They should not let themselves be led astray by empty democratic talk about the freedom of the municipalities, self-government, etc. In a country like Germany, where so many remnants of the Middle Ages are still to be abolished, where so much local and provincial obstinacy has to be broken down, it cannot under any circumstances be tolerated that each village, each town and each province may put new obstacles in the way of revolutionary activity, which can only be developed with full efficiency from a central point.

. . . Least of all can a so-called free system of local government be allowed to perpetuate a form of property which is more backward than modern private property and which is everywhere and inevitably being transformed into private property; namely communal property, with its consequent disputes between poor and rich communities. Nor can this so-called free system of local government be allowed to perpetuate, side by side with the state civil law, the existence of communal civil law with its sharp practices directed against the workers. As in France in 1793, it is the task of the genuinely revo-

lutionary party in Germany to carry through the strictest centralization.[1] . . .

NOTE

1. In an 1855 note, Engels corrected his 1850 viewpoint: he and
Marx, fooled by the "Bonapartist and liberal falsifiers of history," had established an erroneous link between centralization and the revolutionary
process, while, in fact, Bonaparte's reactionary creation of prefects put an
end to a truly revolutionary autonomy on the part of the communes and
departments.

21

Minutes of the Central Committee Meeting
of 15 September 1850

The failure of the republican petite bourgeoisie and of the "socialist democrats" (Ledru-Rollin, Louis Blanc), in France and in Germany in 1848–49, had as its consequence a reinforcement of the Blanquists. Their influence in revolutionary organizations centered on an idea of immediate and rapid revolution directed by a conscious and decided minority. Within the Communist League this tendency was represented by Karl Schnapper and August Willich. Marx called to Schnapper's attention the necessity of a long maturation of the objective conditions for social revolution on the one hand and, on the other, the impossibility of the workers' alone taking and occupying power when faced with a much more numerous petite bourgeoisie and peasant class. He came to the conclusion that what was necessary was the autonomous organization of the proletariat and long-term action, and, starting from the example of the Paris Commune of 1792–94, pointed to the possibility of affecting political events while remaining outside of governmental organs. In the following text, Marx contrasts his own position to the position of the French and German Blanquists.

• • •

. . . The *will,* rather than the actual conditions, was stressed as the chief factor in the revolution. We tell the workers: If you want to change conditions and make yourselves capable of government, you will have to undergo fifteen, twenty or fifty years of civil war. Now they are told: We must come to power immediately or we might as well go to sleep. The word "proletariat" has been reduced to a mere phrase, like the word "people" was by the democrats.

MEW 8:498, 500. *The Revolutions of 1848* (see source note to selection 14), 341, 343. Translated by Joris de Bres.

. . . We are devoted to a party which would do best not to assume power just now. The proletariat, if it should come to power, would not be able to implement proletarian measures immediately, but would have to introduce petty-bourgeois ones. Our party can only become the government when conditions allow *its* views to be put into practice. Louis Blanc provides the best example of what happens when power is assumed prematurely. The Paris Commune is proof that it is not necessary to be part of the government in order to get something done. . . .

22

The Eighteenth Brumaire of Louis Bonaparte

In this book, written in London between December 1851 and March 1852 and published in May 1852 in New York in *The Revolution,* the journal of his German émigré friend Joseph Weydemeyer, Marx developed at length a comparison between the phases of the 1789 revolution and those of the 1848 revolution in France. The 1848–51 movements often appeared a pitiful caricature of the revolutions of 1789–99; this seemed to signify to Marx the end of the era of political revolutions and the transition to an era of social revolutions, both slower and more profound than political revolutions.

This comparison is extended, toward the end of this work, into a general tableau of the political and social evolution of France from the absolute monarchy up to Louis Napoleon Bonaparte; Marx emphasized the continued reinforcement of executive power and state power (bureaucracy) during the period under consideration.

• • •

Hegel remarks somewhere that all the great events and characters of world history occur, so to speak, twice. He forgot to add: the first time as tragedy, the second as farce. Caussidière in place of Danton, Louis Blanc in place of Robespierre, the Montagne of 1848–51 in place of the Montagne of 1793–5, the Nephew in place of the Uncle. And we can perceive the same caricature in the circumstances surrounding the second edition of the eighteenth Brumaire!

Men make their own history, but not of their own free will; not under circumstances they themselves have chosen but under the given and inherited circumstances with which they are directly confronted. The tradition of the dead generations weighs like a nightmare on the minds of the living. And, just when they appear to be engaged in the revolutionary transformation of themselves and their material sur-

MEW 8:115–18, 135, 196–98. *Surveys from Exile* (see source note to selection 18), 146–50, 169–70, 237–38. Translated by Ben Fowkes.

roundings, in the creation of something which does not yet exist, precisely in such epochs of revolutionary crisis they timidly conjure up the spirits of the past to help them; they borrow their names, slogans and costumes so as to stage the new world-historical scene in this venerable disguise and borrowed language. Luther put on the mask of the apostle Paul; the Revolution of 1789–1814 draped itself alternately as the Roman republic and the Roman empire; and the revolution of 1848 knew no better than to parody at some points 1789 and at others the revolutionary traditions of 1793–5. In the same way, the beginner who has learned a new language always retranslates it into his mother tongue: he can only be said to have appropriated the spirit of the new language and to be able to express himself in it freely when he can manipulate it without reference to the old, and when he forgets his original language while using the new one.

If we reflect on this process of world-historical necromancy, we see at once a salient distinction. Camille Desmoulins, Danton, Robespierre, Saint-Just and Napoleon, the heroes of the old French Revolution, as well as its parties and masses, accomplished the task of their epoch, which was the emancipation and establishment of modern *bourgeois* society, in Roman costume and with Roman slogans. The first revolutionaries smashed the feudal basis to pieces and struck off the feudal heads which had grown on it. Then came Napoleon. Within France he created the conditions which first made possible the development of free competition, the exploitation of the land by small peasant property, and the application of the unleashed productive power of the nation's industries. Beyond the borders of France he swept away feudal institutions so far as this was necessary for the provision on the European continent of an appropriate modern environment for the bourgeois society in France. Once the new social formation had been established, the antediluvian colossi disappeared along with the resurrected imitations of Rome—imitations of Brutus, Gracchus, Publicola, the tribunes, the senators, and Caesar himself. Bourgeois society in its sober reality had created its true interpreters and spokesmen in such people as Say, Cousin, Royer-Collard, Benjamin Constant and Guizot. The real leaders of the bourgeois army sat behind office desks while the fathead Louis XVIII served as the bourgeoisie's political head. Bourgeois society was no longer aware that the ghosts of Rome had watched over its cradle, since it was wholly absorbed in the production of wealth and the peaceful struggle of economic competition. But unheroic as bourgeois society is, it still required heroism, self-sacrifice, terror, civil war, and battles in which whole nations were engaged, to bring it into the world. And

its gladiators found in the stern classical traditions of the Roman republic the ideals, art forms and self-deceptions they needed in order
to hide from themselves their enthusiasm at the high level appropriate
to great historical tragedy. A century earlier, in the same way but at a
different stage of development, Cromwell and the English people had
borrowed for their bourgeois revolution the language, passions and
illusions of the Old Testament. When the actual goal had been
reached, when the bourgeois transformation of English society had
been accomplished, Locke drove out Habakkuk.[1]

In these revolutions, then, the resurrection of the dead served to
exalt the new struggles, rather than to parody the old, to exaggerate
the given task in the imagination, rather than to flee from solving it in
reality, and to recover the spirit of the revolution, rather than to set its
ghost walking again.

For it was only the ghost of the old revolution which walked in
the years from 1848 to 1851, from Marrast, the *républicain en gants jau-
nes* who disguised himself as old Bailly, right down to the adventurer
who is now hiding his commonplace and repulsive countenance beneath the iron death-mask of Napoleon.

An entire people thought it had provided itself with a more
powerful motive force by means of a revolution; instead, it suddenly
found itself plunged back into an already dead epoch. It was impossible to mistake this relapse into the past, for the old dates arose again,
along with the old chronology, the old names, the old edicts, long
abandoned to the erudition of the antiquaries, and the old minions of
the law, apparently long decayed. The nation might well appear to
itself to be in the same situation as that mad Englishman in Bedlam,
who thought he was living in the time of the pharaohs. He moaned
every day about the hard work he had to perform as a gold-digger in
the Ethiopian mines, immured in his subterranean prison, by the ex-
iguous light of a lamp fixed on his own head. The overseer of the
slaves stood behind him with a long whip, and at the exits was a
motley assembly of barbarian mercenaries, who had no common language and therefore understood neither the forced labourers in the
mines nor each other. "And I, a freeborn Briton," sighed the mad
Englishmen, "must bear all this to make gold for the old pharaohs."
"To pay the debts of the Bonaparte family," sighed the French nation.
As long as he was in his right mind, the Englishman could not free
himself of the obsession of making gold. As long as the French were
engaged in revolution, they could not free themselves of the memory
of Napoleon. The election of 10 December 1848 proved this. They
yearned to return from the dangers of revolution to the fleshpots of

Egypt, and 2 December 1851 was the answer. They have not merely acquired a caricature of the old Napoleon, they have the old Napoleon himself, in the caricature form he had to take in the middle of the nineteenth century.

The social revolution of the nineteenth century can only create its poetry from the future, not from the past. It cannot begin its own work until it has sloughed off all its superstitious regard for the past. Earlier revolutions have needed world-historical reminiscences to deaden their awareness of their own content. In order to arrive at its own content the revolution of the nineteenth century must let the dead bury their dead. Previously the phrase transcended the content; here the content transcends the phrase.

The February revolution was a surprise attack, it took the old society *unawares*. The people proclaimed this unexpected *coup de main* to be an historic deed, the opening of a new epoch. On 2 December the February revolution was conjured away by the sleight of hand of a cardsharper. It is no longer the monarchy that appears to have been overthrown but the liberal concessions extracted from it by a century of struggle. Instead of *society* conquering a new content for itself, it only seems that the *state* has returned to its most ancient form, the unashamedly simple rule of the military sabre and the clerical cowl. The answer to the coup *de main* of February 1848 was the *coup de tête* of December 1851. Easy come, easy go! However, the intervening period has not gone unused. Between 1848 and 1851 French society, using an abbreviated because revolutionary method, caught up on the studies and experiences which would in the normal or, so to speak, textbook course of development have had to precede the February revolution if it were to do more than merely shatter the surface. Society now appears to have fallen back behind its starting-point; but in reality it must first create the revolutionary starting-point, i.e. the situation, relations, and conditions necessary for the modern revolution to become serious.

Bourgeois revolutions, such as those of the eighteenth century, storm quickly from success to success. They outdo each other in dramatic effects; men and things seem set in sparkling diamonds and each day's spirit is ecstatic. But they are short-lived; they soon reach their apogee, and society has to undergo a long period of regret until it has learned to assimilate soberly the achievements of its period of storm and stress. Proletarian revolutions, however, such as those of the nineteenth century, constantly engage in self-criticism, and in repeated interruptions of their own course. They return to what has apparently already been accomplished in order to begin the task again;

with merciless thoroughness they mock the inadequate, weak and wretched aspects of their first attempts; they seem to throw their opponent to the ground only to see him draw new strength from the earth and rise again before them, more colossal than ever; they shrink back again and again before the indeterminate immensity of their own goals, until the situation is created in which any retreat is impossible, and the conditions themselves cry out:

Hic Rhodus, hic salta![2] Here is the rose, dance here!

. . . In the first French revolution the rule of the Constitutionalists was followed by the rule of the Girondins, and the rule of the Girondins by the rule of the Jacobins. Each of these parties leaned on the more progressive party. As soon as it had brought the revolution to the point where it was unable to follow it any further, let alone advance ahead of it, it was pushed aside by the bolder ally standing behind it and sent to the guillotine. In this way the revolution moved in an ascending path.

In the revolution of 1848 this relationship was reversed. The proletarian party appeared as the appendage of petty-bourgeois democracy. It was betrayed and abandoned by the latter on 16 April, on 15 May, and in the June days. The democratic party, for its part, leant on the shoulders of the bourgeois–republican party. As soon as the bourgeois republicans thought they had found their feet, they shook off this burdensome comrade and relied in turn on the shoulders of the party of Order. The party of Order hunched its shoulders, allowed the bourgeois republicans to tumble off, and threw itself onto the shoulders of the armed forces. It believed it was still sitting on those shoulders when it noticed one fine morning that they had changed into bayonets. Every party kicked out behind at the party pressing it forward and leaned on the party in front, which was pressing backward. No wonder each party lost its balance in this ridiculous posture, and collapsed in the midst of curious capers, after having made the inevitable grimaces. In this way the revolution moved in a descending path. Before the last February barricade had been cleared away and the first revolutionary authority constituted, the parties found themselves enmeshed in this retrogressive process. . . .

The executive power possesses an immense bureaucratic and military organization, an ingenious and broadly based state machinery, and an army of half a million officials alongside the actual army, which numbers a further half million. This frightful parasitic body, which surrounds the body of French society like a caul and stops up all its pores, arose in the time of the absolute monarchy, with the decay of the feudal system, which it helped to accelerate. The seignorial privileges of the landowners and towns were transformed into attributes of the state power, the feudal dignitaries became paid officials, and the variegated medieval pattern of conflicting plenary authorities became the regulated plan of a state authority character-ized by a centralization and division of labour reminiscent of a fac-tory. The task of the first French revolution was to destroy all separate local, territorial, urban and provincial powers in order to create the civil unity of the nation. It had to carry further the centralization that the absolute monarchy had begun, but at the same time it had to de-velop the extent, the attributes and the number of underlings of the governmental power. Napoleon perfected this state machinery. The Legitimist and July monarchies only added a greater division of la-bour, which grew in proportion to the creation of new interest groups, and therefore new material for state administration, by the division of labour within bourgeois society. Every *common* interest was immediately detached from society, opposed to it as a higher, *general* interest, torn away from the self-activity of the individual members of society and made a subject for governmental activity, whether it was a bridge, a schoolhouse, the communal property of a village community, or the railways, the national wealth and the na-tional university of France. Finally, the parliamentary republic was compelled in its struggle against the revolution to strengthen by means of repressive measures the resources and centralization of gov-ernmental power. All political upheavals perfected this machine in-stead of smashing it. The parties that strove in turn for mastery regarded possession of this immense state edifice as the main booty for the victor.

However, under the absolute monarchy, during the first French revolution, and under Napoleon, bureaucracy was only the means of preparing the class rule of the bourgeoisie. Under the Restoration, Louis Philippe, and the parliamentary republic, on the other hand, it was the instrument of the ruling class, however much it strove for power in its own right.

Only under the second Bonaparte does the state seem to have attained a completely autonomous position. The state machine has established itself so firmly *vis-à-vis* civil society that the only leader it needs is the head of the Society of 10 December, an adventurer who has rushed in from abroad and been chosen as leader by a drunken soldiery, which he originally bought with liquor and sausages, and to which he constantly has to throw more sausages. This explains the shamefaced despair, the feeling of terrible humiliation and degradation which weighs upon France's breast and makes her catch her breath. France feels dishonoured.

But the state power does not hover in mid-air. Bonaparte represents a class, indeed he represents the most numerous class of French society, the *small peasant proprietors*.

Just as the Bourbons were the dynasty of big landed property and the Orleans the dynasty of money, so the Bonapartes are the dynasty of the peasants, i.e. of the mass of the French people. The chosen hero of the peasantry is not the Bonaparte who submitted to the bourgeois parliament but the Bonaparte who dispersed it. . . .

NOTES

1. One of the twelve minor Hebrew prophets. In denouncing the tyranny that reigned during his time, he foretold the submission of the people of Israel by the Chaldeans and their subsequent liberation, in which he saw the definitive victory of good over evil. He probably lived during the seventh century B.C.

2. "Here is Rhodes, leap here." A Latin proverb inspired by a fable of Aesop's that means: this is the moment to show what you are capable of.

23

Letter to Engels, 27 July 1854

. . . A book that has interested me greatly is Thierry's *Histoire de la formation et du progrès du Tiers État,* 1853. It is strange how this gentleman, *le père* of the "class struggle" in French historiography, inveighs in his Preface against the "moderns" who, while also perceiving the antagonism between bourgeoisie and proletariat, purport to discover traces of such opposition as far back as the history of the *tiers-état* prior to 1789. He is at great pains to show that the *tiers-état* comprises all social ranks and estates save the *noblesse* and *clergé* and that the bourgeoisie plays the role of representative of all these other elements. Quotes, for example, from Venetian embassy reports:

> Questi che si chiamano li stati del regno sono di tre ordine di persone, cioè del clero, della nobiltà, e del restante di quelle persone che, per voce comune, si puó chiamare *populo.* [These that call themselves the Estates of the realm are of three orders of persons, that of the clergy, of the nobility, and of the rest of those persons who, in common parlance, may be called the people.]

Had Mr. Thierry read our stuff, he would know that the decisive opposition between bourgeoisie and *peuple* does not, of course, crystallise until the former ceases, as *tiers-état,* to oppose the *clergè* and the *noblesse.* But as for the *"racines dans l'histoire . . . d'un antagonisme né d'hier,"* his book provides the best proof that the origin of the *"racines"* coincided with the origin of the *tiers-état.* By the same token, this otherwise intelligent critic would have to conclude from the *Senatus populusque Romanus* that in Rome there was never any opposition save that between the *senatus* and the *populus.* I was interested to discover from the documents he quotes that the term *"catalla, capi-*

MEW 28:381–83. *Collected Works* (see source note to selection 7), 39:473–74.

talia," capital, came into being with the rise of the communes. He has, by the by, unwittingly demonstrated that the victory of the French bourgeoisie was delayed by nothing so much as the fact that it did not decide until 1789 to make COMMON CAUSE with the peasants. Although he does not generalise, he depicts very nicely, 1. how from the beginning, or at least since the rise of the towns, the French bourgeoisie has gained undue influence by constituting itself a parliament, bureaucracy, etc., and not, as in England, by commerce and *industrie* alone. This undoubtedly holds true even of present-day France. 2. From his account it may be readily shown how the class rises as the various forms in which its centre of gravity has lain at different times are ruined and with them the different sections whose influence derives from these forms. In my view, this sequence of metamorphoses leading up to the domination of the class has never before been thus presented—at least so far as the material is concerned. In regard to the *maîtrises, jurandes,* etc., in short, the forms in which the industrial bourgeoisie develops, he has, alas, restricted himself almost wholly to general, and generally known, phrases, despite the fact that here too he alone is familiar with the material. . . .

24

Letter to Engels, 2 December 1856

. . . By the by, in my recent studies of Polish history, what led me *décidément* to plump for Poland was the historical fact that the intensity and the viability of all revolutions since 1789 may be gauged with fair accuracy by their attitude towards Poland. Poland is their "external" thermometer. This is demonstrable *en détail* from French history. It is conspicuous in our brief German revolutionary period, likewise in the Hungarian. Of all the revolutionary governments, including that of Napoleon I, the Comité du salut public is an exception only in as much as it refused to intervene, not out of weakness, but out of "mistrust." In 1794 it sent for the *employé* of the Polish insurgents and asked this *citoyen* the following questions:

> How is it that your Kosciusko,[1] a popular dictator, tolerates the existence alongside himself of a king of whom, moreover, he cannot but know that he was put on the throne by Russia? How is it that your dictator does not dare effect the *levée en masse* of the peasants for fear of the aristocrats, who do not wish to be deprived of any of their "hands"? How is it that the revolutionary complexion of his proclamations pales in proportion to the distance his march removes him from Cracow? How is it that he *immediately* punished with the gallows the popular insurgents in Warsaw, whereas the aristocratic "*traîtres de la patrie*" are allowed to remain at large, or are given refuge in the lengthy formalities of a trial? Answer!

Whereat the Polish "*citoyen*" could only remain silent. . . .

MEW 29:88–89. *Collected Works* (see source note to selection 7), 40:85–86.

SELECTION 24

NOTE

1. Tadeusz Andrzej Kościuszko (1746–1817) was the leader of the national liberation movement in Poland during the last years of the eighteenth century. He participated in the American Revolutionary War, became a general in 1784, and headed the Polish insurrection of 1794.

25

Theories of the Plus Value

This piece, written by Marx between January 1862 and July 1863, constitutes the fourth book of *Capital*. *Theories of the Plus Value* was published for the first time by Kautsky between 1905 and 1910, and then by the Institute of Marxism-Leninism of the Communist Party of the Soviet Union, 1954–61.

Marx mentions the French Revolution here in conjunction with the Physiocrats.

• • •

. . . One sees, therefore, just how little modern economists [such as] Eugène Daire[1], who published the work of the Physiocrats along with his prize-winning essay about them, really understood physiocracy, when they find that their specific theories the productivity exclusive to agricultural labor, on ground rent as the unique plus value, on the outstanding position of the landed property-holder in the system of production, are unrelated and only accidentally connected with their proclamation of free competition, the principle of large-scale industry, of capitalist production. At the same time, one grasps how the feudal appearance of this system, along with the aristocratic tone of its argumentation, was bound to make masses of feudal lords into enthusiastic supporters and propagandists of a system that essentially proclaimed the bourgeois system of production on the ruins of the feudal system. . . .

The contradictions of the economists' whole system. Among others, Quesnay is for absolute monarchy.

> Let authority be unique. . . . The system of checks and
> balances in a government is a pernicious opinion that reveals

MEW 26.1:23, 36–37. 319.

only the discord among the great and the crushing of the small."[2]

Mercier de la Rivière:

Solely by virtue of being destined to live in society, man is destined to live under despotism.[3]

And now who should be the "friend of the people" but the marquis de Mirabeau! Mirabeau the father! And it is just this school that, through *laissez faire, laissez aller,* overthrew Colbertism, eliminated all government intervention in the activities of bourgeois society. It allows the state to survive only in the pores of this society, as Epicurus allowed his gods to survive only in the pores of the world! The glorification of landed property is translated into practice by exclusively taxing income from the land—a virtual confiscation of landed property by the state, akin to the proposals of the radical section of the Ricardians. The French Revolution, over the objections of Roederer and others, embraced this theory of taxation.

Turgot himself, that radical bourgeois minister who initiated the French Revolution. With all their spurious feudal appearance the Physiocrats working hand in hand with the Encylopedists!

Turgot sought to anticipate the measures of the French Revolution; by means of the *février 1776* edict he abolished the *corporations.* (This edict was revoked three months after its publication.) Similarly, he overturned the peasants' road-construction corvée. Attempted to introduce taxes to be levied uniquely on income from the land. . . . When Smith, for his part, said of the Physiocrats, "Their works have certainly been of some service to their country,"[4] he was in an immoderately modest way describing the efficacity of a *Turgot,* for example, one of the direct ancestors of the French Revolution.

NOTES

1. The reference is to *Physiocrates: Quesnay, Dupont de Nemours, Mercier de la Rivière, Baudeau, Le Trosne, avec une introduction sur la doctrine des physiocrates, des comentaires et des notices historiques par Eugène Daire,* part 1 (Paris, 1846).

2. Quesnay, "Maximes générales du gouvernement économique d'une royaume agricole, in *Physiocrates.*

THEORIES OF THE PLUS VALUE

3. Paul-Pierre Mercier de La Rivière, *L'Ordre naturel et essentiel des sociètès politiques* (London and Paris, 1767).

4. Adam Smith, *Inquiry into the Nature and Causes of the Wealth of Nations* (New York: Random House Modern Library Edition, 1937), 642.

26

Letter to Engels, 30 January 1865

. . . It is once more clear what sort of guys these Progressives[1] are by their behavior over the question of coalitions.[2] (*En passant,* the Prussian anticoalition law, like all Continental laws of this type, stems from the decree of the Assemblée Constituante of 14 June 1791, whereby the French bourgeoisie punishes "anything of the sort, even workers' associations of any kind, very severely—for example, with loss of civil rights for one year—under the pretext that this would be *restoration of guilds* and would contradict *liberté constitutionnelle* and the *"droits de l'homme."* It is very characteristic of Robespierre that, at time when it was a guillotinable crime to be a *constitutionnel* in the sense of the Assemblée of 1789, all the laws *against* the workers remained in force.)

NOTES

1. Members of the Progressive party, a liberal bourgeois party hostile to Bismarck's politics.
2. The battle for the right to form coalitions—banned in Prussia—was very active at the beginning of 1865, especially among Berlin printers who were influenced by Wilhelm Liebnecht. The Progressive party thus felt obliged to bring a motion demanding the suppression of certain planned penalties. In order to play the worker card against the bourgeois opposition, the government momentarily pretended that it wished to rescind the penalties as set out by the law.

MEW 31:48.

27

Capital, Volume 1

Volume 1 of the *Capital* was the only one to have been completed and published during Marx's lifetime, in 1867. Volumes 2, 3, and 4, never completed, were published after his death.

• • •

. . . Nomad races are the first to develop the money-form, because all their worldly goods consist of moveable objects and are therefore directly alienable; and because their mode of life, by continually bringing them into contact with foreign communities, solicits the exchange of products. Man has often made man himself, under the form of slaves, serve as the primitive material of money, but has never used land for the purpose. Such an idea could only spring up in a bourgeois society already well developed. It dates from the last third of the 17th century, and the first attempt to put it in practice on a national scale was made a century afterwards, during the French bourgeois revolution. . . .

During the very first storms of the revolution, the French bourgeoisie dared to take away from the workers the right of association but just acquired. By a decree of June 14, 1791, they declared all coalition of the workers as "an attempt against liberty and the declaration of the rights of man," punishable by a fine of 500 livres, together with deprivation of the rights of an active citizen for one year.[1] This law which, by means of State compulsion, confined the struggle between capital and labour within limits comfortable for capital, has outlived revolutions and changes of dynasties. Even the Reign of Terror left it untouched. It was but quite recently struck out of the Penal Code. Nothing is more characteristic than the pretext for this bourgeois *coup*

MEW 23:103–4, 769–70. Karl Marx, *Capital* (New York: International Publishers, 1976, 1977), 88–89, 741.

d'état. "Granting," says Chapelier, the reporter of the Select Committee on this law, "that wages ought to be a little higher than they are, . . . that they ought to be high enough for him that receives them, to be free from that state of absolute dependence due to the want of the necessaries of life, and which is almost that of slavery," yet the workers must not be allowed to come to any understanding about their own interests, nor to act in common and thereby lessen their "absolute dependence, which is almost that of slavery"; because, forsooth, in doing this they injure "the freedom of their cidevant masters, the present entrepreneurs," and because a coalition against the despotism of the quondam masters of the corporations is—guess what!—is a restoration of the corporations abolished by the French constitution.[2]

MARX'S NOTES

1. Article I. of this law runs: "l'anéantissement de toute espèce de corporations du même état et profession étant l'une des bases fondamentales de la constitution française, il est défendu de les rétablir de fait sous quelque prétexte et sous quelque forme que ce soit." Article IV. declares, that if "des citoyens attachés aux mêmes professions, arts et métiers prenaient des délibérations, faisaient entre eux des conventions tendantes à refuser de concert ou à n'accorder qu'à un prix déterminé le secours de leur industrie ou de leurs travaux, les dites délibérations et conventions . . . seront déclarées inconstitutionnelles, attentatoires à la liberté et à la déclaration des droits de l'homme, &c."; felony, therefore, as in the old labour-statutes. ("Révolutions de Paris," Paris, 1791, t. III, p. 523.)

2. Buchez and Roux: *Histoire Parlementaire,* t. X., p. 195.

28

Letter to John Malcolm Ludlow, 10 April 1869

Ludlow—lawyer, journalist, and Christian-inspired socialist—was active in the English cooperative movement. In the following passage, Marx attacks certain of the German socialist Lassalle's conceptions about state-aided cooperatives.

• • •

. . . His practical recipe—cooperative societies with state aid—I would out of politeness call *his* product. In reality, it comes from Monsieur *Buchez,* an ex-Saint-Simonian, author of *Histoire Parlementaire de la Révolution française,*[1] who zealously propagated it at the time of Louis-Philippe. Monsieur Buchez, who glorified Robespierre *and* the Holy Inquisition, advocated his views, in the periodical "L'Atelier,"[2] for example, in *opposition* to the radical views of French communism of that time. . . .

NOTES

1. Buchez and Roux, *Histoire parlementaire de la Révolution française, ou journal des assemblées nationales, depuis 1789 jusqu'en 1815,* 40 vols. (Paris 1834–38).

2. *L'Atelier: Organe spécial de la classe laborieuse, rédigé par des ouvriers exclusivement* was a monthly journal, with Christian-Socialist leanings, published in Paris between 1840 and 1850.

MEW 32:600. (Unable to locate the English original of this letter, I was obliged to retranslate from the German.—Trans.)

29

Letter to César de Paepe, 14 September 1870

This letter was written ten days after the republic was proclaimed in France. César de Paepe (1842–90) was a militant in the Belgian workers' movement and a very active member of the International Workers' Association founded in 1864. The original French text of this letter was published for the first time by Maximilien Rubel, "Trois lettres inédites de Karl Marx présentées par Maximilien Rubel," in *L'Atelier de l'Histoire,* no. 25 (Oct.–Dec. 1958), 22–32. Mr. Rubel and Mr. Janover kindly sent me a copy of this article.

• • •

. . . On 5 September, our central committee[1] in Brunswick had published a call to "German workers" to oppose the annexation of French territory, for peace with the Republic. . . . The German workers . . . despite the cries of bourgeois patriots, conducted themselves admirably.

I am afraid I cannot say the same of our French comrades. Their manifesto was an absurdity.[2] "Repassez le Rhin!" They forget that the Germans need not *recross* the Rhine to get home, but need only withdraw into the Palatinate and the (Prussian) Province of the Rhine. You will understand how this chauvinistic phrase was exploited by Bismarck's official journals! The whole tone of this manifesto is absurd and not at all in keeping with the spirit of the *Internationale*.

. . . This whole state of things will disappear, I hope, before the impending and *inevitable* capitulation of Paris. The misfortunes of the French, even of the workers, are the *grands souvenirs!* Events must, once and for all, smash this reactionary cult of the past! . . .

For source, see above, this page.

NOTES

1. The central committee of the Social-Democratic Worker's Party (*Sozialdemokratische Arbeiterpartei*) founded in Eisenach in 1869 around Wilhelm Liebknecht and August Bebel. It was different from the General Association of Workers (*Allgemeiner Deutscher Arbeiterverein*) created by Ferdinand Lassalle in 1863. The two organizations would merge at the Gotha Congress in 1875.

2. Marx is referring to the call put out on 5 September 1870 by the *conseil fédéral* of Paris "in the name of workers' organizations, the French sections of the International Workers' Association, to the German people, to the Socialist Democracy of the German nation."

30

The Civil War in France

This piece was written by Marx In April and May 1871 and published in London in June, in English, under the title *The Civil War in France;* it was published in German for the first time in the journal *Der Volkstaat* (in Leipzig), 28 June to 29 July 1871. It was an "address" of the General Council of the International Workers' Association to all members of the association in Europe and in the United States. Marx played a very active role at the heart of the International Workers' Association from the time of its creation in 1864. He had followed the events of the Paris Commune, with attention and excitement, by means of the press, correspondence, and direct contacts.

The following text returns to a theme already present in *The Eighteenth Brumaire:* the continuous reinforcement of executive and state power (army and bureaucracy) in France from the absolute monarchy to the Second Empire. Here another theme is added (also present in 1851–52): the need for the working classes to break the bourgeois state machine in order to start up their own revolution, and not to be satisfied with merely seizing that machine as was the case during the purely political revolutions (1789, 1830, 1848).

Marx wrote and twice rewrote the pages of *The Civil War* devoted to the history of the French state between the French Revolution and the Commune. We here publish the three successive versions of this passage.

• • •

MEW 17:538–41, 607–10, 336–38. Karl Marx, *The First International and After,* edited by David Fernbach (Pelican Marx Library, 1974; New York: Vintage Books, 1974), 206–8 (first draft), 246–48 (final version). ©1974 by New Left Review. Reproduced by permission of Penguin Books, Ltd., and Random House, Inc. (Second draft newly translated.—Trans.)

THE CIVIL WAR IN FRANCE

First draft

The centralized state machinery which, with its ubiquitious and complicated military, bureaucratic, clerical and judiciary organs, entoils (enmeshes) the living civil society like a boa constrictor, was first forged in the days of absolute monarchy as a weapon of nascent modern society in its struggle of emancipation from feudalism. The seignorial privileges of the medieval lords and cities and clergy were transformed into the attributes of a unitary state power, displacing the feudal dignitaries by salaried state functionaries, transferring the arms from medieval retainers of the landlords and the corporations of townish citizens to a standing army; substituting for the checkered (parti-coloured) anarchy of conflicting medieval powers the regulated plan of a state power, with a systematic and hierarchic division of labour. The first French revolution with its task to found national unity (to create a nation) had to break down all local, territorial, townish and provincial independence. It was, therefore, forced to develop what absolute monarchy had commenced, the centralization and organization of state power, and to expand the circumference and the attributes of the state power, the number of its tools, its independence, and its supernaturalist sway over real society which in fact took the place of the medieval supernaturalist heaven, with its saints. Every minor solitary interest engendered by the relations of social groups was separated from society itself, fixed and made independent of it and opposed to it in the form of state interest, administered by state priests with exactly determined hierarchical functions.

This parasitical [excrescence upon] civil society, pretending to be its ideal counterpart, grew to its full development under the sway of the first Bonaparte. The Restoration and the monarchy of July [1830] added nothing to it but a greater division of labour, growing at the same measure in which the division of labour within civil society created new groups of interests, and therefore new material for state action. In their struggle against the revolution of 1848, the parliamentary republic of France and the governments of all continental Europe were forced to strengthen, with their measures of repression against the popular movement, the means of action and the centralization of that governmental power. All revolutions thus only perfected the state machinery instead of throwing off this deadening incubus. The fractions and parties of the ruling classes which alternately struggled for supremacy, considered the occupancy (control) (seizure) and the direction of this immense machinery of government as the main

228

SELECTION 30

booty of the victor. It centred in the creation of immense standing armies, a host of state vermin, and huge national debts. During the time of the absolute monarchy it was a means of the struggle of modern society against feudalism, crowned by the French revolution, and under the first Bonaparte it served not only to subjugate the revolution and annihilate all popular liberties, it was an instrument of the French revolution to strike abroad, to create for France on the Continent, instead of feudal monarchies, more or less states after the image of France. Under the Restoration and the monarchy of July it became not only a means of the forcible class domination of the middle class, and a means of adding to the direct economic exploitation a second exploitation of the people by assuring to their families all the rich places of the state household. During the time of the revolutionary struggle of 1848 at last it served as a means of annihilating that revolution and all aspirations at the emancipation of the popular masses. But the state parasite received only its last development during the Second Empire. The governmental power with its standing army, its all-directing bureaucracy, its stultifying clergy and its servile tribunal hierarchy had grown so independent of society itself that a grotesquely mediocre adventurer with a hungry band of desperadoes behind him sufficed to wield it. It did no longer want the pretext of an armed coalition of old Europe against the modern world founded by the revolution of 1789. It appeared no longer as a means of class domination, subordinate to its parliamentary ministry or legislature. Humbling under its sway even the interests of the ruling classes, whose parliamentary show work it supplanted by self-elected Corps Législatifs and self-paid Senates, sanctioned in its absolute sway by universal suffrage, the acknowledged necessity for keeping up "order," that is the rule of the landowner and the capitalist over the producer, cloaking under the tatters of a masquerade of the past, the orgies of the corruption of the present and the victory of the most parasite fraction, the financial swindler, the *debauchery* of all the reactionary influences of the past let loose—a pandemonium of infamies—the state power had received its last and supreme expression in the Second Empire. Apparently the final victory of this governmental power over society, it was in fact the orgy of all the corrupt elements of that society. To the eye of the uninitiated it appeared only as the victory of the executive over the legislative, of the final defeat of the form of class rule pretending to be the autocracy of society by its form pretending to be a superior power to society. But in fact it was only the last degraded and the only possible form of that class ruling, as humiliating to those classes themselves as to the working classes which they kept fettered by it.

Second draft

The centralized state power with its omnipresent organs—standing army, police, bureaucracy, clergy, and judicature, created according to the plan of a systematic and hierarchical division of labor—derives from the time of absolute monarchy, when it served the emerging bourgeois society as a powerful weapon in its struggles for emancipation from feudalism. The French Revolution of the eighteenth century swept away the rubble of seigniorial, local, municipal, and provincial privileges and thus purified the social ground of its last medieval obstacles standing in the way of the state superstructure. It received its final form under the first Empire, which had been born of the coalition wars of the old, half-feudal Europe against modern France. During the succeeding parliamentary regimes, possession of governmental power, by virtue of the irresistible attraction of its authority, profits, and patronage, not only became the apple of discord for the competing factions of the ruling classes; its political character simultaneously changed along with the economic changes of society. To the same extent that the progress of industry developed, expanded, and deepened the class conflict between capital and labor, so government power increasingly took on the character of a national domination of capital over labor, of a political force organized in order to compel social suppression, the character of a mere machine for class domination. In the wake of each popular revolution that marks a new advance in the way (in the development) (in the course) of the struggle of classes (class struggle), the repressive character of state power emerges more merciless and more exposed. The July revolution transferred the direction of the state machinery from the landowner to the capitalist and thus from a distant to an immediate opponent of the workers. This is why the state power takes on a more clearly expressed position of hostility and oppression toward the working class. The February revolution hoists the standard of the "social Republic" and thus proves from the start that the real meaning of state power has been exposed, that its pretext—armed might being for the protection of the public welfare, the embodiment of the general interests of society, rising above competing private interests and relegating them to their proper spheres—is seen to be a sham; that its secret—namely, that it is a tool of class despotism—has been exposed, that the workers no longer want the republic as a political modification of the old system of class rule but as a revolutionary means of destroying class rule itself. Considering the threat of the "social republic," the ruling class instinctively feels that the anonymous regime of a parliamentary republic can be transformed into a joint stock company, of their competing factions, while the monarchies of the past, by virtue of their names alone, bring to expression the victory of one faction and the defeat of another, the dominance of the interests of one part of the ruling class over the interests of the other part, of landed property over capital—or of capital over landed property. In contrast to the working class, the hitherto ruling class, regardless of the specific forms in which it may appropriate the labor of the masses, has one and the same *economic* interest: to maintain the servitude of labor and to reap its fruits, whether directly as landowner and capitalist, or indirectly as state parasites of the landowner and capitalist—to obtain by force that "order" of things in which the productive mass, the "vile multitude," serves as a mere source for the wealth and domination of the "upper classes." This is what binds together the Legitimists, the Orleanists, the bourgeois republicans, and the Bonapartist adventurers, so keen to prove themselves as defenders of property—especially property they have stolen—and to merge into the "party of Order" the practical result of the revolution carried out by the proletariat to the enthusiastic calls for a "social republic." The parliamentary republic of the party of Order is not only the reign of terror of the ruling class: in its hands, state power becomes the *undisguised instrument of civil war* of the capitalists and landowners, their state parasites, against the revolutionary endeavors of the producers.

Under monarchical regimes the repressive measures and the existent government's proclaimed principles were denounced before the people by the fractions of the ruling classes that were not in power; the opposition circles of the ruling class endeavor to interest the people in their partisan quarrels by invoking the people's own interests, posing as peoples' tribunals that insist on the restoration of the people's liberty. But under the anonymous domination of the republic, in which the repressive methods of the regimes of the past melt into each other (which draw the tools of oppression from the arsenals of all the regimes of the past) and are mercilessly applied, the various fractions of the ruling class celebrate an orgy of renegadism. With cynical shamelessness they dispute promises made earlier, trample upon their "so-called" principles, damn the revolutions that they themselves provoked in the name of those principles, and even damn the name of the republic, although its anonymous power offers them sufficient space to draw them into the common crusade against the people.

So this most cruel form of class domination is at the same time the most abhorrent and outrageous form of class domination. Using state power only as a tool of civil war, it can retain power only when perpetuating civil war. With parliamentary anarchy as its summit, crowned by the incessant intrigues of every fraction of the "party of order," each fraction striving for the restoration of its own favorite regime, in open war against the whole body of society outside of its own narrow circle—the domination of the party of Order becomes the most intolerable rule of disorder. In its war against the masses, having crushed all means of the people's resistance, and having delivered the people, helpless, to the sword of executive power, the party of Order itself along with its parliamentary regime, is removed from the staff by means of the sword of executive power. The parliamentary republic of the party of Order can only be an interregnum. Its natural result is the *imperial regime,* regardless of what number empire it would be. State power in its imperial form, with the saber as a scepter, pretends to rest on the peasantry—that great mass of producers that apparently stand outside of the class war between labor and capital; it pretends to save the working class while smashing parliamentarism and with it the direct subordination of state power to the ruling classes; it pretends to save the ruling classes by the suppression of the working classes without offending the latter; it guarantees, if not public welfare, at least national glory. That is how it is proclaimed the "savior of order." Wounding as it may be to the political pride of the ruling class and its state parasites, imperial government in fact proves itself the appropriate regime for bourgeois "order," for it gives full play to all the orgies of its industry, all scandals of its speculations, and all the dissolute splendors of its life. The state, seemingly raised high above civil society, becomes at the same time a hotbed for all the decay in that society. The complete decay of this state and of the society it was supposed to save was laid bare by the Prussian bayonettes; yet the imperial regime is such an unavoidable political form of "order"—the "order" of the bourgeois society—that even Prussia seemed to destroy its center in Paris only to move it to Berlin.

Imperial government, unlike its predecessors—legitimate monarchy, constitutional monarchy, and the parliamentary republic—is not simply one of the political forms of bourgeois society; it is also its most prostituted, perfected, and final political form. It is *the* state power of modern class rule, at least on the European Continent.

Final version

The centralized state power, with its ubiquitous organs of standing
army, police, bureaucracy, clergy, and judicature—organs wrought
after the plan of a systematic and hierarchic division of labour—originates from the days of absolute monarchy, serving nascent middle-
class society as a mighty weapon in its struggles against feudalism.
Still, its development remained clogged by all manner of medieval
rubbish, seignorial rights, local privileges, municipal and guild monopolies and provincial constitutions. The gigantic broom of the
French revolution of the eighteenth century swept away all these relics
of bygone times, thus clearing simultaneously the social soil of its last
hindrances to the superstructure of the modern state edifice raised
under the First Empire, itself the offspring of the coalition wars of old
semi-feudal Europe against modern France. During the subsequent
regimes the government, placed under parliamentary control—that
is, under the direct control of the propertied classes—became not
only a hotbed of huge national debts and crushing taxes; with its irresistible allurements of place, pelf, and patronage, it became not only
the bone of contention between the rival factions and adventurers of
the ruling classes; but its political character changed simultaneously
with the economic changes of society. At the same pace at which the
progress of modern industry developed, widened, intensified the
class antagonism between capital and labour, the state power assumed
more and more the character of the national owner of capital over labour, of a public force organized for social enslavement, of an engine
of class despotism. After every revolution marking a progressive
phase in the class struggle, the purely repressive character of the state
power stands out in bolder and bolder relief. The revolution of 1830,
resulting in the transfer of government from the landlords to the capitalists, transferred it from the more remote to the more direct an-
tagonists of the working men. The bourgeois republicans, who, in
the name of the revolution of February [1848], took the state power,
used it for the June massacres, in order to convince the working class
that "social" republic meant the republic ensuring their social subjection, and in order to convince the royalist bulk of the bourgeois and
landlord class that they might safely leave the cares and emoluments
of government to the bourgeois "republicans." However, after their
one heroic exploit of June, the bourgeois republicans had, from the
front, to fall back to the rear of the "party of Order"—a combination
formed by all the rival fractions and factions of the appropriating class

in their now openly declared antagonism to the producing classes. The proper form of their joint-stock government was the *parliamentary republic,* with Louis Bonaparte for its President. Theirs was a regime of avowed class terrorism and deliberate insult toward the "vile multitude." If the parliamentary republic, as M. Thiers said, "divided them" (the different fractions of the ruling class) "least," it opened an abyss between that class and the whole body of society outside their spare ranks. The restraints by which their own divisions had under former regimes still checked the state power, were removed by their union; and in view of the threatening upheaval of the proletariat, they now used that state power mercilessly and ostentatiously as the national war-engine of capital against labour. In their uninterrupted crusade against the producing masses they were, however, bound not only to invest the executive with continually increased powers of repression, but at the same time to divest their own parliamentary stronghold—the National Assembly—one by one, of all its own means of defence against the executive. The executive, in the person of Louis Bonaparte, turned them out. The natural offspring of the "party-of-Order" republic was the Second Empire.

The Empire, with the coup d'état for its certificate of birth, universal suffrage for its sanction, and the sword for its sceptre, professed to rest upon the peasantry, the large mass of producers not directly involved in the struggle of capital and labour. It professed to save the working class by breaking down parliamentarism, and, with it, the undisguised subserviency of government to the propertied classes. It professed to save the propertied classes by upholding their economic supremacy over the working class; and, finally, it professed to unite all classes by reviving for all the chimera of national glory. In reality, it was the only form of government possible at a time when the bourgeoisie had already lost, and the working class had not yet acquired, the faculty of ruling the nation. It was acclaimed throughout the world as the saviour of society. Under its sway, bourgeois society, freed from political cares, attained a development unexpected even by itself. Its industry and commerce expanded to colossal dimensions; financial swindling celebrated cosmopolitan orgies; the misery of the masses was set off by a shameless display of gorgeous, meretricious and debased luxury. The state power, apparently soaring high above society, was at the same time itself the greatest scandal of that society and the very hotbed of all its corruptions. Its own rottenness, and the rottenness of the society it had saved, were laid bare by the bayonet of Prussia, herself eagerly bent upon transferring the supreme seat of that regime from Paris to Berlin. Imperialism is, at the same time, the most prostitute and the ultimate form of the state power which nascent middle-class society had commenced to elaborate as a means of its own emancipation from feudalism, and which full-grown bourgeois society had finally transformed into a means for the enslavement of labour by capital.

31

Letter to Ferdinand Domela Nieuwenhuis, 22 February 1881

The Dutch socialist leader Nieuwenhuis had written to Marx asking him which legislative measures should be taken by a socialist government—on the political and economic level—to assure the victory of socialism; the Dutch socialists planned to ask that this question be made part of the agenda of the international socialist congress planned for Zurich. In his response, Marx indicated that it was wrong to ask such a question because everything depended on the particular historical conditions; for a socialist government, the essential thing was to inspire sufficient fear in the bourgeoisie as to have the time to act effectively. According to Marx, the Paris Commune was not a convincing example because it involved only one city and was not primarily socialist. He then draws a parallel between the future proletarian revolution and the French Revolution.

• • •

. . . The general demands of the French bourgeoisie before 1789 were established with almost the same precision, *mutatis mutandis,* as in our day the first immediate demands of the proletariat are established quite uniformly in all the countries of capitalist production. But did any eighteenth-century Frenchman have, *a priori,* the slightest idea as to the way in which the demands of the French bourgeoisie would later be realized? The doctrinal and necessarily imaginative anticipation of the program of action of a future revolution only leads away from the present battle. The dream of the imminent destruction of the world fired the primitive Christians in their battle against the Roman world empire and lent them their certitude of victory. Scientific insight into the inevitable and—visibly—continuous disintegration

MEW 35:160–61.

of the dominant social order, the masses that are increasingly being whipped into passion by the ghosts of the old regime itself, the simultaneous development, advancing in giant strides, of the means of production—all this is sufficient to guarantee that the moment a real proletarian revolution breaks out, even the conditions of its (though hardly idyllic) direct, immediate modus operandi will be givens. . . .

Index

(This index covers part 1 only. For details of part 2, see the table of contents.)